THE

FRENCH STAGE

IN

THE EIGHTEENTH CENTURY.

VOL. II.

MLLE. CLAIRON

AS THE MUSE OF TRAGEDY.

THE

FRENCH STAGE

IN

THE EIGHTEENTH CENTURY.

BY

FREDERICK HAWKINS.

IN TWO VOLUMES.

VOL. II.

1750—1799.

GREENWOOD PRESS, PUBLISHERS
NEW YORK

Originally published in 1888
by Chapman and Hall

First Greenwood Reprinting 1969

SET SBN 8371-2746-7
VOL. 2 SBN 8371-2748-3

PRINTED IN UNITED STATES OF AMERICA

THE FRENCH STAGE

IN

THE EIGHTEENTH CENTURY.

CHAPTER I.

1750—1753.

VOLTAIRE'S delight at the homage he received abroad did not make him unmindful of friends at home. Perhaps with some difficulty—for experience in provincial theatres was almost a *sine qua non* in these matters— he induced the Duc d'Aumont, First Gentleman of the Chamber, to grant his "enfant chéri" an order for a début at the Comédie Francaise. Lekain began his period of trial on the 14th of September, when, as a compliment to his benefactor, he played Titus in the *Brutus* of 1730. Those who had not previously seen him at the Hôtel de Jabac or in the Rue Traversière must have experienced a strong feeling of disappointment in his first scene. Nature had raised many formidable obstacles to his success on the stage. His figure was short and ungraceful, his face flat and round, his voice harsh and hollow. Collé condemned the youth's appearance as "hideous," a pair of extremely thick eyebrows giving him a "sombre and fierce look." But, like Dumesnil and Clairon, he had within him a power which, once fairly appealed to, effected a sort of metamorphosis. His figure dilated; his face acquired a strangely fascinating expression; his voice became almost melodious. Poetic warmth, wise judgment, natural dignity, perfect elocution, a singular eloquence of illustrative action,—these qualities were already apparent in his performance, and with further training could hardly fail to raise him to the first rank. Much of his future eminence seems to have been foreseen by the pit, which gave him an encouraging reception throughout. But this encouragement, though continued at his subsequent essays, did not lead to his immediate enrolment among the company. Fine ladies and gentlemen in the boxes, heedless of histrionic excellence save in combination with such physical graces as Baron and Quinault-Dufresne had possessed, listened to and watched him in chilling silence. More than one player took advantage of their apathy to bar his way for private reasons; Clairon was aghast at the idea of playing to "ce monstre à voix humaine," and Grandval, the tragedy-hero of the theatre, saw in him a too formidable rival. In the end, after a successful début, he was

adjudged unfit, at least for the present, to be made one
of his majesty's players.

Probably as the outcome of an intrigue behind the
scenes, an actor of more agreeable presence than Lekain,
but less fortunate in other respects, was brought forward
as a candidate for the *emploi* to which the latter aspired.
Bellecourt, *né* Colson, was the son of a mediocre por-
trait-painter, and, having received a good education at
Toulouse, was placed in Carl Vanloo's studio as a pupil.
Here he became an artist of another sort. His majesty's
painter-in-chief spent much of his time in playgoing,
in getting up amateur performances, and in entertaining
players at his house. In all this he had a willing
partner in his wife, formerly an operatic singer under
the name of Sommis, who is said to have been the first
to make Italian music really popular in France. One
of the pieces represented under their auspices was *Zaïre*,
and Colson, the Nérestan, won so much applause that
he determined to go on the stage. His master, thinking he would do better with the brush, urged him to
abandon the idea, but to no purpose. Two of the
guests, not content with wishing him success, did something towards providing him with a wardrobe. From
Armand he received a pair of red-heeled shoes, with
mock-diamond buckles, and from Clairon a pair of black
velvet breeches which she had worn in a piece requiring
her to don a man's costume. It was at Besançon, again

as the young chevalier in *Zaïre*, that he acted for the
first time in public. He had little reason to congratulate himself upon the result. Stage-fright nearly
deprived him of the power of speech, and the titter so
excited was changed to screams of merriment by the
breeches just mentioned going to pieces as he threw
himself at Lusignan's feet. Presently we find him at
Bordeaux, where, by dint of unremitting labour, he rose
high enough to be gratified with an invitation to Paris.
For his opening début at the Comédie Française he
acted Achille and Léandre in the *Babillard*. In tragedy
he was " crushed " by the comparison with Lekain ; but
as fine gentlemen in comedy, especially if they happened
to be *entre deux vins*, he acted with surprising spirit,
force, and refinement of style. He was speedily received, though for a department differing widely from
that which he had been expected to take. Nor was
this the only disappointment he inflicted upon a few
behind the scenes. He conceived a high regard for
Lekain, and was ever ready to uphold his claims to the
first place among living tragedians.

Bellecourt had scarcely entered the Comédie when
two of its players disappeared under exceptional circumstances. Genest's *Pénélope*, revived at the end of 1745,
was to be represented before the whole Court, and the
Queen expressed a wish that Roselli should be the
Télémaque. Ribou, having coveted the part, was so

exasperated at the preference thus shown that he struck the more fortunate actor, who, though markedly inferior to him in swordsmanship, sent him a challenge. No effort was spared by the company to avert the meeting; but Ribou, apparently bent upon the death of his rival, refused to utter a word of apology, and Roselli was not one to put up tamely with such an insult as he had received. They fought; and after two or three passes Roselli was carried home mortally wounded. Exhorted by a curé to renounce the hateful art of the theatre, he at first replied by murmuring a line in Crébillon's *Catilina*—

N'abusez point, Probus, de l'état où je suis—

but was prevailed upon to make the declaration required to save his remains from a riteless interment. His premature end was regretted in all quarters; and Ribou, fearing the vengeance of the Queen, never ventured to show his face in Paris again.

In *Zarès*, the only noteworthy novelty then in the hands of the players, we have the first work of a man who holds an honourable and conspicuous place in the history of eighteenth century thought, inasmuch as, undismayed by the apparent hopelessness of such a mission, he boldly strove to stem the current of infidelity that was now passing over the country. In 1746, before completing his sixteenth year, Charles Palissot, son of a

conseiller to the Duc de Lorraine, went from Nancy to
continue his studies at the Paris Oratoire. Fame preceded him there; at the mature age of twelve he was
a master of arts, and three years later became a bachelor
of theology. His precocity, indeed, was so marked that
Dom Calmet numbered him among the *enfants célèbres* of
the Bibliothèque. M. Palissot gave him the choice of
three professions, medicine, law, and the church. Instead of adopting any of these, however, he gave himself
up to dramatic literature, partly in consequence of an
acquaintance with Mlle. Gaussin. His earliest play,
founded upon an episode of Jewish history, did not find
acceptance at the Comédie Française, but earned for
him a free admission to that theatre. Eighteen years
of age, he married a penniless girl of good birth, and,
making Paris his home, set to work in good earnest to
write a *Sardanapalus*. "Estimable fellow this," remarked
Voltaire; "young men usually follow the example of
Sardanapalus rather than write about him." Eventually
the piece was named after its hero, a natural but
unrecognized son of Sardanapalus, one Zarès, who is
enamoured of a woman carried off by his father. The
players, after having it in their possession for two years,
produced it on the 3rd of June, with Mlle. Gaussin as
Altazire. It was accepted as of rich promise for the
future; but Palissot, unnerved by a long study of
Racine, abruptly transferred his attention to comedy.

In doing so, it appears, he was not wholly actuated by a literary purpose. Impressed with a deep sense of the truth of Christianity, he thought to check the anti-religious movement by satirizing the persons and doctrines of the philosophers, and it occurred to him that he might make as much use of the drama as Voltaire had for the dissemination of particular opinions. Palissot's courage was here more conspicuous than his discernment. He had no special talent for satire, and the weakness of his attacks, joined to a peculiar acerbity of temper in controversy, was likely to do little but harm to the cause he espoused.

It is significant of the declining power of the priest-hood that a tragedy proscribed only nine years previously as an indirect attack upon Christianity should now be restored to the stage. Perceiving that *défenses* made in the presumed interests of religion were no longer allowed to pass without fierce criticism, two of Voltaire's staunchest friends, the Comte d'Argental and the Abbé Chauvelin, "moved heaven and earth," as Collé terms it, to bring about a revival of *Mahomet.* Crébillon, however, still declined to "approve" the piece. He would not acknowledge that his previous decision was wrong. D'Argenson, devoted to Voltaire's interests, thereupon looked about for another censor. His choice fell upon D'Alembert, then deep in the scientific in-vestigations which laid the foundations of his immense

reputation. Glad to have an opportunity of doing
Voltaire a service, the young philosopher accepted the
commission, made a few unimportant excisions for form's
sake, and finally gave the manuscript his approbation.
He also offered to confute Crébillon's reasons for holding
back the piece if they were reduced to writing, but the
challenge was not accepted. *Mahomet* reappeared on
the 30th of September, the Prophet, as before, being
represented by Lanoue. It was "acclamé avec un
enthousiasme réparateur" by "une chambrée des plus
complètes," and the murmurs elicited by its supposed
application did not prevent it from becoming one of
those tragedies upon which the players could always
rely to draw a paying audience.

In some measure, perhaps, this success was due to
Lekain, who, provided by the Duc de Gêvres with
an order for a second début, had the gratification of
appearing as Séide. Indeed, the power he had acquired
was so exceptional that playgoers daily expected to hear
of his admission to the Comédie, and were at a loss to
understand why the company kept him on probation so
long. It was the custom at the theatre for an actor
to appear at the close of the performance to announce
the programme for the morrow. If a Comédien du Roi,
he said, "Nous aurons l'honneur"; if a débutant, "on
aura l'honneur." Lekain had this duty intrusted to
him after a performance of Voltaire's *Œdipe*, in which

he rose to greatness as the fate-driven hero. "Messieurs," he said, advancing to the footlights, "on aura l'honneur" —"Nous aurons," cried several spectators in the pit. Lekain was not disposed to alter the formula. "Messieurs, on aura l'honneur"—"Nous aurons," interrupted the pit in a body. "Messieurs," he then said, "not having yet been received here, I cannot rightly employ the phrase you suggest; yet, out of the respect I owe you, I will say that to-morrow we shall have the honour of representing" such-and-such a play. Even this demonstration, however, failed to move the authorities; and the young actor, dispirited by their inaction, would have joined Voltaire at Berlin if a woman able to appreciate his value, the Princesse de Robecq, had not urged him to remain.

Madame's discernment was vindicated a little sooner than she might have imagined. Louis XV. had given orders for a performance at Court of *Zaïre.* Lekain, anxious to know his fate, asked Grandval to let him play Orosmane on the occasion. "What!" exclaimed the older actor, "do you want to ruin your prospects in a moment?" "It is high time," Lekain replied, "that my position at the Comédie should be defined. I have considered the matter well, and am prepared to abide by the consequences." "Well," said Grandval, "I consent; and if the result be unfavourable remember that you have yourself only to blame." It was indeed

a hazardous step for the young player to take. He
had been disparaged at Court by Voltaire's enemies,
and the Duc de Richelieu, for reasons unexplained,
had joined in the outcry against him. When he
appeared, therefore, the stately audience were, if anything, more listless and frigid than usual. "How very
ugly he is!" some lords and ladies were heard to
whisper. Before long, however, his physical disadvantages were unheeded by that glittering throng. From
indifference they passed to interest, from interest to
admiration, from admiration to enthusiasm. Never
had the fiery, magnanimous, and tender Orosmane, who
enlists sympathy even as he slays his beautiful captive,
been impersonated with such exquisite sensibility and
art. Involuntary applause broke forth at intervals, and
the changes wrought in the actor's countenance by his
self-abandonment to the illusion of the scene were so
great that many of those who had been inclined to
deride his ugliness now deemed him "handsome." But
the most signal proof of his triumph was yet to come.
Even the King was deeply impressed. "How is it,"
he said to the Duc de Richelieu, "that the sublime
talents of this man have been so unjustly depreciated?
He has made me weep—I, who scarcely ever weep.
Convey to him an assurance of the pleasure he has
afforded me, and let an order for his reception at the
theatre be made out forthwith."

In this way, almost by chance, did the French
stage become possessed of the greatest tragic actor then
living. His progress to the first place at the Comédie
was swift and decisive. By seniority, of course, Grandval had an exclusive right to the most important
characters; but a sense of his inferiority to the new-
comer, strengthened by a disinclination to stand in the
way of a royal favourite, led him to resign them one
by one. Lekain made full use of the opportunities thus
presented to him. No one could approach the vividness
with which he embodied the heroes of Corneille and
Racine; it may even be said that he gave them an
additional vitality. For those of Voltaire, however, he
evinced a warmer predilection, chiefly by reason of
the affection and enthusiasm inspired in him by his
preceptor, friend, and philosopher. Painters despaired
of transferring to canvas the terrible aspect he assumed
on staggering as Arsace from the tomb of Ninus— at the
moment when, amidst the play of realistic thunder and
lightning, with "his arms bare and bloody, his hair
dishevelled, his face haggard, his knees trembling," he
stopped awe-stricken at the portal, "wrestling, so to
speak, with the bolts of Jove himself." Of the principal
characteristics of his acting an appreciative sketch is
given in the well-known *Réflexions sur l'Art Théâtral*.
Like Molière and Baron, Lecouvreur and Dumesnil, he
had a robust faith in natural truth. Filled with "a

burning and communicative energy, his action, at first
impassioned and irregular, delighted the young, who
were enchanted by his ardour and the warmth of his
delivery, and, above all, were moved by the accents of
his profoundly tragic voice. Amateurs of the ancient
psalmody criticized him severely, nicknaming him 'the
bull.' They did not find in him that pompous declamation, that chiming and measured declamation, in which
a deep respect for the caesura and the rhyme made all
the verses fall into a regular cadence. His gait, his
movements, his attitudes, his action had none of those
graces which then constituted the *bel acteur*. He felt
that the art of elocution did not consist in reciting
verse with more or less emphasis, that it might be
made to impart a sort of reality to the fictions of the
stage. To attain this end an actor must be endowed
with an extreme sensibility and a far-reaching intelligence, and Lekain had these qualities in an eminent
degree. His countenance was common, his figure short ;
but his exquisite feeling, the movements of an ardent
and impassioned soul, the faculty of plunging entirely
into the situation of the personage he represented, the
perception, so delicately fine, that enabled him to bring
out all shades of character,—these embellished his
irregular features and gave him an inexpressible charm.
His voice was heavy and by no means flexible ; by dint
of application, however, he contrived to overcome its

stiffness, to enrich it with all the accents of passion, and to render it amenable to all the delicate inflexions of sentiment. It became an elaborate instrument, from which he could draw forth at will every sound he needed. At first, like all young actors, he gave way to boisterous cries and violent movements, believing that by this means he triumphed over difficulties. But in time he found that of all monotonies that of the lungs is the most insupportable ; he resolved to study only that part of the public who were worth pleasing " (*a*). Less versatile than Baron and Quinault-Dufresne— for comedy to him was practically a sealed book—he rivalled them in the power of enchanting an audience, and the fact that he accomplished this feat without the aid of such physical advantages as they possessed may be taken as a sufficient reason for accounting him superior to both in force of imagination and thought. Off the stage, too, he helped to dignify his art. His conversation was marked by wide reading, good sense, even wit ; and had it not been for an irritability which hurried him into acts soon afterwards to be regretted by himself—a fault he had in common with Voltaire, of whom, by the way, he ever spoke with affectionate grati- tude—his character might be deemed beyond reproach.

Lekain's reception was not the only event that trans- ported Voltaire in the spirit from Berlin or Potsdam to the Comédie Française. *Rome Sauvée* appeared there

on the 24th of February. Its success was almost a
foregone conclusion ; a strong reaction in favour of the
persecuted author had set in, and his superiority to
Crébillon in this instance was too obvious to be disputed with any show of reason. In addition to being
technically excellent, the tragedy vindicated what
Crébillon had so needlessly outraged, the truth of
history and the dignity of the Roman senate, and
embodied a lofty conception of the characters of Cicero,
Caesar, and Cato. " Voltaire," writes Chesterfield to
his son, "has really no equal." Indeed, some of the
poet's depreciators were won over to his side. " Perhaps," says one of them, Clément, in his *Cinq Années
Littéraires*, " there is no piece by Voltaire more radiant
than this. Let it be said no longer that his fire
has died out; I recognize here all the brightness
of his colouring." He then gives warm praise to the
chief characters, adding that he only reflected the
" general impression." Marmontel thought that the
eloquent style and historic fidelity of the picture were
lost on the mass of the public, but this could hardly
have been the case at a time when the plays of Corneille
and Racine were frequently represented. Be that as it
may, *Rome Sauvée* had a satisfactory run, and the contest
forced upon Voltaire by the attempt to set Crébillon
over his head was accordingly determined on all points
to his advantage. Mindful of Boileau's well-known

sarcasm upon Corneille, an epigrammatist of the day, speaking of *Oreste*, had said—

> Cette pièce est votre *Attila ;*
> Souffrez que l'on vous dise " Holà ! "

How far *Rome Sauvée* verified the implied prediction he was careful not to point out.

Enmity of a kind similar to that which Voltaire had so bravely overcome was to be experienced by a dramatist quite unable to meet it with equal genius, self-reliance, and strength of purpose. Marmontel's fourth tragedy, the *Héraclides*, appeared under less favourable conditions than his previous pieces. His success, though clouded by the collapse of *Cléopâtre*, was large enough to bring upon him the ill-will of the literary coffee-houses, especially as, yielding to imprudent advice, he had ceased to visit them, and as he " took no pains to conceal his aversion and contempt for the herd of scribblers who, in the words of Voltaire, 'converted the noble profession of letters into a trade as base and despicable as themselves.' " Nor were his prospects improved by the fact that the friends of Gaussin and Dumesnil showed a bias against him. " Clairon," he writes, " was perpetually bearing away a part from one of these actresses, and I, her faithful poet, became an object of their ill-will." In other quarters, too, he " had to contend with the enemies of Voltaire, besides the enthusiasts who, less generous than himself, could

not even tolerate merit inferior to his." In these
circumstances, therefore, a considerable section of the
audience on the first night of the *Héraclides* assembled
in a hostile mood. For a time it seemed likely that
the play would overcome the intended opposition.
Poorly written, but marked by considerable pathos and
tenderness, it made satisfactory progress. Dumesnil,
the Déjanire, was "applauded with transport," while
Clairon found in Olympe a part by no means unworthy
of her powers. In the first entr'acte, however, the
former, "heated with exertion," drank what she supposed to be wine-and-water, but which chanced to be
wine undiluted. It got into her head; the thickness
of her utterance turned pathos into ridicule, and the
performance ended in confusion. As a result, *Les
Héraclides* had only six representations, though the
unlucky actress endeavoured to repair the misfortune
she had caused. Marmontel was so affected by it that
he thought of abandoning the stage altogether. Having
ingratiated himself with Madame de Pompadour he
asked her for a public office. "No," she replied, "you
are born to be a man of letters; your disgust with
poetry is want of courage. Instead of quitting the
game you should take your revenge, and, like Voltaire,
rise from your fall by successful effort."

Madame de Pompadour's compliment to the author
of *Rome Sauvée* on his stout-heartedness and resolution

in the teeth of disappointment—qualities indeed signally
illustrated by the history of *Mariamne, Sémiramis,* and
Oreste—was further justified by the next tragedy
brought out at the Comédie Française.   " *Le Duc de
Foix,* tragédie, par M. de Voltaire," was the announcement made in the bills for the 17th of August, and we
may fairly conclude—I have no precise information
upon the point—that a host of playgoers came together
in the expectation of assisting at yet another production of his pen.   Intense, therefore, must have been
the surprise of many amongst the number at the discovery that they were simply listening to a revival under
different names of that *Adélaïde Duguesclin* which had
been hissed down eighteen years previously by a cabal
composed in the main of persons who for different
reasons were annoyed by the *Temple du Goût.*   Did
some spectators then whisper to others that M. de
Voltaire had never lost faith in the attractiveness of
the play, and that, distracted as he may have been
by recent occurrences at Berlin, he had found time to
go over the manuscript anew, make some trifling alterations, and send it to M. Lekain with some hints as
to the manner in which it ought to be played?   For
this appears to have been the fact.   And the hopes of
the poet were fully realized by the event.   *Le Duc de
Foix,* with the help of a fine performance of Vendôme
by Lekain, became a popular drama.   Its varied charms,

high among which may be placed a sympathetic reflection of the spirit of chivalry, were recognized with an
enthusiasm sufficient to drown the clamour always raised
at the Café Procope against the productions of Voltaire.

By the way, that famous nursery of genius, described
by Longchamp as a "gloomy cavern," with "a set of
lank and sallow poets, having somewhat the air of
apparitions," putting heads together therein, became
the scene of an incident to which subsequent events
gave a peculiar interest. It was on the evening of the
18th of October, about an hour after an anonymous
one-act comedy in prose, *Narcisse, ou l'Amant de Lui-
même,* had been decisively condemned at the theatre
on the other side of the street. "Messieurs," said a
stranger at one of the tables to the assembled critics,
who were vainly guessing at the authorship, "the piece
has failed, deservedly failed. In order that it may not
be attributed to anybody else, know that I wrote it—
I, Jean Jacques Rousseau, 'Rousseau of Geneva.'" By
the feeble light of a lamp suspended from the ceiling,
apparently to make darkness more visible, the company
found themselves in the presence of a man about
forty years of age, poorly dressed, diffident to awkwardness in his manner, spare and pale and prematurely
worn, and with an expression in his dark and dreamy
eyes which indicated something like insanity. Few of
the group were unacquainted with his name, though

the *Contrat Social* and *Emile* had yet to be written
His early life—his neglected childhood in the shadow of
the Alps, his misery as an apprentice, his wanderings,
his privations, the acts of baseness to which he confessedly descended—all this was indeed unknown. But
since 1746, when he carried off the prize of the Dijon
Academy with an essay to the effect that arts and
science had contributed only to the corruption of morals,
he had been marked out by the discerning as one likely
to leave an ineffaceable mark on French literature and
thought. His paradoxical reasoning was not without
a charm at that time, while even those who derided
it were captivated by the nervous and high-toned
eloquence of the work throughout. Established in Paris
as a music-copier, he wrote three operatic pieces—*Les
Muses Galantes, L'Engagement Téméraire,* and *Le Devin
du Village.* Instinct with unartificiality in both the
language and the score, the last was represented at
Fontainebleau before the King, who desired that the
author-composer, then behind the scenes, might be presented to him. Rousseau, painfully conscious of his
gaucherie, fled from Court as soon as the royal pleasure
was made known to him, never stopping until he found
himself in his garret at Paris. Ordinary men marvelled
that he could have been such a fool. By this time he
was often to be found in the set which comprised
Diderot, D'Alembert, Holbach, Marmontel and Helvétius.

"Grimm," writes Marmontel, "used to give us a dinner every week at his own house, and a frank liberty reigned thereat. But this was a dish of which Rousseau tasted very little. No one ever observed more strictly than he the melancholy maxim of living with his friends as if they were one day to be his enemies. He had not then announced any ambition to form a sect. Either his pride was unborn, or he concealed it under the show of a timid politeness, occasionally even obsequious and bordering on humility. But in his fearful reserve distrust was evidently visible. His eye secretly observed everything with a suspicious attention. He was very rarely affable; he never opened his heart. He was not the less amicably received, as we knew that he indulged a restless self-love. Irritable and easily hurt, he was treated with the same consideration and delicacy that we should show towards a beautiful woman, very vain and very capricious, whose favour we wished to win. Nothing could be more sincere than our goodwill to him personally or our esteem for his talents. It is the recollection of these days "— Marmontel wrote his *Mémoires* many years afterwards— "that made me indignant against him when I saw him, for wrongs of his own creation, calumniate men who treated him so kindly, would have been so happy to love him." Evidence from all sides tends to bear out this description of Jean Jacques, besides suggesting that his genius was "to madness near allied." He was at least subject to the strangest hallucinations and impulses. His mental vision was defective; scarcely anything presented itself to him in its actual colours. But the infirmity of mind here shown did not prevent him from setting forth a string of audacious sophisms in a specious form. Emboldened by the success of his paradoxical essay, he resolved to attack the whole order of things as they stood, and his *Discours sur l'Origine de l'Inégalité*, now in preparation, was animated by an eloquence which announced the advent of a new power in literature. In no respect did *Narcisse* foreshadow the Rousseau of the future. Its characters were supplied by the society he dreamt of destroying, and the piece generally was weak enough to justify the verdict so decisively pronounced upon it.

Let us here note two events of histrionic importance —the reception at the Comédie of a roguish-looking and ambitious young actress, Mlle. Hus, and the death of François Arnould Poisson. Prepared for the stage by Clairon, the former, after a second début, persuaded the players that nature had designed her for tragedy, which was scarcely the fact. Poisson, who passed away in his fifty-eighth year, was the last descendant at the theatre of the Poissons of the Molierean epoch, and we have no reason to doubt that he fully upheld the fame of his progenitors. Except as the Lafleur of the

Glorieux, perhaps, he had not been fortunate in original characters; but it was feared that many whimsical figures of the drama before his time, notably those of Turcaret, Don Japhet d'Arménie, Bertrand de Cigarrol, the Roi de Cocagne, Bernadille in the *Juge Femme et Partie*, the Marquis in the *Mère Coquette*, Pascal in the *Sœur Ridicule*, and, above all, the Crispins and the Jodelets, had virtually passed away with him. His humour, his quaint figure, his comic expression,—all had made his hereditary stutter forgiven, if not unnoticed.

Poisson lived long enough to witness a welcome change in Clairon's method of acting. Marmontel had frequently urged her to aim at less artificiality, pointing out that force without suppleness and truth was nearer to rant than sensibility. "You have," he would say to her, " all the means of excellence in your art ; and, great as you are, it would be easy for you to rise above yourself by managing more carefully the talents of which you are so prodigal. You cite to me your brilliant successes; you cite to me the opinion of M. de Voltaire, who recites his verse with emphasis, and who pretends that declamation requires the same pomp as the style. I have an irresistible feeling that declamation, like style, may be noble, and majestic, and tragic, with simplicity ; that expression, to be lively and profoundly penetrating, requires gradations, shades, unforc-

seen and sudden traits, which it cannot have when
stretched and forced." "I see," she sometimes replied,
"that you will never let me rest until I have assumed
a familiar and comic tone in tragedy." "No," he said,
"that you will never have; nature has forbidden it.
You even have it not while you are speaking to me;
the sound of your voice, the air of your countenance,
your pronunciation, your gestures, your attitudes are
naturally noble; by changing your style you will only
be more impressive." Suddenly, in the course of an
engagement at Bordeaux, she resolved to try the effect
of what he recommended. In her own words, it had
the greatest success, murmurs of "mais cela est beau!"
being raised in the first scene. On her return she
had to play Roxane before the Court at Versailles.
Marmontel went to see her at her toilette. "Yes," she
said, after relating her experience at Bordeaux, "and
I am going to try the new style here. If I succeed
as well, farewell to my old declamation." Marmontel
did not fail to see the performance. "The event,"
he writes, "surpassed our expectations. It was no
longer the actress, it was Roxane herself, whom the
audience thought they heard. The surprise, the illusion, the enchantment was extreme." Paris hailed the
novelty with equal warmth; the actress found increasing
inducement to keep her word, and another invigorating
influence made itself felt in the theatre.

Marmontel's connexion with the Comédie did not last long after he did it this important service. Out of complaisance for Madame de Pompadour, he tells us, he had undertaken to produce another tragedy. Perceiving that the masters of the art had employed all the great springs of terror and pity, he racked his brains to invent a plot of an unconventional kind, and at length framed one on a subject of pure imagination. It "offered an exhibition of imposing majesty (the *Funerailles de Sésostris*); it gave me great characters to paint in favourable contrast, and an intrigue so nicely veiled that its conclusion could not be foreseen. This blinded me to the disadvantages of a story without love, composed wholly of politics and morality, and requiring all the resources of poetic eloquence to sustain it with warmth during five acts." Madame de Pompadour read the tragedy as soon as it was finished. One morning, while it was in her possession, the author presented himself at her toilette, at that moment surrounded by courtiers. Taking him into her cabinet, she returned to him the manuscript, on which she had pencilled what are described as some very just criticisms. In a few minutes she went back to the toilette, and Marmontel quietly resumed his place there. "I suspected," he writes, "the effect this singular incident would have, but the impression it made on the whole company far exceeded my expectations. All eyes were fixed upon

me ; on all sides I was greeted with little imperceptible
salutations and gentle smiles of friendship; I was invited
to dinner for at least a week. Shall I say it ? a titled
man, one decorated with the ribbon, whom I had sometimes met at M. de Lapoplinière's, whispered to me,
'What, you won't know your old friend ?' I bowed
in confusion at his meanness, and said to myself, 'Ah !
what then is favour if only its shade gives me such
importance ?'"   In regard to the tragedy, by name
Ægyptus, "the players, like Madame de Pompadour,
were impressed at the reading by the fine morality
with which I had embellished the last acts. But on
the stage their feebleness was manifest, particularly
because I had charged the first with more vehemence
and warmth. My combat of generosity and virtue had
nothing tragic. The public were weary of not being
moved, and the piece fell. This time I was satisfied
that the public were in the right. I went home determined to write no more for the stage "—a determination
to which he adhered as far as original work for the
Théâtre Français was concerned. *Ægyptus,* however,
brought him good fortune in another way. Madame
de Pompadour was at supper with the King at Bellevue
when the news of her protégé's failure reached her.
"The new piece," she said, "is unsuccessful. Do you
know, sire, who it is that tells me so ? The author
himself. Unhappy young man ! I would willingly

have some place to offer him as a consolation." Her
brother, the Marquis de Marigny, who was present, at
once made the unhappy young man a secrétaire des bâti-
ments, and the certainty of a somewhat easy existence
accordingly fell to his lot.

Voltaire, himself so dauntless under defeat, might
have had a good deal to say about Marmontel's faint-
hearted abandonment of the theatre if more important
matters had not absorbed his thoughts.   His disillusion-
izing visit to Frederick came to an end; the ill-will
with which he had long been regarded at Versailles
culminated in a hint that he would do well not to
reappear in Paris, and he was now flitting from place
to place near the frontier with a vague idea of settling
in Switzerland.   It is not the least cogent illustration
of the narrowmindedness of Louis Quinze that the
man thus capriciously exiled had recently penned that
enduring memorial of French greatness, the *Siècle de
Louis Quatorze*.   In vain did Madame de Pompadour
endeavour to change the King's mind on the point.
" She still loves you," said Marmontel to the poet some
time afterwards, "and has often told me as much.   But
she is too weak to effect all she wishes; the King no
longer cares for her."   Voltaire, as may be supposed,
felt the blow in all its severity.   Exclusion from Paris
was a sort of moral death to one of his lively and
sociable temperament, which continued proof against

the inroads of time. Nevertheless, he could look forward
to the future with no ordinary pleasure. He delighted
in country life; the additional leisure he would now
have was in itself a boon to so industrious a writer, and
the influence he possessed would have satisfied a vanity
less egregious than that ignorantly laid to his charge.
For he was already marked out as the sovereign writer
of the age. "Letters reigned over Europe; Voltaire
reigned over letters." In his own land, too, the prophet
found increasing honour. The detraction to which he
had been exposed was passing away except among some
of those who disliked him simply on account of his
scepticism. In the words of Marmontel, Envy, apparently weary of the pursuit, began to spare him as he
drew near the grave.

CHAPTER II.

1753—1760.

In the Faubourg St. Germain, immediately behind the Comédie Française, there was a thoroughfare which from the time of Louis VII. had been styled the Rue des Mauvais Garçons. From a dilapidated house here, on an autumn evening in 1733, five motherless boys rushed away to avoid some ill-treatment by their father—M. Dubus, intendant to the Princesse de Bourbon, the abbess of the Petit Saint Antoine—and with a determination never to darken his door again. For a few days they sought employment in all quarters, sleeping at night in the Marais or the Luxembourg gardens. It then became evident that they had made a dire mistake; nobody would take them in, a few sous they had hoarded up disappeared, and starvation stared them in the face. In this strait it was proposed by one that they should return to their father, whatever the consequences might be. Three faintly voted in favour of the motion, but the youngest continued to hold out. "I am able," he said, "to work, and have no doubt that I shall earn enough to live upon." Remonstrance and argument were alike thrown away upon him; and

his brothers, probably too hungry to indulge in any
marked display of fraternal affection, went back in fear
and trembling to the home they had abandoned.

Pierre Louis Dubus, as the boy they left behind
was named, mechanically walked about until he found
himself at the convent of the Chartreux, from which
some masons were coming out for breakfast. He
promptly asked them for work, adding that he was
starving. Some of the masons took pity upon him, fed
him from their own scanty store, and on their return
made him a hod and mortar carrier. In this capacity
he was found so useful that one of them took him as
an apprentice. Dom Népomucène, the procureur of the
convent, happened to look in at that moment to see
how the work was progressing. Impressed by the boy's
appearance and manner, which argued at least a decent
training, he kindly asked him who he was. Pierre
Louis, after a little hesitation, told his story without
reserve. Dom Népomucène urged him to reconsider his
intention, and, finding him obdurate upon the point,
thought it right to apprise M. Dubus of the runaway's
whereabouts. But the intendant—

> a sordid man
> Who love nor pity knew—

was then in his hardest mood. "Had my son come
back with the others," he said, "he might have been
forgiven; as it is, I leave him to his own devices."

Pierre Louis was not to continue his informal apprenticeship to masonry. Dom Népomucène apparently had to leave Paris, and his brother, M. de Vaumorin, took the friendless boy by the hand. He gave him a home, sent him to a school near the Estrapade, and, possessed of much intelligence and refinement of taste, exercised a salutary influence over the formation of his character. In one respect only did he disappoint the expectations of this excellent friend. He longed to be a player. From his childhood, when he would lie awake at night to hear the roars of applause at the Comédie Française, the stage for him had had a peculiar fascination, and at school he had distinguished himself as a clever reciter of poetry. In the hope that he might be cured of this dangerous ambition, M. de Vaumorin placed him in the office of a notary named Macquer, at the same time forbidding him to go to the theatre again until he was a lawyer. He obeyed; indeed, it is said that if his way lay through the Rue des Fossés St. Germain he would make a détour to avoid the temptation held out to him by the sight of the doors of the Comédie.

But, as Voltaire used to say, nature is stronger than education. M. de Vaumorin died; and some months afterwards, with the aid of some raillery, Dubus was prevailed upon to accompany his fellow-clerks to see a performance of the ever-green *Légataire Universel*. On

the following day, in an interval of office work, he
acted Crispin as Poisson had acted it.   His hearers were
delighted.   By closing their eyes, it was declared, they
could persuade themselves that M. Poisson himself stood
before them.   At supper they repeated this eulogium
to M. Macquer, who said that he would like to judge for
himself whether it was really merited.   Dubus accordingly gave his imitation of Poisson again, though at the
disadvantage of being less at his ease than he had been
in the office.   "Mon cher Pierre," the lawyer gravely
and regretfully remarked at the end, "it is clear that
you will never belong to my profession.   You are
destined to the stage.   I am sorry for you ; Thalia and
Fortune seldom go together."

Dubus left the notary's office, went into the country
as a strolling player under the name of Préville, and
on the death of Poisson became a candidate for the
place thus made vacant.   It was soon evident that he
would more than repair what had been deemed an irreparable loss.   Of less than medium height, with sharp
features and remarkably expressive eyes, he opened his
début on the 20th of September as Crispin in the
Légataire—the character in which he had delighted his
fellow-clerks at M. Macquer's—and as St. Germain in
the *Famille Extravagante*.   Many *laudatores temporis acti*
joined the rest of the audience in greeting him at the
fall of the curtain with enthusiasm.   Few hesitated

to credit him with an extraordinary aptitude for comedy.

> Poisson, qui si longtemps amusait tout Paris,
> Descendait dans la tombe, escorté par les Ris;
> Préville vient, paraît; il ranime la scène,
> Et Momus aisément fait oublier Silène.

He next played the Marquis in the *Joueur*, Crispin in the *Folies Amoureuses*, and Strabon in *Démocrite*. In the first and last he was unsatisfactory; the other enabled him to confirm the advantage he had won. But it was reserved for Boursault's *Mercure Galant*, revived in four acts on the 8th of October, to illustrate anything like the full measure of his power. His impersonations of the six characters in one were so happily individualized that six different men seemed to come forward. In the same month he repeated the achievement at Court, besides playing Sosie in *Amphitryon*. " M. Préville," said the King, " must be of the Comédie Française."

In truth, with the possible exception of Jean Baptiste Raisin, Préville was the most brilliant comedian yet secured for that theatre. Looking down the list of characters associated with his name—characters often essentially different from one another—we cannot refuse him the credit of singular versatility and power. In humour and tenderness he was equally at home, and all his portraitures seem to have been marked by keenness of perception, natural truth, appropriate warmth of colouring, freedom from extravagance, and a sufficient mastery of the resources of his art to illustrate the finest shades of character. His power of self-absorption is shown by an amusing anecdote. Having to play the drunken Larissolle at Court, he assumed the part a few moments before his appearance, just as representatives of Richard III. and Macbeth lash themselves into excitement behind the scenes for their final combats. So perfect was the simulation that the master of the dramatic ceremonies barred his way. " For heaven's sake," he pleaded, " do not appear; let it be announced that you are ill; do you want me clapped in prison ? " Préville, who was of a grave cast of mind, did not forget old friends in his prosperity. He at once sought out Dom Népomucène. "Mon père," he said, "your principles will make you condemn me for going on the stage ; be assured, however, that honour and probity will always be, as they always have been, the rules of my conduct." It is not too much to add that he kept his word, a choleric temper and an excessive devotion to table-pleasures being the principal faults with which he could be reproached (*b*).

Préville's success lent a fresh attractiveness to old plays, but did not abate the demand for novelties. Early in the ensuing year came a tragedy by Mailhol, *Paros.* It had been received mainly at the instance of

Mlle. Hus, who, overshadowed by Clairon and Dumesnil
in the interpretation of the great tragic dramatists, had
conceived the idea of having a repertory of her own,
and had induced the author, a needy poetaster, to assign
her the leading character in return for more than its real
value.　Infatuated with her beauty, a rich financier
organized a *claque* to applaud her, which they did so
thoroughly as to create a passing impression that a great
poet and a great actress had been discovered at one
stroke.　More than two years previously an *Antipater*
by one Portelance had been hissed with right good
will ; "hissed like *Antipater*," indeed, became a sort of
proverb.　Now, in conjunction with a short-lived young
scholar, Claude Patu, he wrote *Les Adieux du Goût*—a
piece hardly designed to flatter the national vanity,
inasmuch as it represents Taste taking leave of Paris
in despair.　Probably the fall of *Antipater* had something to do with his choice of subject.　Pierre Rousseau
brought out a comedy under the title of *Les Méprises*,
and, extremely anxious not to be confounded with Jean
Jacques, whose recently-published work on French music
had given offence far and wide, appended to his name in
the bills the words "de Toulouse, pour se distinguer de
celui de Genève."　Still a power in the theatre, the
Chevalier de la Morlière joined the little array of
dramatists with a comedy called *La Créole*, which proved
a dismal failure.　One of the characters had to describe

a fête as "not worth a curse." "Just like the piece itself!" roared several of the pittites in chorus; and the curtain had to be lowered.

The players had more than one misfortune to deplore as the year rose and fell. Lachaussée and Destouches died within a few months of each other, at the ages of sixty-two and seventy-four respectively. In them the French stage lost the most distinctive representatives in their time of two different kinds of comedy. For the space of forty-four years, except during his brief but not uneventful career as a diplomatist, Destouches had occupied himself with more or less merry illustrations, *à la* Molière, of everyday character—illustrations strengthened by no inconsiderable humour, skill, refinement, and attractiveness of style. *Lo Philosophe Marié* and *Le Glorieux*, the first-fruits of his retirement at Fortoiseau, had deservedly taken classical rank. In one respect he did not fall short of his otherwise unapproachable model. His *théâtre* is remarkably free from pruriency of incident or language, and *castigat ridendo mores* was a principle which he kept steadily in view from the beginning. Esteemed by all for his fine social qualities, he worked on gaily to the last, leaving behind him four comedies—the *Depôt*, the *Mari Confident*, the *Fausse Agnès*, and the *Tambour Nocturne* —in a finished state. Lachaussée was also under the inspiration of Molière, but to a different end. Bearing in mind the pathetic note struck in the *Misanthrope* and the *Ecole des Femmes,* he opposed himself to an idea which the author of those plays had involuntarily helped to confirm—namely, that the province of Thalia did not extend beyond the confines of the diverting—and accordingly invented or revived a *comédie attendrissante.* Notwithstanding the jeers levelled at it by Piron, who seems to have meditated a similar innovation, the new school had already made appreciable progress, as Lachaussée had much of the sensibility and eloquence it needed, and as several influential writers, including Voltaire, had given his theory a practical support.

Nobles condescended at times to write for the theatre ; the Marquis de Ximénès threw off an *Amalazonte,* and an anonymous little piece, *Le Souper,* was attributed, apparently not without reason, to the Comte de Tressan. Palissot had not yet braced himself to the task of satirizing the philosophers on the stage. His second piece, *Les Tuteurs,* a comedy in two acts, is purely and simply dramatic. Its heroine can inherit her dead father's wealth only on the condition that she marries with the unanimous consent of three old men whom he has made her guardians. Each of the trio, amusing "originals" all, delights to be at variance with the others ; but a lover of the girl, by a stratagem similar to that ascribed to the Marquis de Létorière, contrives to obtain both her hand and possessions. *Les Tuteurs,* while pleasing the town, commended its author to the notice of the Duc de Choiseul, who, as a means of developing his talents for comedy, introduced him to the glittering society of Versailles. Eighty years of age, Crébillon had just completed in his malodorous garret another tragedy, *Le Triumvirat*, in which he sought to repair the wrong he had done to Cicero in *Catilina*. It was given for the first time on the 23rd of December, and, though weak save in a few isolated passages, was received, if not with warmth, at least with the respect due to the creator of *Electre* and *Rhadamiste*. His partisans extolled it as a further proof of his superiority to all contemporary dramatists, but found that their voices were no longer heeded beyond the walls of the coffee houses.

News of this deserved *succès d'estime* found Voltaire on the picturesque shores of the Lake of Geneva, in the vicinity of which he intended to pass the remainder of his life. Not long afterwards, with a half-finished tragedy in his pocket, the exiled poet, in addition to having a house at Lausanne for the winter, bought what from the first he rapturously called the *Délices*—a little mansion near the confluence of the Rhone and the Arves, surrounded by exquisite gardens, and commanding a fine view of the romantic scenery about it. From his bed, we are told, he could see the lake, the rivers, and the snow-crowned Alps in the far distance. " The great

drawback of the house," he writes, " is that it was built
by a man who thought only of himself, and who totally
neglected to provide suitable accommodation for his
friends." Voltaire, as before, was the very soul of
hospitality, and had begun to look forward to a time
when, the work of the day done, he might find himself
at supper every evening with more or less kindred
spirits. However, the limited capacities of the place
were utilized to the utmost, and its master frequently
had the gratification of entertaining a few welcome
visitors. The delight he took in such society was not
suffered to interfere with his literary labours. For
instance, in less than two months from the date
on which he first slept at the Délices, the tragedy
hereinbefore mentioned, *L'Orphelin de la Chine*, with
Genghis Khan as its most prominent figure, was ready
for transmission to the Comédie Française.

Lekain, for whom the character of the great Mongol
warrior had been expressly written, arrived at Geneva
in the spring, after playing at Dijon and other places
on his way. He was received by Voltaire " with open
arms," not only as " un artiste célèbre auquel on doit
personnellement plus d'un succès," but as " son propre
fils "—a title probably dearer to him than the other.
Dramatic performances were immediately given on a
stage constructed in the largest room of the house, the
perennial *Zaïre*, with Lekain as the Soldan, Voltaire

as Lusignan, and Madame Denis as the heroine, being played there in the presence of nearly the whole of the Council of Geneva. " Never," says the happy author, " have I seen more tears shed ; never have the Calvinists proved so tender-hearted." In regard to the new tragedy, " take care," he said to Lekain, " that you do not allow the naturally soft inflexions of your voice to appear in the part of Genghis Khan. In him I have sought to depict a tiger which thrusts its talons into the loins of the tigress it is caressing. If your comrades find any of the speeches too long, they have my permission to use the pruning-knife, as there are citizens who must be sacrificed to the well-being of the republic." In a subsequent conversation he abandoned to the company his rights in the piece, which he pleasantly called " ses magots." It was proverbially difficult to extract a manuscript from the most fastidious of writers, but that of *L'Orphelin de la Chine* had been confided to Lekain when he regretfully left Geneva for Paris.

Nearly four months later, on the 20th of August, an overflowing audience assembled at the Comédie Française to see the first performance of the tragedy. No surprise was felt by the author's friends that he should have gone to the far East for a background. He had long evinced an insatiable curiosity as to the Chinese, partly because they appealed to his sense of the picturesque, but in the main, as may be supposed, because they were supposed to have shown of old that pure morals could exist in the absence of revealed religion. In one monument of their early civilization, a play written about six centuries before the Christian era, the *Orphan of Tchao*, which had been imperfectly done into French by Père Prémare, he had found a dramatic *motif* of no ordinary value. He at once turned it to account, and, by way of adding to the attractiveness of the story, sought to illustrate in his work, as in *Zaïre* and *Alzire*, the contrast between two different races of men. For this purpose he shifts the incidents to the thirteenth century, just after the conquest of China by the Tartar hordes of Genghis Khan. That mediæval Napoleon is persuaded that he will not sit firmly on his new throne unless the last prince of the old Chinese dynasty, an infant, has been " removed." Zanti, to whom the care of the child has been left, loyally proposes that his own child shall be passed off as the threatened heir ; his wife, Idamé, opposes the idea with all the energy of maternal devotion. Persecuted by the conqueror, who aspires to her favour, the mother conjures her husband to stab her and then himself to the heart ; and Genghis, chancing to be an unseen witness of the scene, is so much impressed by her heroism that he ceases to molest her or aim at the life of the young prince. *L'Orphelin de la Chine* was at first in three acts only, but the author, with all his former respect for anything like sound criticism, allowed himself to be persuaded by the Comte d'Argental to extend it.

Inferior in depth and power to Voltaire's chief tragedies, if not to the primitive drama itself, the new play yet took possession of the stage from the moment it appeared. He had at least gone far to meet the requirements of the subject, while the acting was of a quality to throw a veil over his shortcomings. Lekain, apparently in consequence of a cold, was unable, it is true, to do himself or the poet justice on the first evening. According to Collini, not a word of what he said could be heard. By the second representation, however, he had recovered his voice, and a fine portraiture of a barbarian softened by virtue and beauty was then presented to the audience. " My uncle," writes Madame Denis to the Comte d'Argental, " has received a letter, with which he is delighted, from M. Le Kein (*sic*), who confesses that he played badly at first, but that he is playing well now. All the letters we receive confirm this." No less admirable than the Genghis was the Idamé of Clairon. Her exquisite art, with its new admixture of natural truth, is said to have reached here a point little short of perfection. Lekain, with his usual frankness, acknowledged that the actress to a certain extent had overshadowed him. " Mlle. Clairon," he quaintly said, " plays Genghis; I am reduced to play only Idamé."

L'Orphelin de la Chine was to be associated with an important theatrical reform. "Ah!" said Clairon to Marmontel at Versailles when he congratulated her upon the change in her style of declamation, "don't you see that it ruins me? In all my characters the costume must now be observed; the truth of declamation requires that of dress; all my rich stage wardrobe is from this moment laid aside. I have spent twelve hundred guineas upon it, but the sacrifice is made. You shall see me here within a week playing *Electre* to the life." Marmontel went. It was the *Electre* of Crébillon. "Instead of the ridiculous hoop and the ample mourning robe in which we had been accustomed to see her in this character," he writes, "she appeared in the simple habit of a slave, her hair dishevelled, her arms loaded with long chains. She was admirable in it, and some time afterwards she was still more sublime as the Electre of Voltaire." Perceiving what her predecessors, with the possible exceptions of Adrienne Lecouvreur and Marie Favart, had entirely overlooked, that "a new degree of probability and interest was given to theatrical action by truth of costume," the actress at length set herself to accomplish a revolution in that respect, and thereafter was an unwearying student of statues, monuments, and portraits in old manuscripts. Her project found an ardent supporter in Lekain, who soon aroused himself to a sense of the

absurdity of dressing the characters of ancient Greece
and Rome in a half-modern fashion. *L'Orphelin de la
Chine* was the first piece in which they ventured to act
upon their ideas. Clairon appeared in it without the
huge panier in vogue; Lekain had the no less unequivocal courage to discard the conventional wig. Subsequently, having to play Oreste in *Andromaque*, the
latter donned a costume not widely dissimilar from that
of old Greece. " Beautiful! " Dauberval exclaimed in
naïve warmth; "the next time I play a Roman part
it shall be in something like that." Marmontel says
that the players were obliged from this time to abandon
their old fantastic apparel; the fact was that the
innovation of Lekain and Clairon found increasing
acceptance among them.

Few words are needed to record the events of the
year that followed. Like its immediate forerunner, it
yielded only one noteworthy play. I refer to a five-act
comedy in verse, the *Coquette Corrigée*, by Lanoue. It
was coldly received down to the closing scenes, when
an unusual briskness of action saved it from apparently
inevitable failure, and the author, who represented
his hero, from being hissed in person on the stage.
Before long it became extremely popular, in some
measure, we are gravely told, because the Duchesse
d'Orléans applauded it throughout at the second performance. Its reputation, I think, was in excess of its

deserts. Bitten by the increasing taste for metaphysical subtlety in comedy, Lanoue here cured a heartless coquette by means of a pretended marriage of the man she loves to one of her relatives—is heartless coquetry curable at all?—and was unable to redeem the improbability of the story by any of the chastened wit and humour which Marivaux had scattered over many similar paradoxes in dramatic form. Not long afterwards, in consequence of failing health, Lanoue left the Comédie to divide his time between play-writing and the fulfilment of his duties as director of theatricals at Court, but died without having completed two or three pieces he had projected.

It was fortunate for the players that they possessed the largest and most popular of repertories in Europe, as but few new plays were in their hands. One of these, *Iphigénie en Tauride*, came from Guimond de Latouche, son of a wealthy and lettered Procureur du Roi at Châteauroux. Born at that place in 1723, he had been in the Jesuit Order for about fourteen years, but had recently withdrawn from it to study law in Paris. Here he gave himself up to literature, *Iphigénie en Tauride* being his first serious essay therein. His father, apprised of this, wrote him a letter at which many parents would have stood aghast. It was to the effect that if the piece succeeded he should remain in Paris upon an annual allowance of 1500 livres, then a

comfortable income.   In the result, *Iphigénie*, thanks
in part to Clairon, whom he had met at Madame de
Grafigny's, afforded high satisfaction to a representative
audience, and at the close was so rapturously applauded
that he fainted from ecstasy.   He did not live long to
enjoy his income from Châteauroux, dying at Paris in
his thirty-seventh year.   Like Voltaire, he was ready to
profit by criticism.   For instance, at the suggestion of
the players, he reconstructed the fifth act of his tragedy
as the curtain rose for the first performance.   It was a
hazardous thing to do, but Clairon assures us that the
amended section, finished in less than an hour, went off
as smoothly as though it had been learnt and rehearsed
at leisure (*c*).

In view of the retirement of Sarrazin, who had long
been in feeble health, the company brought forward two
provincial players.   Pierre Brizard, the elder of the pair,
demands very respectful consideration.   He came of a
good family at Orleans, and was born there in 1721.
In his youth, after receiving a liberal education, he was
placed with Carl Vanloo, as Bellecourt had been, to
be initiated into the mysteries of painting.   His progress
was so rapid that his master advised him to compete
for the Grand Prix; but instead of endeavouring to
realize his promise in this way he resolved to go on the
stage.   His career in the country was marked by at
least one curious incident.   It is said that a boat in

which he was crossing the river capsized in mid-stream, that he saved himself by clinging to the stonework of a bridge, and that the fright given him by the immersion —for he could not swim—caused his hair to whiten in a few hours. He was certainly able to impersonate veterans without a wig. In 1756, at Lyons, with about ten years' experience to aid him, he attracted the attention of Dumesnil and Clairon, who were fulfilling an engagement in that city, and who did not fail on their return to speak of him at the theatre. For the opening of his début at the Comédie (July 30) he appeared as Alphonse in *Inès de Castro*, and during the remainder of the term as Brutus, Mithridate, and other exacting characters. He was then elected to succeed Sarrazin in *rois* and *pères nobles*. To a burning and communicative sensibility, always managed in the spirit of a fine artist, he united the charms of a dignified presence, handsome features, and a sympathetic voice. His acting in general was marked by a noble simplicity, and had the delightful freshness arising from a readiness to catch at the inspiration or suggestion of the moment if it happened to be in harmony with the conception he sought to embody. "It is clear," the King of Denmark said to him, "that you do not study your characters before a mirror."

The players were now in possession of a little piece with which a curious story is connected. Its author, Antoine Poinsinet, had earned some credit by writing

a parody of the opera of *Titon et l'Aurore,* but was
enough of a simpleton to become the favourite butt of
the small wits and practical jokers of the coffee-houses.
"Messieurs," he said one evening at the Procope, "congratulate me ; a little comedy of mine, *L'Impatient,* is to
be represented at the Comédie Française, and I am to be
there at the meeting to-morrow at eleven o'clock in the
morning." Some of those present, aware that if he
failed to keep the appointment the piece would be
shelved for six months, promptly concerted a stratagem
for keeping him away. Ostensibly to "commemorate
the important event he had announced," they asked him
to join them at supper in a well-known little hostelry on
the outskirts of Paris, and the invitation was smilingly
accepted as a testimony to his fact rising reputation.
Over the table, apparently by mere chance, the conversation turned upon recent exploits of assassins and
robbers in that neighbourhood, perhaps the worst lighted
in the city. Poinsinet listened to it all with staring
eyes, and, unconsciously playing into the hands of the
conspirators, determined to remain for the night in the
hostelry. Before going to bed he anxiously enjoined
the hostess to wake him at nine o'clock, so that he
might not be too late for the "assemblée des comédiens." It was an hour after that before the poet's
slumbers ended. "Morbleu !" he cried, "I have not a
moment to lose ; fetch a perruquier." His wig dressed, he

proceeded to draw on his breeches, which then resolved themselves into two divisions. Nearly every stitch in them had been severed during his sleep. In an agony of distress he had recourse to the cook, who consented to patch them up after a fashion, but who, having been taken by his tormentors into their confidence, did her work in such a way that he could not get his legs through the unfortunate garment. Beside himself with fury, he next sent a commissionaire to his house with a note asking for another pair of breeches to be sent to him without delay. It was duly intercepted, and the plotters, in explanation of the non-arrival of what he expected, pleasantly suggested that the commissionaire, a shabbily-dressed person, had appropriated the parcel to his own use. Midday had now come, and Poinsinet, making the best of his irreverently treated clothing, slunk home with the mournful idea—which was fully realized—that six months more would elapse before his piece saw the light. For the rest, *L'Impatient* was produced only to be withdrawn, the audience, as a wit in the green-room remarked, assisting in the performance of the title-part from beginning to end.

Boissy passes away from us at this point. In his closing days, by a mere accident, he found himself elevated to comparative opulence, though not until he had drunk the cup of poverty to its very dregs. " Do

you know," said Madame de Pompadour to Marmontel
one evening at Fontainebleau, "that Labruère," the
author of the *Mécontents*, "is dead? I mean he who
held the patent of the *Mercure*. Now, this patent was
worth £1,000 a year to him; there is enough to make
more than one happy man, and we intend to saddle the
new patent with a few pensions for men of letters.
Name to me those who deserve such pensions." Marmontel, inwardly coveting the patent for himself, mentioned, among others, the unfortunate Boissy, whom
he scarcely knew. "Is not Boissy rich?" Madame
asked. "I thought him at least in easy circumstances.
I have seen him always well dressed." "No, madame,
he is poor, but disguises the fact. In short —shall I
say it?—he is so far from rich that but for the intervention of a friend he would have perished last winter
from want. Without bread, and too proud to ask for
it from anybody, he and his wife and son were going
to kill themselves in each other's arms when this helping friend forced in his way upon and saved them."
Madame de Pompadour, with "tears in her eyes," went
to recommend the starving poet to the King, who gave
him the patent of the *Mercure* itself. For a time the
paper did not thrive in his hands. He was not a
heaven-born editor, but Marmontel, on whom one of
the pensions had been conferred, came to his rescue with
the first of those *Contes Moraux* which have obtained so

wide and deserved a reputation.   Boissy did not live
long to enjoy this gleam of prosperity ; he died on the
19th of April in the present year.

Marmontel, still befriended by Madame de Pompadour,
became the new editor of the *Mercure*, and in this
capacity was the means of widely extending the scope
and influence of French journalism.   He turned the
periodical into a systematic and pleasing record of the
progress of literature, art, and science, with the whole
of its criticism marked by a judicial and kindly tone.
" To men of letters," he wrote in the preface to his first
volume, " I purpose to speak the language of truth,
decorum, and esteem ; and my attention in exalting
the beauties of their works will justify the freedom with
which I shall observe their defects."   In one respect,
perhaps, the spirit underlying these words was felt with
particular force.   Dramatic criticism worthy of the name
had not yet been created in France.   What passed for
it was simply a brief and arid report, often coloured
by envy, hatred, and all uncharitableness.   Marmontel
rose superior to this in principle and practice.   He
strove to blend deserved censure with equally deserved
eulogy.   If he ever showed undue tenderness it was in
the case of young authors, partly because the kindly
encouragement he received from Voltaire had enabled
him to achieve more than the student at Toulouse had
dared to hope for.   " It should be the public care,"

he said, speaking of three a little above the rest, " to protect them, to give them heart, to console them for the ebullitions of envy. The arts need the spur of criticism and the spur of glory." Marmontel's policy may not have been theoretically unassailable, but the good he did by it can hardly be overrated. He was the founder of dramatic criticism in Paris, the precursor of the Gautiers and Janins of a much later time.

One of the first plays to experience this pleasant frankness of treatment was a *Hypermnestre* by Antoine Marin Lemierre, a spurmaker's son, born at Paris in 1733. Already had he been talked of in the coffee-houses as a sort of prodigy. In his teens, having shown a remarkable quickness and taste for learning, he was sent to a college of the University, although his parents could barely afford to give him a less expensive education. He amply justified their confidence, prize after prize fell to his lot, and on turning out into the world he was made secretary to Fermier-Général Dupin. Making an exemplary use of his leisure, he threw off a variety of short poems, many of which were deservedly crowned by the French Academy. It may be assumed that the " fair hopes " thus raised as to his future were not largely disappointed by his *Hypermnestre*. By no means a work of capital importance, it yet contained, as Marmontel duly remarked, one or two scenes of conspicuous

force, and was distinctly ahead of the tragedy by Riupérous on the same subject. In writing a play, however,
Lemierre laboured under two heavy disadvantages—an
incurable tendency to make his characters reason on the
principles of the new philosophy, which found in him
an ardent advocate, and a singular insensibility to
melody and refinement of style. " Lend me a pen,"
he once said to a player, intending to make some
changes in a part designed for the latter. " Why not
seek to find Racine's ? " he was not impertinently
asked.

Madame de Grafigny's connexion with the first
theatre in the realm was to be very brief. Not content with the success of *Cénie*, she had written another
pathetic comedy in prose, *La Fille d'Aristide*. It was
barely heard to the end ; and the amiable authoress,
then in feeble health, died shortly afterwards " of a
broken heart." According to one sketch of her career,
the piece had been reconstructed about twenty times,
and in its final form was far less effective than at any
previous stage of the process. Madame de Grafigny,
whose best title to fame lies in the *Lettres d'une Péru-
vienne*, left behind her four or five comedies, each in one
act. They were represented at the Court of Vienna by
the children of the Emperor, but did not appear at the
Comédie Française.

In the last days of the year an actor of celebrity

abroad came to Paris to make a début at the Comédie,
though only to figure there as a dramatic author.
Pierre Laurent Debelloy was born at St. Flour, Auvergne,
in 1727.   In early life he became an orphan, and his
uncle, M. Buirette, an avocat au Parlement in the
capital, brought him up for the law.   How far he liked
the profession intended for him may be inferred from the
fact that at the age of twenty he turned strolling player.
Having succeeded beyond his expectations, he ventured
to make a tour of northern Europe, and for some years
was one of the favourite actors of the Empress Elizabeth
at St. Petersburg.   For all this, however, his heart
yearned towards his native country.

> Ah ! de ses fils absents la France est plus chérie ;
> Plus je vis l'étranger plus j'aimai ma patrie,

he once burst out.   Eventually, after writing a *Titus*, he
set out for Paris in the hope of distinguishing himself
both as a dramatist and as a player.   Buirette, ashamed
of his nephew's connexion with a calling under the ban
of the Church, at once obtained, on what pretext we are
not informed, an order for his arrest, but promised to
withhold it if he forbore to appear on the stage.   Infirmity of purpose was not among the old advocate's
shortcomings, and Debelloy, overawed by the threat
held out to him, returned for a season to the banks of
the Niemen.   Before doing so, however, he interested
the players in his tragedy, which had but a single

representation. " Ahem," remarked Favart, mindful of his Roman history, " Titus perdit un jour ; un jour perdit *Titus.*"

Destouches' *Fausse Agnès*, which bears more than an accidental resemblance to the *Folies Amoureuses*, and which, in its turn, afforded Mrs. Cowley some of the materials for the *Belle's Stratagem*, was the last novelty produced before the Easter recess, when Sarrazin, Mlle. Lamotte, and Lathorillière took leave of the stage. Exactly thirty years had elapsed since the first left the priesthood to become a player, and during the whole of this period his reputation as a *roi* and *père* had stood deservedly high. He had not all the physical force needed for the former, but was never wanting in sensibility, refinement, and distinction. His Lusignan in *Zaïre* seems to have silenced criticism itself. He retired in consequence of a bronchial complaint, which carried him off in 1762. Lathorillière, as we have seen, began his career of thirty-seven years as a tragedian, but found his true vocation in *financiers, rôles à manteaux*, and *pères comiques*. His departure, soon to be followed by his death, excited a regret for reasons apart from his histrionic talents ; he was the grandson of Molière's Lathorillière, and his name formed a sort of link between the Golden Age and the less fruitful present. In Mlle. Lamotte, still one of the prettiest of actresses, the public lost an eminent representative of characters for

which the grace of her manner in private life might
have been thought to unfit her—the ridiculous old
women formerly played by men. No performance of
Tartuffe had been deemed complete without her Madame
Pernelle.

By far the most important of the few reforms required
at the Comédie Française was suddenly accomplished at
the reopening of the theatre. From that evening inclusive the stage was cleared of the swarms of dandies who
had so long been permitted to sit there in sight of the
audience in the *salle*. For many years past, but more
especially since the production of *Sémiramis,* Voltaire
had never been tired of recording protests, both in
writing and in conversation, against this very curious
custom. Did it not confound the movements of the
players with the vanity and giddiness of the privileged
spectators, make illusion well nigh an impossibility, and
tend to restrict the scope of the drama ? His arguments,
with the help of the increased effect produced by *Sémiramis* when the seats were temporarily abolished, gradually brought thinking amateurs of the theatre over to
his opinion, and a widespread desire for the suppression
of so grave an abuse at length became manifest. Even
then, however, the players as a body hesitated to make
the change by which they had so much to gain in an
artistic sense. It might at once diminish their receipts
—a consideration not to be overlooked—and lead to

a destructive riot in the theatre. In reply to these
representations, a frivolous but clever frequenter of the
green-room, the Comte de Lauragais, offered to give the
company 12,000 livres if they granted the coveted boon.
His offer was accepted; and the mass of gaily be-
dizened spectators at each side of the stage, with their
supercilious airs, their affectations of languor, their
insolent ogling of the pit, their often audible whispers
in the middle of an impressive scene, vanished from
sight without making an effort to retain their old
privilege. Henceforward the dramatist was in a position
to aim at greater breadth of effect, the player to illustrate the full power of his art, and the audience to
understand what theatrical illusion really meant.

Some young actresses went through débuts under
these improved conditions. First in order of time, as
of merit, was a Mlle. Rosalie, who displayed so much
force as Camille and other robust characters that her
admission to the company was deemed a certainty.
Prepared for the stage by Clairon, Mlle. Dubois,
daughter of an actor of that name, represented Didon,
Hermione, Camille, and Constance in the *Préjugé à la
Mode*. Her acting was a feeble and colourless imitation
of her teacher's, and would have been condemned without mercy if she had not possessed singular beauty. Of
the third débutante, Mlle. Camouche, no record is
preserved. Now, only one place in the theatre had to

be filled, and the company gave a performance of
Iphigénie for the purpose of testing the comparative
merits of the trio. Mlle. Rosalie was the Eriphile,
Mlle. Dubois the heroine, and Mlle. Camouche the
Clytemnestre. Nobody could doubt that the first-named
carried away the palm, but the established players,
apparently at the instance of the Gentlemen of the
Chamber, decided to elect Mlle. Dubois. Mlle. Rosalie,
sensible of the injustice with which she had been treated,
did not reappear at the Comédie, contenting herself with
the laurels to be gathered in provincial theatres by an
actress of unquestionable ability.

Rotrou's *Venceslas* was among the old tragedies which
now had the advantage of being performed on a stage
unencumbered with fops. But a false taste prevented
it from reappearing as it left the poet's hands. Madame
de Pompadour, wishing to see it at Court, had prevailed
upon Marmontel, much against his inclination, to weed
out its real and fancied crudities of diction—in other
words, to bring it up to the standard of eighteenth-
century refinement. None of the players objected to
the alterations except Lekain, who, cast for the fiery
Ladislas, was lured by an unreasoning dislike of the
adapter into taking a very singular course. He privately
employed Colardeau to re-write the part for him, and,
without acquainting any of the players with his inten-
tions, played it according to the interpolations and

excisions then made.   Consequently, from the beginning
to the end of the performance, which took place at
Versailles, the utmost confusion existed among the
company.   Lekain's irritable and impulsive temperament often made him do foolish things, but this was
the worst of all.   Marmontel complained loudly of the
actor's "insolence," and Madame de Pompadour gave
orders that on the piece being represented in Paris it
should be without Colardeau's verses.   Lekain, not entirely to be beaten, took advantage of the vagueness of
this message to follow the original text in Ladislas as
closely as the changes effected in the other characters
would allow—a step which led to a lively controversy
in the press respecting the *Venceslas* of Rotrou and the
Venceslas Retouché.   In the end, at the instance of the
Duc d'Aumont, who stood by Lekain, Marmontel was
arbitrarily commanded to hold his peace, and an actor
had to undergo a short imprisonment at For l'Evêque
for having written to the *Mercure* on the subject without
the knowledge of his comrades.

Passing to absolute novelties, we find two youthful
poets, Poinsinet de Sivri and Claude Joseph Dorat,
leaping suddenly into fame.   In a *Briséis*, the former
connected some of the most dramatic incidents of the
Iliad with a skilful and sympathetic hand, and a peculiar
brilliancy with which the leading parts were sustained
by Lekain and Mlle. Gaussin left nothing wanting to

his triumph. " Obligé de se montrer sur la scène, il
y parut avec modestie, au bruit d'un applaudissement
général," one of the journals said. Sivri was then only
twenty-six, but had already done some honour to his
Alma Mater, the Collége de la Marche, by writing a
variety of poems, chiefly amatory, and translations from
Anacreon, Moschus, and Bion. His father is said to
have been a *huissier du cabinet* to the Duc d'Orléans.
Dorat, who came of a good family, and who, after a
vain attempt to fall in love with the law and then with
military life, had begun to devote himself to literature
of all kinds, met with as much success as Sivri, though
not quite as soon. His first essay at the theatre was
a tragedy entitled *Zulica*. Before its representation
it had been read and praised in many a salon. " One
may easily imagine," he writes, " how great was my
intoxication, how high ran my hopes. In imagination
I felt the piece extolled to the skies. I aspired to
nothing less than immortality. At the first representation the scales dropped from my eyes. It was the stroke
of the wand that changed the gardens of Armida into a
desert. Four acts were received with transport; the
fifth, on which I depended the most," and in which
Crébillon the younger had persuaded him to make
radical changes, " brought the representation to a dis-
astrous end." But the actors did not leave him to
despair. M. de Latouche had reconstructed a defective

act at the shortest notice : could not M. Dorat do the
same ?   He undertook to do so ; and from the 12th of
January, when it was played for the second time,
Zulica became a highly popular piece.   In one sense,
there can be no doubt, Dorat's success did him more
harm than good.   It rekindled his aspirations to the
point of making him believe that he was the long-
sought rival to Voltaire.   In this he largely overrated
his powers.   " His little tales," as Fleury says, " were
remarkably clever, his poetic epistles really elegant
and graceful.   He might have earned a creditable share
of reputation at a period when a quatrain for a lady's
fan would confer it.   Instead of being content to soar
upon the wings of the dove, however, he attempted to
take the eagle's flight," with what result we shall
presently see.

Meanwhile, happily unconscious of the tribulations
intended for him, the author of the *Henriade*, after
" refining in a visible degree the manners of Lausanne,"
had finally settled at Ferney, on the western shores of
Lake Leman.   He built in this spot a pretty little
château, decorated it throughout in his usual taste, and
surrounded it with gardens laid out in the English style.
Enriched by literary success and shrewd speculations,
he began to live in it as a seigneur of the old school,
extending the most genial and munificent hospitality
to friends and strangers alike.   Nothing afforded him

keener delight than to regale his guests with a dramatic performance—for a theatre, it need hardly be said, was among the adjuncts of the new home—and afterwards with a supper and a ball. He often sat at the side of the stage to prompt and inspire the players, and on one occasion, during a representation of *Zaïre*, was so far carried away by excitement as to wheel his chair by degrees up to the hero and heroine. "Even now," wrote one of the spectators half a century later, "I seem to see him in his ordinary dress—gray stockings and shoes, a woollen waistcoat coming down almost to his knees, an ample wig squeezed into a little black velvet cap turned up in front, and finally a large dressing-gown, the corners of which he would sometimes tuck into the bands of his small-clothes. In such a costume anybody else would have looked like a caricature, but Voltaire's appearance never suggested an idea of the ridiculous." For in his presence it was difficult to be conscious of anything but the unimpaired brilliancy of his wit and fancy. His generous impulses seem to have gathered a new strength with time. For example, learning that a grand-niece of Corneille was in poverty, he received her into his family, treated her as a daughter, and, in order to provide her with a dowry in a form as little like a gift as possible, prepared an edition, with more or less valuable *Commentaires* of his own, of her ancestor's plays. "An old soldier," he said, "may well be glad to have an opportunity of being useful to his general's child." Of his exertions in behalf of the desolate and oppressed, such as the Calases and the Sirvens, it is unnecessary to speak. Nor were these the only ways in which his pleasure in doing good manifested itself. He drained the adjacent land, studded it with cottages for Genevese artizans of good character, and so converted a miserable hamlet into a populous and thriving colony. Yet, despite all these distractions, his pen was as active as before. He invariably had literary work of some kind on hand, besides getting through an amount of correspondence that might have exhausted two or three ordinary men. Indeed, it was not until after he had settled in his present retreat, whither pilgrimages were made in constantly increasing numbers, that the sort of royalty which he had so long exercised over Europe rose to its full height.

Ferney came to be associated in some degree with a radical change of national thought. Voltaire was now appearing before the world in a new character. His attitude towards Christianity had previously been one of unbelief tempered with respect. In the *Epître à Uranie* he had spoken of the Saviour in a tone almost of reverence :—

> Ses exemples sont saints ; sa morale est divine ;
> Il console en secret les cœurs qu'il illumine ;
> Dans les plus grands malheurs il leur offre un appui ;
> Et si sur l'imposture il fonde sa doctrine,
> C'est un bonheur encore d'être trompé par lui.

Zaïre and *Alzire*, too, had depicted religious enthusiasm
in the brightest colours. But the failure hitherto of
the poet's attempts to extirpate some of the abuses of
ecclesiastical power led him by degrees into a very
different course. He assailed the faith of his forefathers with peculiar energy and bitterness, generally
employing for his purpose the arguments of the English
deists, and bringing to his task a genius for mockery
which has been not untruly described as the most
terrible of all the intellectual weapons ever wielded by
man. His voice was not as of one crying in the
wilderness; each of his polemics, trivial in form as it
might be, sent an electric shock through the whole
frame of civilization. In his anti-Christian zeal, however, he never rejected the claims of natural religion.
He believed as firmly in the existence of a Supreme
Ruler as any of the bigots who craved to hear of his
death. He would often rise at daybreak, toil feebly
up a hill near his house to see the sun rise over the
lake, and then, drinking in the exquisite beauty of the
scene, with his meagre figure bent before it in a spirit
of simple piety, give vent to exclamations which, it has
been remarked, strike upon the ear like a hymn—
" Almighty Framer of the skies, I bow down and worship
thee !" Equally fervent, though with far less effect
on his practice, was the deism of another declared
enemy of the priesthood, Jean Jacques Rousseau. But

a band of profound thinkers who had begun by sitting at Voltaire's feet—Diderot, D'Alembert, Holbach,
Helvétius, Raynal, and the rest—came to reject his
creed with almost as much contempt as they heaped
upon Christianity itself.   In the *Encyclopédie*, perhaps
the most representative work of the century, they
moved to a standpoint not distinguishable from that
of pure atheism.   Much to the astonishment of David
Hume, who met them under an impression that he
would not be found the least sceptical of the party, they
laughed at him for supposing the existence of a God to
be even probable.   Their principles amounted to a
direct negation of the highest yearnings of the human
heart.   It was in vain that Voltaire sought to rein in
these hardy materialists; they left him further and
further behind.   In one respect, however, they entirely
agreed with their sometime master.   He had said that a
Church so infamous as that of France must be destroyed,
and *Ecrasons l'Infâme*, "down with the abomination,"
forthwith took the first place on the banner they unfurled.   The clergy, on their side, were not disposed to
fall without striking a blow.   Foiled in an attempt to
gag their adversaries, who had friends at Court in
Madame de Pompadour and the Duc de Choiseul, they
met argument with argument, ridicule with ridicule,
paradox with paradox.   In this conflict they were as a
child in the grasp of a giant.   No Bossuet or Fénélon

rose among them to stem the tide of infidelity. Except
the scholarly and ironical Guénée, their spokesmen
were at best of the secondary order. In the way of
outside support they had nothing better to depend
upon than that of a Palissot or a Fréron. Lastly, while
consciously weakened by the effects of the revocation of
the Nantes edict, they daily became more hateful to the
people on account of their continued hostility to the
spread of education, their bitter and relentless persecu-
tion of heterodoxy in any shape, and the nearly undis-
guised profligacy in which so many of their number
lived. In all these circumstances, of course, the philosophers had no difficulty in making it appear that they
achieved an absolute victory. They seemed to fill the
whole public mind with their thought. Orthodoxy
became a byword of derision ; the services in the
churches were gradually abandoned to a few. France,
the mother of the reverent and elaborate Mystery,
identified herself with denial in its most chilling aspect,
but a denial which brought good as well as evil in its
train. Of the philosophical sect, as of their nominal
patriarch at Ferney, it may be said that no human
teachers ever left behind them "so vast and terrible
a wreck of truths and falsehoods, of things noble and
things base, of things useful and things pernicious."

But the onslaught thus made upon religion was merely
part of a movement that made itself felt throughout the

land. Men had begun to yearn for the reconstruction
of society upon a new basis.   Every existing institution
was an object of hatred, ridicule, and scorn.   For the
origin of this revolutionary spirit we are obviously
indebted to Voltaire.   His banishment from France in
1726 may be regarded as an event of great historical
importance.   If the authorities had foreseen the consequences of that step they would have sacrificed twenty
Chevaliers de Rohan rather than let him go to London.
His admiring *Lettres sur les Anglais* had done more than
infect his countrymen with a taste for the literature and
philosophy of their ancient enemy.   England, until then
as little known to them as the far East, was here represented in all the vigour of her ordered freedom, with the
happiness and material prosperity it engendered.   The
spectacle awakened them to a sense of the degrading
and hurtful conditions under which they lived.   Facts
long glossed over by the splendours of Versailles—the
arbitrary nature of the government, the enslavement
of the people, the fetters imposed upon liberty of discussion, and last, but not least, the special privileges
of the nobles, who, while exempted from taxation, had
an almost exclusive claim to posts of honour and profit
and utility — seem to have been forced upon every
reflecting mind.   Before long a party in favour of
limited monarchy dared to raise its head, Montesquieu
aiding it with his *Grandeur et Décadence des Romains,*

printed in the same year as the *Lettres sur les Anglais*, and again in his *Esprit des Lois* (1748). Grimm speaks of the latter work as effecting a complete revolution in the ideas of the nation. " Government," he adds, " is becoming more and more a matter of philosophic treatment and argument." How fast the agitation spread may be gathered from an oft-quoted sentence in a letter written by Lord Chesterfield in 1753—" all the symptoms I have ever met with in history previous to great changes and revolutions in governments now exist and daily increase in France." Neither Voltaire nor Montesquieu aimed at anything beyond moderate reform ; both were of aristocratic sympathies, and would have recoiled from any political system that did not secure the ascendency of education, wealth, and demonstrated intelligence. For the rights of the *canaille*, as the former hastily called the mass of the people, they unquestionably cared very little. In this they were not at one with a man who followed them to the forum. Jean Jacques Rousseau, emboldened by the success of his declamations against literature and art, profited by the unsettled state of the public mind to embody his dark dreamings of revolution. He ascribed the misery of the world to the despotism of kings, the rapacity of nobles, the pretensions of priests, and the so-called benefits of civilization in general. Men, he contended, were born free, equal, and innocent. In the untutored

savage you had a model of all the virtues. Rightly
understood, society rested upon a sort of contract, under
which the will of the people at large ought to be supreme.
They might at times be misled, but were always to be
obeyed. " Despots," he continued, " reign only by the
might of the strongest. The insurrection which sends
a sultan to the scaffold is as lawful an act as his disposition of the lives and property of his subjects. It
is manifestly contrary to natural law that a child
should govern a man, that the imbecile should guide
the wise, and that a few should revel in luxury while
the many are in absolute want." Penned with impassioned eloquence, the book fully expounding these
theories, the *Contrat Social* excited an enthusiasm to
which no parallel can be found. It inflamed the awakening democracy with fresh ideas and aspirations. It
turned their demand for constitutional monarchy into
one for republicanism pure and simple. It became to
them what the Bible had been to the English Puritans
of the previous century. Most of the Encyclopædists
strove to better the instruction it conveyed ; Diderot
assailed the principle of property in land—a principle
as to which Rousseau was apparently unable to form a
decided opinion—and the Abbé Raynal wrote, or helped
to write, a *Histoire des Indes* in order to hold up a
seductive picture of mankind in an uncivilized state.
" Imbeciles," was one appeal made to the people in the

latter work, " you are content to groan when you ought
to roar !" And this current of hostility to the old
system was accelerated rather than retarded by those
whom it threatened to overwhelm. Louis XV., to do
him justice, had the intelligence to perceive the approaching danger, but could not be diverted from
courses that could scarcely fail to aggravate it. He
continued to steep the Court in the mire of corruption,
made the position of his mistress an office of State,
allowed girls of tender age to be dragged from their
homes to the Parc-aux Cerfs for the gratification of his
lust, and used all the machinery at his command—the
censorship, lettres de cachet, and the Bastille—to prevent
as far as possible the dissemination of anti-monarchical
ideas. His sole anxiety was that the " deluge " should
not come in his time. Moreover, like moths hovering
about a flame just lighted, many of the nobles, while
insolently maintaining the invidious distinction between
themselves and the rest of the community, thought fit
to coquet with the most advanced doctrines, partly on
account of their agreeable novelty, but chiefly because
one of them sanctioned licentiousness in the name of
liberty. On the whole, the state of France at this
period was such as to suggest that society there was fast
crumbling to pieces. Nine-tenths of the populace seem
to have hungered for more or less drastic changes ; a
love of innovation for its own sake appeared in nearly

all walks of life ; the pole-star of reason was to be
followed in preference to the teachings of the past.   In
one sense the Girondists and the Mountain had already
come upon the scene, the former being represented by
Voltaire, who retained to the end his admiration of
English constitutionalism, and the other by Rousseau,
with the difference that he would have refused to
purchase national happiness at the cost of a single life.
Nothing but hopeless confusion in the finances was
needed to bring matters to a crisis, and into such
confusion, with the rising sect of the Economists to
explain its real causes, the finances were rapidly falling.
"Yes," Voltaire would remark with alternate hope and
misgiving, "a revolution will assuredly come, though
not until I am in the grave.   Happy are the young,
they will see great things!"   For to him, as to a
few other keen observers, the cloud rising above the
horizon had only one meaning.   It might be no
bigger at present than a man's hand, but was to
spread and spread until it enveloped the whole world
in darkness.

From the time when this portent appeared the history
of the stage has an other than dramatic and histrionic
interest.   It deserves to be studied by those who would
mark the progress of the democratic passion lately
excited in the country.   By what may seem a special
irony of fate, the Théâtre Français added largely to

the forces arrayed against the absolutism which it had been formed to strengthen. From their own point of view the powers that were would have done well to subject its repertory to a thorough overhauling. Many tragedies of high poetic value abounded in idealized pictures of republican antiquity, besides cogent arguments as to the merits and demerits of different principles of government. No exceptional sagacity, it may be thought, was needed to perceive the inevitable effect of the representation of such pieces on a people notoriously susceptible to beauties of thought and style, embittered against the Bourbon *régime*, enraptured with the utopia opened out before them in the *Contrat Social*, and not always capable of discriminating between the fanciful and the true. But the Court overlooked the peril; the tragedies in question continued to be played as often as the company pleased, and the " gospel according to Rousseau " derived fresh weight and influence from the visions they conjured up of the virtues of a republic. It was less out of books than at the theatre in the Rue des Fossés St. Germain that the rising generation imbibed the taste for classical illustration which lent so distinctive a colouring to the oratory and literature of the Revolution. Not unfrequently, too, a new play contained passages of a nature to fan the fast-spreading antagonism to the throne and the altar, the censor appointed to examine it being either careless, wanting

in penetration, or an iconoclast in disguise. Death was
to be the punishment of those who attacked religion or
the monarchical principle, but a dramatist offending in
this way seems to have been exempt from any sort of
penalty save the frowns of the Court. Of the influence
exerted by the drama a very inadequate conception existed
at Versailles. Nor is it simply as disclosing a comparatively unchecked incentive to revolution that the
records of the Comédie Française invite our attention.
Parisians of all grades flocked to what may be termed
the last refuge of free discussion in the country ; a flash
of genius gave them less pleasure than a satirical glance
at the abuses of power, and their attitude towards a
play or a player was often determined by political
sympathies alone. In the moods of the parterre at
particular moments, indeed, we may see as in a mirror
the gathering of the most terrible social storm that had
broken over Europe since the collapse of the Roman
empire.

CHAPTER III.

1760—1766.

In the winter of 1753 4 a curious thing happened at the bureau in Paris of M. de Gagny, Intendant des Finances. Perched upon a stool at a desk, with a mass of accounts before him, was a handsome and buoyant-looking young clerk, by name François René Molet. But his thoughts were not with the work on which he seemed to be engaged. He aspired to theatrical honours, and in imagination was receiving the applause of the critical audience of the Comédie Française. In his desk one might have discovered a rich variety of plays, programmes, and books relating to the stage. Presently, in the belief that M. de Gagny had gone for the day, he put aside his accounts, placed the chairs so as to form a dummy auditorium, arranged the table-cloth over his shoulders in the way of a tragic mantle, and then, springing on to the table itself, began to recite some of the finest bursts of poetry in the French drama. In the middle of this practice, just as he had struck a most impressive attitude, his master,

having forgotten to give him a necessary order, noiselessly entered the room.

Before saying how the Intendant acted in these grave
circumstances, which he had no reason to anticipate,
we may possess ourselves of the previous history of the
ambitious youth on the table. He was born in Paris
in 1734, the youngest of three sons. His father had
been in a good social position, but had brought himself
to the necessity of living by an art which in happier
days he had cultivated for his amusement, that of
engraving. He did not succeed; friends fell away one
by one, and the family were often reduced to the
hardest straits. Death came to his release in 1750, and
his remains would have been consigned to the *fosse*
if François René, stung to the quick by the prospect
of such a humiliation, had not prevailed upon a flinty-
hearted old miser in the neighbourhood to lend him
ten louis on his own security. Not long afterwards he
had the good fortune to obtain employment at M. de
Gagny's—employment which may not have been to
his taste, but which enabled him at least to give his
mother a helping hand, to repay the ten louis (Harpagon,
admiring the boy's spirit, would not take any interest
for the loan), and to pay an occasional visit to the
theatre in the Rue des Fossés St. Germain.

For a few minutes the Intendant looked about him
in mute bewilderment. His clerk enveloped in the

ample folds of the table-cloth, declaiming a tirade from one of the great tragic dramatists, with the chairs displaced to form an imaginary *salle*—could he believe such things to be possible? This, then, was the way in which the Sieur Molet attended to his duties during his master's absence? But the discovery did not prove so unlucky for the youth as might have been expected. M. de Gagny, himself a cultured playgoer, had conceived a liking for his active-minded clerk, and was far from being insensible to the humour of the situation. "It is quite clear," he at length remarked, "in what direction your tastes lie. You are going to be an actor. Fate has decreed it. Well, to facilitate your progress I will give you a little more leisure without reducing your emoluments."

Molet profited by this kindness not only to pay more visits to the theatre, which he was usually the first to enter and the last to leave, but to join a band of amateur players in the Temple, where, as at some soirées in M. de Gagny's house, he distinguished himself so favourably that the Gentlemen of the Chamber voluntarily sent him an order for a début at the Comédie Française. He began on the 7th of November 1754, not having completed his twentieth year. Behind the scenes he could hardly persuade himself that it was not a dream. Many of the players whom he had reverently admired from the pit—the impassioned

Clairon, the tragic Lekain, the queenly Dumesnil, the richly comic Préville, the elegant Bellecourt, the sparkling Marie Dangeville, the still beautiful and voluptuous Gaussin—these and others were present, some to be with him on the stage, others simply to look on, all to give him a word of encouragement. Both at this and subsequent essays he carried the audience with him; but the judges, thinking that he had much to learn by experience, especially in the management of his voice, which was by no means strong, relegated him for a time to the provinces.

From the night of his reappearance, the 28th of January this year, Molet (now Molé) occupied a well-defined position at the theatre. Nature seemed to have formed him to represent the young heroes of tragedy and comedy. His acting, it is true, was somewhat unequal, his delivery not altogether pleasing. But, as one of his rivals remarked many years later, he could hardly have been improved by the correction of his faults. In all his impersonations there was an indescribable charm. He was a personification of youth, grace, and vivacity, with a fine appreciation of the poetical and the humorous. " Some of his most admirable touches," Fleury says, " occurred when he chanced to forget his part; while recovering his memory he would draw down his ruffles, play with his cravat, search for his snuff-box, or pass his hat from one hand to another with a peculiar drollery of manner." Indeed, it may be said that he owed little to his handsome figure and countenance, though these made him a sort of idol to the gentler sex. His success did not blind him to the importance of continued study. Petted at Court and in Paris, he profited with the eagerness of a true artist by the opportunities thus given him of noting the airs and graces of the counterparts in real life of characters which he preferred—courtiers, rakes, *petits-maîtres*, and the like—and reproduced those airs and graces with brilliant fidelity. By and by the relative positions of the model and the copyist were reversed; the young noblesse flocked to the theatre for the purpose of improving their deportment by his. Edmund Burke, it may be remembered, used at the same period to borrow tricks of oratory by listening to Garrick at Drury-lane. When we find what sort of person Molé was—self-satisfied, fond of society, ever ready for an amorous intrigue, and by no means indifferent to the pleasures of the table—the time and thought he certainly devoted to his art will appear more remarkable (*d*).

Molé's début was speedily followed by the first palpable indication of the revolutionary change now coming over the public mind. The players, after producing a rather impressive tragedy by Saurin, *Spartacus*, accepted a comedy by Palissot, *Les Philosophes*. Here, prompted by Madame de Robecq and Madame de

Lamarck, both of whom had a personal grudge against Diderot, the young dramatist had at length ventured to hold up some of the *philosophes* to derision and contempt. *Les Femmes Savantes* and *Les Précieuses Ridicules* appear to have provided him with his plot. Infatuated with three philosophers of the most advanced ideas, a stupid woman in society hopes that one of them will become her son-in-law, although her daughter loves and is loved by Damis. In the sequel, finding that they have requited her hospitality by lampooning her, she visits them with the profoundest humiliation. Now, in this trio of characters we have serious caricatures of Diderot, Helvétius, and Jean Jacques Rousseau, the last of whom, in allusion to one of his special doctrines, is made to appear on all fours. Clairon, quick to perceive the truth, induced her comrades to reject the piece; but the Court, chancing to hear of its drift, eagerly ordered it to be played. Played it was on the second of May, with a representative audience filling every nook and corner of the house. Neat and witty as the satire often was, it aroused many deep murmurs of resentment in the pit, and all the exertions of the Court-party were needed to give *Les Philosophes* the semblance of being successful. Palissot had personal reasons for not including the most conspicuous of the philosophers among those so assailed. Four years previously he had made a sort of pilgrimage to Voltaire at the Délices, and, though a stranger to his host, had been received there with a kindness which completely won his heart. Besides that, he may have shrunk from laying himself open to such blistering ridicule as that of *Doctor Akakia.*

This comedy against the philosophers was to be succeeded by one satirizing the most powerful of their lay adversaries. I speak of Fréron, the conductor of the *Année Littéraire.* It is strange that this sarcastic ex-Jesuit had not previously met with such a castigation. For about fifteen years he had aspired to play the part of an Aristarchus in Paris, first in contributions to Desfontaine's *Observations sur les Ecrits Modernes,* afterwards in *Lettres de la Comtesse de* ——, and lastly in the more famous periodical just mentioned. Influenced less by respect for religion than a desire to extend the sale of his work by assailing the great, he made himself a thorn in the sides of the philosophers from the outset of their career, fastening upon Voltaire with a particular acrimony of insult. His disinterestedness was not unimpeachable, and it would be difficult to overrate the harm he did to the cause of Christianity in France by standing forward in its behalf. One of his many victims, instead of wisely ignoring his existence, was at length irritated into making reprisals. In the present summer there was printed a five-act comedy, *Le Café, ou l'Ecossaise,* "by M. Hume, Pasteur de

l'Eglise d'Edimbourg," and " translated into French by
M. Jérome Carré." According to the quidnuncs of the
town, this M. Hume had already produced two excellent
tragedies at Drury-lane, and was related to " the cele-
brated M. David Hume." Mlle. Livri's peculiar adventure
in London lies at the bottom of the story, though the
incident of the sham lottery is not introduced. Fallen
from wealth to poverty, a Scotch girl, Lindane, secretly
leaves her native country to take employment at a
London coffee-house, where she wins the affections of
a Lord Murray. It is by his parents that her family
has been brought to its present straits, but this circumstance does not prevent the two from being united.
Milord has done generous service to Lindane's father, by
whom she is traced, without being aware of his relation-
ship to her, and gratitude goes with inclination to make
her accept the proffered hand. Fréron experienced a
painful shock on reading the piece. In a subordinate
but clearly drawn personage, under a name which had
the double advantage of suggesting his own and of
signifying hornet (Frelon), he found himself painted
with but a slight exaggeration of the truth—that is to
say, as a journalist selling his pen to the highest bidder,
as calumniating men of light and leading in order to
attract more attention, and as readily swearing to things
on which a prudent regard for his pocket forbade him
to lay a wager. Burning with fury, he besought the

protection of the police, who, aware that he was in good odour at Court, though not so much as a friend of religion as an opponent of the philosophers, requested the players—for the comedy was then in rehearsal—to give M. Frelon another name.

L'Ecossaise appeared at the Comédie on the 26th of July, M. Jérome Carré taking advantage of the general ignorance of English to call the professional libeller " M. Wasp." The audience that evening was divided into two parties—the friends and foes of the philosophers. In the centre of the orchestra, with a courage that failed him in no emergency, the editor of the *Année Littéraire*, alternately reddening and growing pale before the objurgations showered upon him as the advocate of an "exploded superstition," defiantly awaited the outcome of the performance. Victory could not but declare itself against him *L'Ecossaise*, if not rich in humour, at least bristled with wit; one of its characters, Free-port, was an improvement upon that of the welcome merchant captain in Dufresny's *Faux Honnéte-Homme*, and the satire directed against the unscrupulous journalist seldom failed to hit its mark. " Do not distress yourself," said a friend of Favart's to Madame Fréron, who was in the amphitheatre; " this Wasp bears no resemblance to its presumed original; your husband is neither a libeller nor an informer." " Ah, Monsieur," she replied, " you speak in vain; he will always be seen in the character." In the result, *L'Ecossaise* met with the "greatest success," partly by reason of its intrinsic merits (the cool-headed Grimm thought it would introduce a "simpler and more natural style than was to be found in ordinary comedy"), but chiefly because of its attack upon the arch-enemy of the philosophers. By a powerful effort of volition, Fréron managed to write of it in his paper with a judicious affectation of good temper, but also with a rather obvious conviction that, as his wife had foreseen, he and M. Wasp would be inseparably associated in the public mind. "I have heard a good deal," Voltaire writes to a friend on the 6th of August, "of the comedy *L'Ecossaise*, translated from the English of M. Hume, a Scotch clergyman. It is said that Fréron recognizes himself therein ; but could any one dare to speak ill of one who, like him, has never spoken ill of others ?" Meanwhile, it appears, the air had become thick with a rumour that *L'Ecossaise*, far from being a translation, was of home production— a rumour strengthened by the essentially French tone and *verve* of the whole. Eventually, to the confusion of the quidnuncs who had known so much about him, M. Hume turned out to be a pure myth, and a passing flutter of surprise and excitement was created by the discovery that the author resided at Ferney.

From this unwelcome spectacle of a man like Voltaire crushing an adversary unworthy of his steel—a proof that his morbid sensitiveness to attack had not decreased with years—we turn to a tragedy in which his genius shone forth brightly for the last time. Nearly half a century before this, at the age of eighteen or nineteen, he indited to the Comtesse de Fontaine a set of verses as to her *Comtesse de Savoie*, then only in manuscript. Notwithstanding his youth, she had asked him to give her the benefit of his criticism upon the work, and with his usual grace he thanked her for having "permitted him to see it." Many years later, in the fulness of his power as a dramatist, he thought of making its story the groundwork of a tragedy, but was deterred from doing so by the impossibility of treating it with adequate effect for a stage encumbered with spectators. On the suppression of that abuse he eagerly returned to the project, which took him only twenty-six days to execute. Between the novel and the play, however, there was to be nothing in common except the nature of the plot. Founded upon Ariosto, who had derived it from the French mediæval theatre, the *Comtesse de Savoie* brings before us a high-born woman condemned to death, though on no better evidence than an intercepted letter without an address, on the charge of entering into correspondence with enemies of her native country. By saying for whom the letter is intended she might save her life, but as the declaration would imperil the safety of a lover she holds her peace. Believing her to be guilty, the latter

yet does battle for her in the lists, from which he comes
forth victorious. He then goes off to attack a fancied
rival, returns mortally wounded, and learns that the
letter in question was sent to himself. In *Tancrède*,
as the tragedy was called, Voltaire told this story in
a more enduring form. He does not escape a few
glaring faults of construction and style, but at the same
time gives eloquent expression to the pathos and tenderness and chivalric sentiment bound up in his narra-
tive. Especially admirable, perhaps, is the scene at the
end, in which he rises to a high tragic impressiveness by
the utmost simplicity of means. Most of the characters
are of an elevated cast, those of the hero and heroine,
respectively named Tancrède and Aménaïde, being
worthy of the pre-eminence they take in the group.
Except Corneille, none of the old French dramatists
could have drawn Orbassan, who offers to defend the
condemned princess in single combat on the condition
that if successful he shall be rewarded with her hand—
a condition she firmly refuses—and who, by the exercise
of a rare skill, is made to compel admiration without
awakening sympathy. For the rest, the author pro-
vides a more picturesque background for the piece by
transferring the scene to Syracuse at the period when
that city had thrown off the Saracenic yoke, but when
other parts of Sicily, such as Messina and Palermo,
were still in the hands of hated foreigners.

Marmontel had the privilege of reading the new tragedy before it was sent to Paris. Accompanied by a son of one of the poet's friends, Gaulard, he paid a visit to Switzerland. "Voltaire," he writes, "was in bed when we arrived. He extended to us his arms, he wept for joy as he embraced us. 'You find me dying,' he said; 'do you come to restore me to life or receive my last sighs?' My companion was alarmed at this preface; but I, having heard Voltaire a hundred times say that he was dying, gave Gaulard a gentle sign of encouragement." Early one morning the poet put a manuscript into Marmontel's hands. "Go into my room and read that," he said; "you shall give me your opinion upon it." It was *Tancrede;* and Marmontel returned to him with moistened eyes. "Who should play Aménaïde?" Voltaire asked him. "Clairon," replied the guest; "with her in it I will be warrant for a success at least equal to that of *Zaïre.*" "Your tears," said Voltaire, "tell me eloquently what I most desired to know. But the action—did you find nothing that stopped you in its march?" Marmontel answered that the public would be too much moved to think of such matters. Not long afterwards the parting of the master and pupil came. "Our adieux," the latter writes, "were tender even to tears, but much more so on my part than on his, as was natural. For, independently of my gratitude and all the reasons I had for loving him, I left him in exile."

Marmontel's foresight was abundantly justified by the fate of the tragedy in Paris.   Brought out on the 3rd of September, with Lekain and Clairon as the ill-starred lovers, *Tancrède* "tourna toutes les têtes." More than one author must have awaited the result with special curiosity.   In addition to encroaching upon the unity of place, the poet, so long disposed to maintain the drama as Racine left it, had written the piece in *vers croisés*, though in equal measure,—an innovation which had the effect of decreasing the monotony arising from regular rhyme, especially when an unvarying alternation of the masculine and feminine is followed. Before the curtain rose, Lekain made a short speech to prepare the audience for these changes, and a wit in the theatre wrote an amusing parody of it for an intended burlesque of the piece at the Comédie Italienne.   " Messieurs," the actor is said to have said, "it is necessary to inform you that the author is far away from Paris, as one might wish his play were at this moment.   He has instructed us to warn you that it is in *vers croisés*, as otherwise you might not perceive the fact.   It is also well to let you know that it *is* in verse, as in many places you might think it is in prose.   Lastly, he has taken the liberty of varying his scene, so as to resemble some great writers at least in their defects."   But these innovations, like the shortcomings already noticed, were unheeded in the enthusiasm generated by the play as it went on.   Its refined sensibility left a deep impression ; and while one section of the audience were delighted at being reminded of names and circumstances in their history on which even unbelievers dwelt with pride— of the valour shown by their forefathers in the Crusades —the democratic spirit creeping over the land was flattered by such lines as—

L'injustice à la fin produit l'indépendance—

and a passage in the dialogue between Aménaïde and her confidant :—

A leurs seuls intérêts les grands sont attachés ;
Le peuple est plus sensible. . . . Il est aussi plus juste.

Moreover, the piece is frequently marked by a realism which introduced a new element into classical tragedy, and for that reason was welcomed by a people now pre-disposed in favour of change : Aménaïde appeared in fetters ; Tancrède threw down the gauntlet to Orbassan in defying him to the combat.   As usual, the poet was extremely fortunate in his interpreters.   Lekain gave fine expression to the chivalric sentiment and mental torture of the hero, whether by voice or pantomime. His power in the latter respect was now so high that a look he cast at the walls of Syracuse on his first entrance made it needless for him to deliver the line,

A tous les cœurs bien nés que la patrie est chère !

If possible, Clairon was still more conspicuous as the
noble, tender, and fiery Aménaïde. In some degree
she was like the character itself, and the eulogies
lavished upon her impersonation of it will leave no
doubt that she exercised a species of fascination over
the audience. "Ah, mon cher maître," writes Diderot
to Voltaire, "if you could see her crossing the stage,
half leaning upon the executioners present, her knees
threatening to give way, her eyes closed, her arms
hanging down as though in death—if you could hear
her cry on recognizing Tancrède—you would be convinced more than ever that acting sometimes has a
pathos beyond all the resources of oratory." Favart
tells us that *Tancrède* came to be called "Mlle. Clairon's
tragedy"—a new form of homage to histrionic excellence.
In a word, the poet, aided by two players of rare genius,
again found himself covered with laurels, the general
verdict being that he had produced the most exquisite
play of its kind since the *Cid*. Elated by his victory, he
inscribed *Tancrède* to Madame de Pompadour, not only
in the expectation that she might yet procure him the
liberty to pay an occasional visit to Paris—the line I
have just quoted came straight from his heart—but
because the decline of her power at Court was exposing
her to innumerable lampoons at the hands of the populace. Her one claim to respect should at least be
asserted on his authority. "I owe much to you," he

wrote, "and I ought to say it. I dare to go further—to
thank you publicly for the kindness you have shown to
a very large number of veritable authors, great artists,
and men of merit in more than one way." Had this
tribute been reserved for another time it would have
lost some of its value. *Tancrède* was the last of the
tragedies on which Voltaire's reputation as a tragic poet
depends. His mocking wit outlived his imagination;
the soul and spirit breathed in *Zaïre* and *Alzire* had
begun rapidly to die away.

It was with the hopes and fears proper to a new
dramatist that Diderot sat through the performance of
Tancrède. Already in print, a five-act piece in prose
from his pen, the *Père de Famille*, had been accepted
at the Comédie. Few novelties could have been so
powerfully recommended to notice as this was by the
name of its author, of whom some account must be
given here. Denis Diderot, the "most German of
Frenchmen," came into the world at Langres in 1713,
and was educated by the Jesuits of that busy town.
His father, a successful cutler, wished him to be a
doctor or a lawyer, but failed to make him either.
Feeling that his true vocation lay in literature, he
became a bookseller's hack in Paris, where the influence
of Voltaire superseded any that may have been exercised
over him by the instructors of his youth. His deism
soon ripened into a fanatical hatred of religion in any

form, and the *Lettres sur les Aveugles,* printed in 1749,
caused him to be imprisoned for a short time at
Vincennes. How far he was cowed by this stretch of
authority may be inferred from the fact that he occupied
his enforced leisure in mentally elaborating the design
of the *Encyclopédie,* the first instalment of which
appeared in 1751. None of his contemporaries could
surpass him in breadth of information, fertility of ideas,
and originality of thought, obscured as these qualities
often were by carelessness of style and method. " He
never knew," writes Marmontel, " how to form a whole ;
the operation of first putting everything into its
place was for him too slow and too painful. As he
used to say himself, he penned many beautiful pages,
but never a book." In conversation he was more
himself. " Every branch of human knowledge was
so familiar to him, so present to his mind, that he
always appeared prepared for whatever might be said
to him, and his most sudden perceptions were like
the results of recent study or long meditation. I cannot express what charm the eloquence of sentiment
had in him. His whole soul was in his eyes and on his
lips. Never did the face paint better the goodness of
the heart "—a goodness really beyond denial, but allied
to something like contempt for decency of expression.
Lately, too active-minded to be content with his work
for the *Encyclopédie,* he had turned his attention to the

drama, chiefly because it might furnish him with the means of disseminating social and philanthropic ideas in a popular form. *Le Père de Famille,* in which comedy assumes a more serious tone than Lachaussée himself had ventured upon, amounts to a resolute protest against the supposed rights of birth and wealth. In contrast with a man disposed to push these rights to the furthest point, the Commandeur d'Auvilé, there is a father who allows himself to be swayed by the voice of nature instead of the conventions of society, and attachments formed by a son and daughter for persons in a less elevated position serve to place the nobility and tenderness of his character in the highest light. Excellent in principle, the play did not rise above mediocrity in execution, its scenes being clumsily huddled together, its personages ill-sustained, and its dialogue a little sermonizing. Préville and Bellecourt relieved it of many superfluous speeches, but even with this improvement it would not have survived the first representation (February 18) if the moral thesis underlying it had not been a grateful surprise to the rising democracy. As it was, the pit went into a transport of delight. "Such a success," writes the author to Mlle. Voland, "is not remembered here. Everybody pronounces the work a fine one. I myself am astonished."

Months passed away, and on the following 18th of January a five-act comedy in ten-syllable verse from

the pen of Voltaire, *L'Ecueil du Sage*, came up for
judgment. Nothing could be simpler than the story
here set forth. The period selected is that of Henri IV.
Mathurin, a wealthy farmer, wishes to espouse Acante
while the seigneur of the place, a Marquis, is absent in
Paris, as there is reason to fear that the latter will
exercise the feudal *droit*. Collette, a young villager,
was to have been the anxious lover's wife, but is now
wholly supplanted in his affections. Fortunately, Acante
holds Mathurin in at best a cold respect, and the girls
conspire to make him fulfil his first promise. Everything is put right in the end by the seigneur's return ;
he forces the farmer to marry Collette, and becoming
enamoured at first sight of Acante, who is really of good
birth, makes her his Marquise. *L'Ecueil du Sage*, which
at one time bore the title of *Le Droit du Seigneur*, was
saved from failure simply by the fact that it came from
Voltaire. It had little of his usual vivacity, was written
in an unpopular measure, and gave a little offence by
painting an aristocrat in somewhat flattering colours.
Had it included an onslaught upon the *droit du seigneur*
it would have been received with enthusiasm by the
pit, but the time for breathing a syllable on the stage
against that curious relic of feudalism was yet to come.
Certainly nothing of the kind would have been passed
by Crébillon, who, still unable to forget that Voltaire
had outstripped him in the race for dramatic fame,

abused his power as the censor royal to strike out the
"best pleasantries" in the piece.

It was on the eve of what proved a fatal illness that
the author of *Rhadamiste* afforded himself this regrettable
gratification. Surrounded to the last by his beloved
dogs and cats, with the raven croaking on the back of
his chair, he died in that miserable garret by the Marais
on the 17th of June, in the eighty-ninth year of his age.
On finding that his end was at hand he expressed some
remorse for the annoyance inflicted upon Voltaire in
connexion with *Mahomet* and *L'Ecueil du Sage*, and that
remorse, coupled with the fact that his nature had been
warped and soured by persistent ill-fortune, may serve
to lighten, though not wholly to obliterate, a serious
reproach on his memory. Indeed, there was little in
the lonely old man's retrospect to brighten his closing
days. From almost the outset of his career he had been
face to face with poverty. Notwithstanding the power
of his earlier plays, he had to wait for a trifling pension
from the Court until he was seventy-two, and even then
would have missed it if a cabal had not seen in him a
convenient instrument for diminishing the prestige of
Voltaire. For many years he had to live upon his
earnings as a censor, and these were both scanty and
irregular. He also had the affliction of being treated
with insolent ingratitude by his son, Claude Prosper
Jolyot de Crébillon, who exercised rare literary talents

in creating and pandering to a taste for licentious novels.
" Whichever may be my best work," the poet said with
a groan, "he is certainly my worst." But of one consolation the victim of destiny could not be deprived.
His tragedies, a sumptuous edition of which had been
brought out by the Imprimerie Royale at the public
cost, contained much that deserved to live, though it
is undeniable that his style is painfully harsh, and that
in striving to excite terror, as was generally his object,
he not unfrequently fell into the horrible. *Electre* and
Rhadamiste, his highest achievements, are marked by a
peculiar energy and grandeur of thought. Nor were his
claims to admiration ignored when he passed away. He
was ceremoniously laid to rest within the walls of St.
Gervais, where the King had a monument erected to his
memory. Moreover, at the instance of the players, the
curé of a church not within the jurisdiction of the Archbishop of Paris, that of Saint Jean de Latran, had a
stately service there for the repose of the poet's soul—
a concession for which the reverend gentleman was
rusticated and fined two hundred livres by the Order
of Malta—and a congregation representative of genius
and learning and rank assembled to join in this tribute
to a man who had so long been permitted to starve.
France, as one of her sons remarked in years to come of
England, was an excellent place for a poet to die in.

Crébillon's place in the censorship fell to a person

who was to play some curious parts in life. François
Marin, an illegitimate offshoot of the family of Michel
Ange Marin, was born at Laciotat, in Provence, in 1721.
Early associations with the Church as a chorister gave
him a taste for the ecclesiastical state, but after wearing
the petit-collet for a year or two he became a lawyer.
Established in Paris, he made the acquaintance of
Voltaire, who, finding that he was very poor, did not
allow him to want money, procured for him the post
of tutor to the Marquis de Rosen, and encouraged him
to occupy his leisure in writing.   Among other things,
he produced a *Histoire de Saladin*, which deservedly
brought him into notice, and a prose comedy in three
acts, *Julie*, which appeared this year at the Théâtre
Français with conspicuous ill success. " Marins seem
to be out of luck just now," said a jester in the pit,
alluding to the reverses lately suffered by the French in
the East.   Besides his censorship, Marin held the post
of Secrétaire-Général of the Librairie, and in this capacity
was a terror to everybody concerned in the printing and
dissemination of unauthorized literature.   He allowed
scarcely a day to pass without sending some unhappy
colporteur to Bicêtre or the galleys.   In one respect, however, he undid with one hand what prudence made him
do with the other.   He was really an ardent anti-Christian in the disguise of an ardent Christian.   Feigning
extreme horror at the writings of the new philosophical

school, he caused a zealous watch to be kept for them at all the barriers of the city, but took more care that they should obtain ingress by some means or another. Curiously enough, the sincerity of his professions was never doubted by the authorities, and he found himself an object of bitter detestation to the advocates of the cause which he secretly espoused.

Marin's *Julie* came to the Comédie with a swarm of other pieces. Debelloy, bidding a final farewell to Russia, returned to Paris with a *Zelmire*, in which, somewhat like the Roman citizen, a father left to die of hunger in a cave by his son is suckled by his daughter until he can turn the tables upon his gaoler. However disagreeable its story might be to sensitive persons, the tragedy met with full success, and had the honour of being noticed by Metastasio. Indeed, there were few Parisian plays of mark by which the Italian poet at Vienna did not profit. "Le cher voleur!" Voltaire once exclaimed; "il m'a bien embelli!" In the *Méprises*, a five-act comedy in ten-syllable verse, Palissot made good dramatic capital out of two men who, as in the *Menaechmi*, bear a close resemblance to each other, who are mixed up in a love intrigue, and who may be impersonated by one actor. But his attack upon the philosophers had not yet been forgiven; their adherents hooted down the piece, and when Bellecourt appeared to announce a second performance they compelled him to retire unheard. Marmontel was indirectly to render the players a service apart from his judicious criticism in the *Mercure* of their work. One of his *Moral Tales* supplied the material of a little comedy in verse, *Heureusement*, by Rochon de Chabannes. Fortified by some experience as a writer for the Théâtre Italien and the Opéra Comique, the dramatist here treated a pleasing story with all the effect of which it was susceptible, and nothing that acting could do for the piece appears to have been wanting. Molé, it is certain, represented with delightful effect the young officer Lindor—a part so full of refined vivacity that the author at first thought of allotting it to the still brilliant Marie Dangeville. Noteworthy, too, was the Marquise de Lisban of Mlle. Hus, who introduced into her performance a rather felicitous apropos. "I drink to Cypris," Molé had to say to her in the course of a tête-à-tête between Lindor and the Marquise. At that moment the gallant Condé entered a box. "For my part," said the actress, turning to the Prince with a pretty curtsey, "I drink to Mars!"

The players found themselves in greater strength at the close of the year. Not long previously they had secured a sterling comedian in a Sieur Dauberval. He was now followed to the Comédie by Pierre Bouret, the shortest, the fattest, and one of the most humorous of living actors. In 1756, at a theatre of the Fair, Vadé,

the Dancourt of the Opéra Comique, found himself at
his wits' end for somebody to play a sort of Polichinelle.
By chance he became acquainted with Bouret, who had
lately begun to appear there. " He's the man for me ! "
exclaimed the delighted author, and Bouret justified
this confidence well enough to put himself on the high
road to fame and fortune at a single step. At the
Comédie Française he suffered by comparison with
Préville, but a peculiar excellence in *rôles de niais* made
his début successful. His Sosie and Pourceaugnac
would have delighted Molière himself. It was also to
the advantage of the company that Mlle. Hus had at
length discovered where her strength lay. Early in the
year her comrades decided to revive the *Comte d' Essex*.
" I should like to play Elizabeth," said Clairon. " My
seniority gives me that," replied Dumesnil. " Let me
have the Duchess then," Clairon continued. " No," said
Mlle. Hus ; " the part has been allotted to me, and I
will not resign it." " In that case," said Clairon, resolved
to punish her former pupil for some rudeness, " I will
be the confidant." And the confidant she was, with the
result that the Duchess found herself completely overshadowed. Mindful of this severe lesson, Mlle. Hus
finally abandoned tragedy for comedy, and the sprightliness of her Marquise in *Heureusement* supplied the first
of many proofs that in doing so she had been well
advised.

Dupuis et Desronais, a serious comedy in three acts, introduces us to a new dramatist of the mature age of fifty-three. Bred for the law, but turning from it to take a clerkship under the Receiver-General of Finances, Charles Collé, a notary's son, had long been one of the haunters of the Caveau, where he distinguished himself by a peculiar aptitude for conversation. At a dinner given every week by Pelletier, the *fermier-général*, to eight or ten bachelors, all jovial friends, "the men of the wildest heads," writes Marmontel, "were Collé and Crébillon *fils*. Between them it was a continual war of excellent pleasantry, and all were free to join in the combat. They never indulged in personality. The self-love of talent was alone attacked. But it was attacked without indulgence, and had to be shaken off when you entered the lists. Collé was brilliant beyond all expression, and Crébillon had in a singular degree the power of animating by exciting him. . . . Never was the fire of gaiety of so regular and fruitful a warmth" as in Collé. "I cannot now tell you what we laughed at so much, but I well know that at every turn he made us laugh till the tears came in our eyes. His fancy, once exalted, made everything appear comic and ridiculous." Fortunately, Collé aspired to something more than the applause of listening groups in café and salon. He cultivated a natural talent for song-writing until it bore the richest fruit. Becoming secretary or reader to the young Duc d'Orléans, who loved the drama to madness, he delighted him with a variety of comedies, many of which were printed under the collective title of *Théâtre de Société*. Intended for private representation only, they often set admitted rules at defiance, and for this reason had a tendency to enlarge the bounds of dramatic art. Nevertheless, *Dupuis et Desronais*, which seems to have been one of his earliest productions, found favour in the eyes of the players, and, what is even more surprising, in those of the conservative audience. Collé was less at home in the serious than in the lively, but in this piece he successfully deals with the simple story of a girl overcoming by filial tenderness and respect a selfish opposition on the part of her father to a match in which her affections are engaged.

Following closely upon the tardy advent of this dramatist came the departure of a more distinctive figure in literary history. Marivaux, whose muse had long been silent, died in Paris on the 12th of February, at the sufficient age of seventy-four. In his case, as in that of Swift, " the stage darkened ere the curtain fell; " his only child, a daughter, had left him to immure herself in a monastery, and he might have spent his declining years in poverty if Helvétius had not anonymously made him a regular allowance. It is difficult to think of this fascinating writer except as one going through life in disguise. From the outset of his career he had been the reverse of what he was. He had consistently aped an extreme singularity of ideas, sentiment, and phraseology. He sought to revive the *préciosité* of the seventeenth century in combination with metaphysical subtlety. In society he had a preoccupied air. "Having acquired," says Marmontel, "a reputation for deep and refined wit, he thought himself obliged to give perpetual proofs of that wit, and was continually on the watch for ideas susceptible of opposition or analysis, in order to turn or wind them as his fancy dictated. He would agree that such a thing was true 'as far as a certain point or in a certain view;' but there was always some restriction or distinction to make which no one perceived but himself. Never, I believe, was there a self-love more delicate, more wayward, more fearing. But as he respected that of others we respected his, only pitying him that he could not resolve to be simple and natural." One of his favourite affectations may be briefly noticed. He used to say that he would rather take a back seat among a small band of original writers than head a tribe of imitators. In point of fact, he was often under important obligations to other writers, one of his contributions to the Théâtre Italien, *Les Fausses Confidences,* being an unavowed reproduction of the *Gardener's Dog* of Lope de Vega. It is also true, however, that he set upon all his work the impress of a

clear individuality. He could do much to transform
the old into something new. And the result was of no
inconsiderable value. If the highway of human nature
was less familiar to him than its by-paths, as Voltaire
well pointed out, he utilized his knowledge with a
brightness of wit and a delicacy of thought seldom
to be obscured by his elaborate, mincing, periphrastic,
and conceit-laden style. In the delineation of women,
whether *ingénues* or coquettes, he was particularly
happy.

Four weeks after the death of Marivaux a double
disaster overtook the theatre. Gaussin and Dangeville,
who had become Comédiennes du Roi in the same year,
simultaneously obtained permission to retire. It may
be presumed that they had some difficulty in doing so,
as neither of them had lost the means of preserving her
popularity for some time to come. Gaussin, though
irreverently spoken of by Voltaire as "that old girl,"
retained much of the personal attractiveness and fineness
of sensibility which so readily won for her a place at
the Comédie in 1730. Her figure had lost little of its
symmetry, her dark eyes little of their dreamy eloquence,
her demeanour little of its sensuous grace, her sway
over the audience little of its magnetic power. For
tragedy of the sterner cast she was physically unfitted,
but no common versatility is implied in the fact that
her name long remained identified with Iphigénie,

Bérénice, Monime, Zaire, Alzire, Adélaïde Duguesclin,
Briséïs, and Lucinde in the *Oracle*.   Long of frail
virtue, she suddenly saw the error of her ways, married
a dancer named Tavlaigo, gave up the stage in deference
to religious scruples, and went to live at Laszenay.
Mlle. Dangeville seems to have been even more sorely
missed.   Except Mlle. Quinault, no such comedy queen
had yet been seen in Paris.   Her soubrettes and fine
ladies and "character" personages set all rivalry at
defiance.   It was impossible to withstand her delicate
humour, her spontaneous gaiety, her refined *espièglerie*,
her poetic dancing, her general brilliancy of execution.
By a glance of her roguish eyes she worked marvels;
the wit of Voltaire himself derived a fresh piquancy
and grace as it fell from her. lips.

Mlle. Gaussin died in widowhood four years afterwards, but a long and honoured old age awaited the
"amiable rival of Thalia."   Her retreat at Vaugirard
was the scene of many a delightful assemblage.   "When
I first saw Mlle. Dangeville," says Fleury, "she was
about sixty years of age, but did not look so old.   Her
manners were easy, frank, and unaffected, and were
marked by a charming quietness of modesty."   Many
little conspiracies were hatched at the Comédie to do
her honour.   For instance, on one of her birthdays, a
detachment from the theatre, including Brizard, Molé,
Mlle. Hus, Dauberval, and Madame Drouin, gave a

performance in her garden, a forest scene in the piece
having the natural background of some noble elms.
Lekain, Lemierre, Préville, Dorat, Mlle. Lamotte, Saint-
Foix, Chabannes, and others assembled to dine with
her on another such occasion. At one end of the room
hung the portrait of the still beautiful actress, with the
lines beginning—

> Il me semble la voir, l'œil brillant de gaîté,
> Parler, agir, marcher avec légèreté,

inscribed on the frame. Dinner over, Saint-Foix, according to one of the guests, delivered a rapid eulogy of
their hostess. " It is difficult to believe," he said,
" that the same person should have played the Indiscrète
in the *Ambitieux*, Martine in the *Femmes Savantes*, the
Fausse Agnès, the Marquise d'Olban in *Nanine*, L'Amour
in the *Grâces*, and so many other different parts.
Study and reflection and taste may make a fine actress,
but an actress of genius is very rare, and between the
two there is as much distinction as between Molière
and an author with wit only." " Enough," cried Mlle.
Dangeville ; " you are going too far. Molière ! I have
never been anything save his humble handmaid."
" Lekain seems anxious to speak," said Chabannes.
" Yes," said the tragedian, " the Comédie must present
its bouquet." " Let it be without flattery, then,"
interposed Mlle. Dangeville, " or I will go." " Once
upon a time," continued Lekain, with his eyes fixed

upon the portrait mentioned, "there was a fairy"—
Cries of "Bravo!" interrupted him. "You will force
me to leave the table," said Mlle. Dangeville. Lekain
accused Chabannes of prompting him to tell the story.
"Indeed," said Mlle. Dangeville, "is he the offender?
An old friend, too! But I will have my revenge. I
exile M. Rochon de Chabannes to Dresden." "Madame,
you alarm me," said the poet. "Yes," she continued,
"since I am a fairy I avail myself of a fairy's power
to send you to Dresden as his most Christian majesty's
Chargé d'Affaires. I have appealed to the Minister
against the injustice you have suffered; he has made
you a head taller; go and thank him to-morrow.
Messieurs," she added, as the poet embraced her, "the
Greeks made ambassadors of their actors; in France,
you see, an actress can make a plenipotentiary."

"Humph!" remarked Armand on learning that
Gaussin and Dangeville were on the point of leaving
the stage, "it is high time that so old and feeble a
fellow as myself should think of following their
example." Perhaps mindful of this warning, the company looked to a young actor named Auger, then in
a French theatre at Vienna, as the one most likely to
fill the impending vacancy. He came forward on the
14th of April as Dave in *L'Andrienne* and Labranche
in *Crispin Rival de Son Maître*, subsequently playing
Olive in the *Tuteur*, Mascarille in the *Etourdi*, and other

such characters. It may be doubted whether a better selection could have been made. He had an excellent figure, mobile features, and finely expressive eyes; his acting was shrewd, original, and full of colour. For a time he was disposed to encroach upon decency in his bye-play, but a closer acquaintance with the traditions of the Comédie sufficed to cure him of this tendency. He was warmly received by his future comrades, Clairon declaring that no début within her knowledge had displayed so great a ripeness of talent. Armand, of whom we may now take leave, generously joined in the plaudits. "M. Auger," he said, "will not only succeed me but make me forgotten"—a prediction borne out only on the first point.

No less fortunate were the company in their efforts to find promising substitutes for Gaussin and Dangeville. Mlle. Hus had the right of seniority to the *emploi* of the former, but in this she was overshadowed by a Mlle. Doligny, who opened a début on the 3rd of May with unusual success. Like the original representative of Zaïre, the new actress combined a pleasing presence with the most exquisite sensibility, refinement, and grace. Dorat hailed her arrival in an expressive quatrain :—

> Par les talents et la décence
> Tu fais captives tour à tour,
> Et tu souris comme l'Amour
> Quand il avait son innocence.

From Collé we learn that after she had played only three or four parts " all Paris declared that she would not fall far short of the inimitable actress whom the public still regretted." Nothing is known of her previous history, but we may fairly assume that she had had a wise and careful training. Her private character was spotless. Bachaumont tells us that the Marquis de Gouffier attempted to corrupt her, and, finding her unconquerable, offered her his hand. Probably to the surprise of everybody, she declined to be made even a marchioness, on the ground that while esteeming herself too much to be his mistress she esteemed herself too little to be his wife. Dorothée Luzi, the other new actress, was in her eighteenth year, and had figured at the Opéra Comique from a very tender age. In 1760, at the Foire Saint Laurent, she made herself famous as Crispin in the *Soldat Magicien.* Her début at the Comédie Française, which began on the 26th of May, could not but end in her admission, though the peculiar brilliancy of Dangeville was beyond her reach. Her acting was marked by much intelligence, humour, and sprightliness.

The players did not allow these changes to interfere with their usual business. *Le Bienfait Rendu*, a five-act comedy in verse by one Dampierre, seemed foredoomed to failure ; but the "prodigious" acting of Préville, with a few pleasantries against the noblesse, "captivated the pit," says Grimm, "in spite of itself." In a new tragedy, *Blanche et Guiscard*, David Garrick, now halting in Paris for three weeks on his way to Italy, perceived an adaptation (by Saurin) of one written for himself, Thomson's *Tancred and Sigismunda*, which had been founded upon the episode in *Gil Blas* of the Marriage of Vengeance. It did not survive a third representation, although the cast included Lekain, Clairon, and Brizard. In strong contrast to the fate of *Blanche et Guiscard* was that of a *Comte de Warwick*, in which Lekain played the Kingmaker to Mlle. Dumesnil's Marguerite d'Anjou. It instantly became the talk of Paris, and the author, Jean François Laharpe, a mere stripling, found himself the observed of all observers.

Estimable more for talent than personal character was the young poet thus brought under our notice. Only son of a captain in the artillery, he was born in Paris in 1739, and at the present moment, therefore, had not quite completed his twenty-fourth year. According to his own statement, he was descended from a noble family of Vaud. Be that as it may, the artillery captain was extremely poor, and Jean François, having been left an orphan at the age of nine, might have become a *gamin* if the Sisters of Charity in his native parish, that of St. André des Arts, had not taken him under their protection. Four or five years afterwards he recited some verses in the hearing of the proviseur of the Collége d'Harcourt, M. Asselin, who undertook to educate him gratis. He proved an apt pupil; the most coveted prizes fell to his lot. His residence at the Collége, however, came to an untimely close. He composed, or at least helped to compose, a lampoon upon his benefactor, and for doing so was incarcerated at Bicêtre or For l'Evêque for several months. On regaining his liberty he embarked upon the troubled waters of literature. Colardeau had then brought the *héroïde* into vogue, and two effusions by Laharpe in the same way attracted some attention. He then began the *Comte de Warwick*. M. de Voltaire had utilized mediæval names to good purpose : why should not mediæval history itself be drawn upon for the stage ? In the result, however, history had but a slight share in the youthful dramatist's scheme. What Shakspere had been content to follow was not good enough for him. He devised a plot for himself; and it is beyond dispute that he embodied a rather vigorous conception of the Kingmaker in verse above the average level. Frantically acclaimed at the Comédie, partly because Lekain played the hero, the *Comte de Warwick* soon found its way to the theatre at Versailles, where Laharpe had the felicity of being presented to his most Christian majesty. Forthwith a copy of the tragedy was despatched to the acknowledged president of the republic of letters, who received it in his most gracious

spirit, invited the author to Ferney, and treated him
with an indulgence usually reserved for old and tested
friends.   One little colloquy between the patriarch and
his guest is worthy of preservation.   Laharpe, it must
be premised, was nothing if not critical.   It was practically impossible for him to contemplate the noblest
monument of human genius without discovering a flaw
therein.   And the works of his host did not escape his
animadversion.   "Mon père," he said one evening, just
before taking part in a performance of *Adélaïde
Duguesclin* in the little theatre, "I have altered a
few lines which to me seem a trifle feeble."   "Feeble?"
echoed the patriarch.   "Judge for yourself," replied
the youth.   Voltaire ran his eye over the alterations
with a half-serious, half-amused air.   "Excellent," he
said ; "they are changes for the better ; do not hesitate
to make more ; I can only gain by such emendations."
"I am surprised," said a third person, after Laharpe
had gone, "that you should allow your verse to be
tampered with in this way."   "Nay," said the philosopher, "I do not pretend that what I have written is
unsusceptible of improvement.   Besides that, I admire
the boy ; and he loves me and my works."   But the
affection in which he was held by Voltaire must
not blind us to one or two grave defects in Laharpe.
His lampoon upon Asselin was due not so much to
the thoughtlessness of youth as to an incapability of

gratitude. He could sting any bosom in which he had nestled. And to this callousness he united a morbid and irritable vanity. " Buy Laharpe at his real value, sell him at the price he puts upon himself, and you will be wealthy," was the burden of an epigram of the time.

> Si vous voudrez faire bientôt
> Une fortune immense autant que légitime,
> Il vous faut acheter Laharpe ce qu'il vaut
> Et le vendre ce qu'il s'estime.

Few there were, we are told, who did not owe him a grudge for some offensive display of self-conceit.

More than one dramatic project occupied Voltaire's thoughts as he entertained Laharpe at Ferney. *Olympie* and the *Triumvirat*, tragedies both, had emanated from his ever active brain. In its original form the first was the work of six days. " Then you ought not to have rested on the seventh," said a friend whom he had asked to criticize the piece. For some of the lines were sadly awkward. " Well," the philosopher replied, "the piece shall have due revision ; woe unto him who does not seek advice ! " Carefully written, *Olympie* was represented several times in the little theatre of the château, with Lekain, now "looking like a fat canon," as a reverent spectator on at least one occasion. Voltaire, unlike many others, saw a competent actress in his niece. "Madame Denis," he writes, " plays Statira as Mlle. Dumesnil plays Mérope."

"Yesterday," he adds in a letter to the Comte d'Argental, "Lekain was Zamore in *Alzire*. He was even finer than I had expected. He played the second act in a way to make me blush for having once lauded Baron and Dufresne. I did not believe it was possible to carry tragic art so far. It is true that he was not so brilliant in the other acts. He was very badly supported; my niece did not appear." Having been printed at Frankfort, *Olympie* soon became known to Grimm, who pronounced it feeble. "Nevertheless," he adds, "I am convinced that it will succeed at the theatre. It is full of pictures; Mlle. Clairon will be great in it, and M. de Voltaire in his languor is still superior to our other poets in their vigour." His prognostications were fully verified when, after considerable hesitation, the players produced the piece (March 17). Feebly written it indeed was; but three very dramatic situations—the marriage, the combat, and the burning at the stake—went far to redeem this disadvantage. "*O l'impie*," sneered Fréron, "does he really suppose that for this success he is not indebted mainly to a feeling of gratitude for his former achievements?" Voltaire was not disposed to be applauded on such terms. Nobody in Paris knew that he had written the *Triumvirat*. Might it not be brought out anonymously? He preferred to stand or fall by the intrinsic merit of his work. Consequently, the tragedy was sent to the Comédie Française with a stipulation that the author's name should not be revealed. His wishes were scrupulously respected. Even Grimm did not get at the truth. Voltaire had little reason to be satisfied with the issue. *Le Triumvirat*, though better than that of 1754, was not good enough for the audience, and the author had the additional mortification to find that so inconsiderable a person as Poinsinet had spared no trouble to convince the world that he was innocent of any share in the work.

With *Olympie* and the *Triumvirat* there were a few plays of even humbler pretensions. Lemierre, unlike Voltaire, exposed himself to hazardous comparisons in treating Crébillon's subjects, and the result of an *Idomenée* warned him to avoid them in future. Barthe, a young poet from Marseilles, developed an original idea in a one-act comedy, *L'Amateur*. His hero, Valère, a sculptor living only for his art, becomes enamoured of a statue which a friend has presented to him, and which turns out to be one of the friend's daughter. The story of *Inkle and Yarico*, recently imitated by Dorat, supplied the materials for a one-act comedy, the *Jeune Indienne*, by a native of Auvergne, Nicolas Chamfort, the author in years to come of the immortal *Maximes et Pensées*, but at present known only as a successful scholar at the Collége de Grassins, as a contributor to the periodicals of Paris, and as a victorious competitor for the poetry prize of the Academy. Duclairon, a dabbler in literature, produced a *Cromwell*, the subject of which is not the death of Charles I. (it is needless to say that), but the bitterness of faction in England after the temporary fall of her ancient monarchy. Exaggerated as that bitterness of faction was by the author, who held office under the crown, some thought it preferable to the grinding despotism it followed. In a one-act comedy by Poinsinet, *Le Cercle*, we have an agreeable picture of the frivolity of the age—so agreeable, indeed, that his friends doubted whether it had all come out of his own head. Nor did that doubt prove unfounded. *Le Cercle* was a collection of cribbings from other pieces, especially from a comedy written by Palissot for the theatre at Nancy. "Why do you not lay claim to the credit assumed by Poinsinet?" the author of the *Philosophes* was asked. "Bah!" he replied, "a gentleman does not wear a coat after it has been worn by his valet."

Busy as they were, the players did not allow budding histrionic talent to pass unheeded. Alexandrine Fanier, born at Cambrai in 1745, came forward as the soubrettes of the *Dissipateur* and the *Préjugé Vaincu*, and was received to double Mlle. Luzi in such parts. Grimm says that her voice and demeanour were those of a fish-hawker, but this would appear to have been wide of the truth. Other critics concur in describing her

as vivacious, gay, and refined, with a pretty figure
and a piquant countenance.   In Feulie, a young player
without practical experience in a public theatre, the
company discovered a not unworthy second to the
great Préville himself.   He seemed to have been born
for the Comédie Francaise, uniting as he did a large
measure of liveliness and humour to an instinctive
abhorrence of vulgarity.   "It is rather singular," the
Old Amateur writes, "that an actor so reserved should
have shown a leaning towards the pieces of Legrand
and Scarron, in which comedy is so often wedded to
licence.   But he had the art to make them decent.
Without omitting any of their sallies, and simply laying
stress on those not repugnant to good taste, Feulie,
thanks to a judgment not always allied in his profession to talent, made himself applauded with transport, not only in the *Amazones Modernes*, wherein he
played Crispin, but in the character otherwise indelicate of Don Japhet d'Arménie, wherein he conciliated
the suffrages of the most fastidious spectators" (*e*).

Never had the importance of a new and attractive
subject to the dramatist been more clearly demonstrated
than it was by a tragedy then in rehearsal at the
Comédie.   Few attempts, it may have been seen, had
as yet been made to break down the prejudice against
illustrating modern history on the stage.   Nine out
of every ten poets still clung to the idea that tragedy

found dignified employment only in the illustration of antiquity. If anything, the history of France experienced particular neglect, although Voltaire, in his eagerness to infuse a special warmth and colour into the serious drama, had decorated imaginary personages with names revered by the nation at large. Outstripping the author of *Zaïre* and *Tancrède* in the way of innovation, Debelloy dramatized one of the most impressive events in which his fellow-countrymen had had a share, that of the siege of Calais, and took care to give sonorous expression to the patriotic sentiments incident to his theme. In this he set himself a task beyond his power. He did not rise to a definite and vigorous conception of the greatness of Eustache de St. Pierre, Edward III., and other prominent characters in the piece. Regarded as a whole, the *Siége de Calais* (February 13) is poor in both principle and execution. But its story and grandiloquent speeches, with the aid of a cast including Lekain, Clairon, Brizard, Molé, and Dauberval, made the audience indifferent to its shortcomings. It met with a success almost without precedent in theatrical annals, partly as a matter of patriotism, but chiefly perhaps, because it reminded the democracy that the lasting honour done to France by the resistance of Calais to the redoubtable legions of Edward was due wholly to the courage and constancy of the citizens. By extraordinary good fortune the piece was played three times at Court, where Debelloy had the honour of being presented to the royal family. "Monsieur," said the King, "I am delighted with your tragedy, and still more so, if that is possible, by the enthusiasm it has aroused." "How well you depict French heroism!" exclaimed the Queen. "I, the elder brother of the French, have witnessed the performance with the keenest pleasure," chimed in the Dauphin. "Fall ill whenever you like," said the Maréchal de Brissac to Brizard (Eustache); "I'll play your part." In the country, too, the *Siége de Calais* created a *furore*. It had several representations at Strasburg and Metz. It was frequently played in garrisons to inflame the patriotic ardour of the soldiers, the officers previously distributing copies of it among the spectators. Calais gave the author the freedom of the town in a gold box, with "lauream tulit : civicam recipit" inscribed on the lid, and had his portrait put among those of her benefactors. Nor was the fame of the *Siége de Calais* confined to its native land. Edition after edition of it was bought up in London, Vienna, and elsewhere. Nevertheless, it is now remembered chiefly by an accidental association with events which occurred shortly after its production, and to which our attention must forthwith be directed.

Early in April, during the Easter recess, unusual

commotion might have been observed in the green-room.
An actor named Dubois, " who for the last twenty-nine
years," to quote from Grimm, " had enjoyed the confidence of all the tragic heroes, and who had exercised
himself with success as simple valets on deigning to
exchange the buskin for the sock," had consulted a
surgeon named Benoît in very discreditable circumstances, and on receiving the bill declared most stoutly
that he had paid it. Benoît then brought an action
against him for the amount. His comrades, irritated
to find a Comédien du Roi mixed up in such a dispute,
referred the matter to a Gentleman of the Chamber,
but were requested to decide upon it themselves.
Inquiry and examination followed ; Dubois, driven into
a corner, confessed to having lied through thick and
thin in the matter, and at the suggestion of Clairon
he was ignominiously expelled from the company. But
the story was not to end here. Pretty Mlle. Dubois,
the culprit's daughter, espoused her father's cause with
the most commendable zeal. Next day, sweet as
Aphrodite rising from the sea, she appeared before the
Duc de Fronsac, one of her admirers, and urged him
to have her "respectable père " reinstated at the theatre.
Her prayer was readily granted, as may be inferred
from the fact that an hour or two later, accompanied by
the enamoured Duke and two other sprigs of nobility,
she broke in upon a rehearsal in the green-room with an

order to the effect that Dubois should be permitted
to play his usual parts until the King determined the
question of his fitness to remain a royal player. But
five of his comrades—Clairon, Lekain, Brizard, Molé,
and Dauberval—were not to be diverted from their
purpose. Cost them what it might, they resolved not
to appear with Dubois again.

It was on the evening of the same day that the
Comédie reopened its doors after the recess. *Le Siége
de Calais* had been announced, and Dubois, who played
Melun, firmly refused to let his place be taken by
anybody else. Consequently, the five mutineers were
conspicuous by their absence as the time for raising
the curtain arrived. What could be done? It was
an anxious moment for the players behind the scenes,
as the assembled audience, induced by various hirelings
of Dubois in the house to believe that the absentees had
capriciously declined to fulfil their duties, were getting
into a somewhat vindictive mood. Bouret at length
came forward to announce that owing to the defection
of particular players the *Joueur* would be substituted for
the *Siége de Calais*, and that those who did not care
to see the former might have their admission money
returned. " Messieurs," he began, " we are in despair."
" None of that," gruffly interposed a spectator; " we
want the *Siége de Calais*." Hereupon a deafening
clamour arose, and the actor, finding that he was

not likely to obtain a hearing, returned to the green-room. Préville, giving the signal for the curtain to go up, went on for the first scene in the *Joueur*, but was hissed off the stage. Before long the spirit of tumult reigned supreme, fierce objurgations upon the refractory players being coupled with demands for their immediate incarceration. Clairon seems to have been singled out for particular resentment. Exaggerated stories of her disdainful pride had already qualified her popularity. Cries of "Clairon à prison !" "Frétillon à l'Hôpital!" "Clairon au For l'Evêque !" frequently made themselves heard above the prevailing din.

Subsequent events could not but intensify what Bachaumont calls the "surprising excitement" caused in Paris by this disturbance. In a conference with M. de Sartines, Lieutenant-General of Police, the Gentlemen of the Chamber, always responsible for the well-being of the Comédie Française, decided to make an example of the players on strike by clapping them for an indefinite period in For l'Evêque, the ancient Forum Episcopi, situated in the Rue St. Germain l'Auxerrois. Brizard and Dauberval were conducted thither a few hours afterwards. More difficulty was experienced in discovering Lekain and Molé, who, hearing of the punishment intended for them, had retired to a friend's house at a short distance from the city in the hope that the storm

would soon blow over. On the same day, however,
they were sent to join Brizard and Dauberval. " Better
this," wrote Lekain from his durance, " than to be seen
on the stage with Dubois." Clairon was arrested at the
house of Madame de Sauvigné, wife of the Intendant de
Paris. " In an analogous case in your regiment," the
actress asked an officer present, " would you not have
acted in the same way ? " " Doubtless," was the reply ;
" mais ce ne serait pas un jour de *siége.*" On her road
to prison she loftily remarked that her life and possessions were at the mercy of the King, but not her
honour. Her custodian bethought himself of an old
legal maxim. " Oui," he said ; " où il n'y a rien le
roi perd ses droits"—a jest which, carefully bruited
about by the jester, caused infinite amusement to the
town. But the imprisonment of the actors was really
a triumph for each. Every evening the approaches to
the gaol were blocked with the carriages of those who
came to tender them expressions of sympathy, to cheer
them with a little lively conversation, and also to
partake of delightful suppers over which they presided.

Before long the authorities had cause to reconsider
their decision. As may be supposed, the current of
public feeling turned decisively in favour of the prisoners
as soon as it became known that they had been actuated
simply by a determination to uphold the credit of their
order, and had had the boldness to disregard at least

the intention of an order emanating from the Court. In such a play-loving city as Paris, too, the prospect of their being kept off the boards for even a few weeks was hardly to be endured. Evidently mindful of all this, the Gentlemen of the Chamber thought fit to liberate the offending players, though only by degrees. Lekain, Molé, Brizard, and Dauberval were allowed to play at the theatre, on the condition, however, that they returned to prison at the end of the performance. Nobody now supposed that they had meant any disrespect to the public, but the Lieutenant of Police insisted that before they reappeared an apologetic address which he had drawn up should be delivered from the stage by Bellecourt, and a magistrate went in his robes to be sure that it was spoken according to copy. "If I did not love the Comédie better than myself," said the actor selected for the task, "I should have been unable to get through the words." Five days after her arrest, Clairon, having procured a medical certificate that her health had been gravely affected by prison life, received permission to return home, but was forbidden to go out or see more than four persons at a time. Like her comrades, she still refused to be associated in any way with Dubois, who then found himself compelled to retire on the full pension. Eventually the persecuted players recovered their full liberty, Clairon in twenty-one days, the others in about twenty-four.

If the authorities believed that things at the Comédie would now go on as before they were grievously disappointed. The men resumed their places, but Clairon, stung to the quick by the humiliation she had undergone, resolved to quit the stage for good. Her services as a Comédienne du Roi, extending as they did over more than two decades, entitled her to a pension of 1500 livres a year, and out of her receipts she had saved enough to make a moderate competency. Her application was based on a justifiable plea of ill-health. But the first Gentleman of the Chamber, the Duc de Richelieu, would not readily accede to her wishes. He gave her leave of absence until the following Easter, adding that if she did not recover by that time he would again consider the matter. Clairon took advantage of this *congé* to pay a visit to Voltaire, to whom she theatrically fell upon her knees as, without standing upon ceremony, he ran out of his château to welcome the long-expected guest. In her eyes he had always been a sort of demi-god. On his side, the aged philosopher was quite prepared to view her in a similar light, especially after witnessing in his little theatre the superb combination of art and truth which her acting had presented for the last thirteen years. Among the heroines she played there was the Electre of his *Oreste*. According to Marmontel, this character, which the poet had induced her to declaim with a continual and monotonous lamentation, acquired, when spoken naturally, a charm unknown to himself. "It is not I who wrote that," he exclaimed at the close, with tears in his eyes; "'tis Clairon who has created the part." On her return to Paris it was believed that she would reappear at the Comédie, but no argument or entreaty could do more than temporarily shake her resolution. In the prime of womanhood, with her voice and personal beauty as little impaired by time as her intellect, this wayward and intrepid daughter of genius voluntarily abandoned a profession in which she had been supreme for nearly a quarter of a century.

Few incidents of special interest mark the records of her subsequent life. For some time she lived in a house near the Pont Royal, and on particular days would surround herself with representative throngs. Marmontel speaks of her receptions as "numerous and brilliant." One evening, dressed as a priestess of Apollo, with a crown of laurel in her hand, she might have been found ardently reciting to her guests an ode by the author of *Denis* in praise of Voltaire, a bust of whom was on a pedestal at her side. "Arrived at Paris," writes Walpole, under date August 23, 1767, "at a quarter to seven; at eight to Madame du Deffand's; found the Clairon acting Agrippine and Phèdre. Not tall; but I liked her acting better than I expected." Five years after her retirement, having a friend at Court in the Duchesse de Villeroi, she was selected, though not without a good deal of opposition from the admirers of Mlle. Dumesnil, to head the cast for a performance of *Athalie* in the private theatre at Versailles during the fêtes in honour of the royal wedding—a performance apparently intended to exhibit a masterpiece of dramatic poetry in combination with the finest histrionic talent then procurable. Her acting as the Jewish Queen seems to have fallen below expectation, but we may not unreasonably assume that its effect was interfered with by a spectacular grandeur theretofore unattempted in a French theatre. "No language," we are told in the Fleury memoirs, "could do justice to the magnificence of the chief scene. When the great temple opened, discovering the King of the Jews seated on his throne of gold, with five hundred Levites and warriors marching on from different points, the picture was at once imposing and terrific. It realized all the ideas I had conceived of the splendour of Jerusalem." Meanwhile, with characteristic energy, the actress had striven to relieve her old profession from the ban so long laid upon it by the clergy. In this she failed, as did Saint Florentin, a courtier of the day, in attempting to regain for the players the privileges of *valets de chambre comédiens du roi*. "No," said the King; "in my reign they shall never be what they have been in those of my predecessors; let no more be said to me on the subject."

At the age of fifty Clairon migrated to the Court of the Margrave of Anspach, where she remained seventeen years. During this time she wrote much of her auto-biography, besides some valuable *Réflexions sur la Déclamation Théâtrale.* In 1791, the Margrave dying, she returned to Paris, and before long was reduced to comparative poverty by the general stoppage of Court pensions as the monarchy fell. For this loss she had some consolation in the profits of her *Mémoires et Réflexions*, which came out in 1799, and of which a second edition was called for in a few months. With her mind apparently unimpaired to the last, she died in sleep on the 18th of January 1803, within a few weeks of completing her eightieth year. Her book had revived the tradition of her greatness, and old playgoers may well have experienced a little sentimental regret on hearing that this bright link with the past had been snapped. Nor did the moralist fail to remark upon the contrast between her necessitous old age and her former position in the world—a position so elevated that to have met her in society was one of the proudest boasts which Voltaire put into the mouth of the braggart in *Candide.*

But to return to the point when she made up her mind to leave the stage. No less sensible than she was of the indignity just put upon them, but indisposed for various reasons to follow her example, the players sullenly returned to the even tenor of their way. *Le Siége de Calais* had come down like a rocket-stick, and another tragedy on French history, *Pharamond,* was to take its place. Profound secrecy was observed as to the authorship of the new piece, which had been sent to the theatre itself anonymously. " It is impossible," remarked Bachaumont, " not to admire this sudden modesty of our authors in having recourse to an incognito so difficult to maintain, but rendered as prudent as necessary by the repeated failures which most of them have experienced." *Pharamond* added another item to this already formid- able list. When the curtain fell, the pit, in a spirit of mingled curiosity and mischief, called for the author. Lekain, who had to make the announcement for the morrow, said that the dramatist was not there. " His name ? "   Lekain replied that he did not know it, which was probably the fact. " If *I* had the honour to be the pit," energetically declared a young virago near the orchestra, " I would soon have the secret out." In the result, *Pharamond* had only two representations, both of which were rather stormy. " This tragedy," says Bachaumont, " has a simplicity of plan very rare now- adays—a quality which leads most connoisseurs to believe that the work is by M. de Laharpe." The sagacity of the connoisseurs was not at fault.

In the following month another piece appeared without its author's name. *Phèdre* was announced

for the 30th of September, with Dumesnil in the
part which Clairon had so long made her own. But
when the audience had assembled Préville asked them
to allow an unrepresented five-act comedy in prose to
be substituted for the tragedy, and the change was
assented to without a murmur. *Le Tuteur Dupé*, as
the novelty was called, had the merit of arraying an
old and familiar story, that of the *Ecole des Femmes*,
in a fresh and not unattractive dress. Bounteously
cheered at the Comédie, it soon found its way to
Fontainebleau, where the writer received the honour,
then unprecedented in Court-annals, of being called
before the curtain. Thereupon, with becoming modesty
and self-possession, Jean François Cailhava, a young poet
from Toulouse, faced that brilliant assemblage, made his
best bow, and disappeared. Few could have grudged
him this triumph, as it had been achieved in the teeth
of more than one disappointment. In 1757, having
distinguished himself by a poem on Damien's attempt
to assassinate the King, he turned his attention to the
drama, but for some time without encouragement to
persevere. His first piece was rejected; the second
excited derision. "A youth who has come from
Toulouse expressly to be hissed," was Grimm's description of the aspirant. Many excellent critics, however,
saw in the *Tuteur Dupé* the germ of considerable aptitude. "I hope," wrote Voltaire to the author, "that

you will not rest content with this essay. My greatest consolation in a languishing old age is to see the arts I so passionately love upheld by a man of your talents."

Higher praise awaited another five-act comedy in prose, the *Philosophe sans le Savoir*, in which some of the ideas generated by the *Contrat Social* found vague but not unintelligible expression. Its author, Jean Michel Sédaine, born in Paris as far back as 1719, might be called the Vanbrugh of French literature and art. In his sixteenth year, having lost his father, a struggling architect, he was called upon to do something for the support, not only of himself, but of an invalid mother and a goodly number of younger brothers and sisters. Manfully accepting his responsibility, he obtained employment as a stonemason—a craft of which he had idly picked up a little knowledge—and devoted his scanty leisure to the extension of his very incomplete education. In the dinner-hour one day, his master, the architect Buron, found him poring over a serious book, and, struck by a circumstance so unusual among the men, pleasantly entered into conversation with him. Sédaine had the secret of finding friends wherever he went. Buron made him a pupil free of charge, gave him a sort of partnership, and assisted him in acquiring separate eminence as an architect. But this eminence was not enough for Sédaine. He aspired to literary fame for its own sake. In 1756, after throwing off a

variety of songs, one of which was a humorous apostrophe to his coat, he contributed an opéra comique, the
Diable à Quatre, to the Foire St. Laurent.   Four others,
including the *Roi et le Fermier* and *On ne s'avise jamais
de tout*, came in tolerably rapid succession.   It is permis-
sible to suppose that he was a student of the latter-day
English drama, as the first-named piece, which brought
him 10,000 francs from the Comédie Italienne, is an adaptation of the farce, as yet not translated into French, of
the *Miller of Mansfield*.   *Le Philosophe sans le Savoir*, his
first essay for the Théâtre Français, was a comedy of the
kind advocated by Diderot, to whose theories on most
subjects he lent a willing ear, and for whom he cherished
a warm regard.   He infused the reforming spirit of the
age into a serious story, the principal incident therein
being the anguish of M. Vanderk, a man of quality
metamorphosed into an opulent merchant under another
name, on learning that his son is about to fight a duel.
Like Orbesson in the *Père de Famille*, this father indirectly preaches the doctrine of social equality.   He
holds the assumed privileges of rank and wealth in
something like contempt.   " J'ai déja remis dans votre
famille," he says to his son in recommending him to
devote himself to commerce, " tous les biens que la
nécessité de servir le prince avait fait sortir des mains
de vos ancêtres.   Ils seront a vous, ces biens ; et si vous
pensez que j'ai fait par le commerce une tache à leur

nom, c'est à vous de l'effacer ; mais, dans un siècle aussi éclairé que le nôtre, ce qui peut procurer la noblesse n'est pas capable de l'ôter." *Le Philosophe sans le Savoir* was to have been played in the first instance at Fontainebleau, but the police found so much in it to object to that the intended performance did not take place. Having undergone a formal revision, it at length appeared at the Comédie Française (November 2), with the above-quoted speech, among others of a similar tendency, inadvertently overlooked. Excellent in a dramatic rather than purely literary sense, as all Sédaine's work was, it met with loud applause, especially where passages in harmony with public sentiment were recited. Diderot, ever free from unworthy jealousy, cordially hailed the advent of this powerful disciple. " Mon cher ami," he exclaimed, " if you were not so old I would make you my son-in-law." Mlle. Diderot might easily have done worse than by espousing her father's helpmate, his forty-seven years notwithstanding. Outwardly austere and caustic, he had one of the most generous of dispositions, as was shown by the trouble and expense he went to in preparing Buron's grandson, François David, for his fruitful career as a painter.

Sédaine's imitation of the *Miller of Mansfield* did more than provide the Comédie Italienne with an attractive musical piece. It suggested to Collé an extremely

happy idea. Borrowing the plot without substantial
alteration, he transferred the scene to France, made
Henri Quatre his hero, and drew a faithful and pleasing
picture of that genial monarch's surroundings. For
most of the details, indeed, there was historical warrant.
La Partie de Chasse d'Henri IV., as the piece came to
be named, is in three acts. In the first, representing
the old Louvre, we are shown a group consisting of
the King, Sulli, Rosni, Conchini, and Bellegarde, with
the second vindicating himself from the aspersions so
bitterly cast upon his probity by innumerable enemies.
One of these, Conchini, has just abducted a beautiful
peasant girl, who, however, contrives to escape before
he can attain his object. Sulli's defence concluded,
Henri and his courtiers go a hunting in the forest of
Sénart, where they are overtaken by the night. His
majesty presently finds himself on foot and unattended
—a circumstance on which he dwells with characteristic
pleasantry. Suddenly he is confronted and seized by
Michau, a peasant. "I have him!" the latter triumph-
antly shouts to two others in the rear; "rascal, you
come here to poach upon our excellent King's preserves!"
For the affection in which his majesty is generally held
is so great here that the inhabitants gratuitously serve
him as gamekeepers. He is too sensible of the humour
of the situation to avow who he really is. He gives
himself out as a subordinate member of the royal

household, and is invited to pass the night in Michau's cottage. Now, his captor has a pretty daughter, by name Catau. Henri, unrecognized by any of the family, helps her to get supper ready, sets the table for her, places himself by her side, delights her by innumerable little attentions, pledges her in more than one bumper, and generally makes himself completely at home. Supper over, the good Michau, among other things, sings a loyal song with the following refrain :—

> Vive Henri Quatre,
>   Vive ce Roi vaillant :
> Ce diable à quatre
>   A le triple talent
> De boire et de battre
>   Et d'être vert galant.

His majesty, profoundly touched, then finds it necessary to drink his own health—a duty which he fulfils with sufficient awkwardness to bring upon himself a suspicion of disloyalty. Presently the party is joined by Conchini's intended victim, Agathe, long betrothed to one Richard. Henri waxes wroth on learning of the indignity put upon her by the Marquis, who, with Sulli and Belle-garde, enters in search of him. " Sire ! " exclaims one of the new-comers. Michau, bewildered by the surprise conveyed in that word, falls at the feet of his guest. His majesty acts precisely as might have been an-ticipated. He sends Conchini away in disgrace, gives Catau and Agathe each a comfortable dowry, and then,

having had a long day, goes to sleep in the cottager's
bed.   And therewith the *Partie de Chasse* comes to an
end.   Collé was to be congratulated upon having painted
a striking portrait in agreeable dialogue.   Henri Quatre
seemed to live again in those three different scenes.   His
political sagacity, his strength of character, his martial
ardour, his chivalric spirit, his imperturbable Gascon
humour, his high-bred gallantry, his easy dignity of
bearing, his thoroughgoing *bonhomie,* his open-handed
generosity, his hearty affection for and sympathy with
the people, and also, it must be added, his proverbial
quickness to admire a pretty woman,—all these points
are illustrated or glanced at with good effect.   But the
author's success in this way exposed him to a keen disappointment.   Louis XV., while allowing the piece to
be printed and represented in private, decided to prevent
the run it was certain to have at the Comédie Française.
For there, with the potent and finished art of Brizard,
the selected representative of the hero, to give it
additional vitality, it could not fail to create the most
vivid impression, and might lead the democracy to
institute daily comparisons between the illustrious Henri
and the present occupant of the throne.   It might
indeed rekindle a little enthusiasm for the monarchy,
but the future of the monarchy was a matter of indifference to Louis XV. if the people could be induced to
abstain from any rising against himself.

The players were consoled for this loss by an important accession to their ranks. " Mlle. Clairon's *emploi*," the Old Amateur writes, " had been abandoned to Mlle. Dubois, an actress less clever than beautiful. Mlle. Sainval, an actress less beautiful than clever, was summoned to divide it with her. The new-comer was neither tall nor gracious, but had the art of giving her figure a dignity and her countenance a charm which they did not possess off the stage. Barely twenty years of age, she had yet established a rather high reputation at Lyons, whence she had come. I saw from the first that that reputation was just. Mlle. Sainval had intelligence, warmth, dignity, and pathos. In her, however, I found less analogy with Mlle. Clairon than with Mlle. Dumesnil. Natural and simple, like the latter, Mlle. Sainval sometimes had that *diable au corps* which, according to Voltaire, is necessary to success in any art. How surprising she was as Phèdre, Clytemnestre, and Hermione ! But, also like Dumesnil, how slow and monotonous and insignificant she was when the *diable* abandoned her, as it occasionally did ! Faults which the energy of her acting had obscured or excused then became apparent; the seamy side of her elocution forced itself upon our attention. Born at Aix, she had contracted a Provençal accent, and could never wholly shake it off. In proportion as her talent developed itself the justness of my remark was confirmed.

Enlightened by experience, the *sociétaires* of the Théâtre
Français, perceiving that it was not for her to succeed
Mlle. Clairon, elected her to double Mlle. Dumesnil,
who had already been " nearly " thirty years at the
theatre."

But against the advent of Mlle. Sainval the players
had to set four successive disappointments.   In the first
place, a *Barneveldt* by Lemierre was suppressed by the
police, on the ground that certain tirades at the expense
of the tribunal by which the hero was condemned would
be susceptible of dangerous applications.   Laharpe was
not fortunate in an attempt to surpass even Piron in
a *Gustave Vasa*.   " It was my lot," ironically wrote
Fréron, always ready to wound a philosopher, " to be
a witness of this disaster, which caused me considerable pain, but seemed to delight the spectators
around me.   I asked them why it did.   They replied
that it was not wrong to rejoice in the humiliation of
a young man who, as they said, had boasted of having
written a tragedy much superior to M. Piron's."   In
no way daunted by the loss of *Barneveldt*, Lemierre
hastened to complete *Artaxerxe,* an adaptation of Metastasio's tragedy, and a *Guillaume Tell*, perhaps the
best of its author's many works.   Both fell, the latter
being weak enough to damp the ardour with which the
pit were predisposed to hail the appearance of the
mythical patriot.   Lekain, who played the character,

had been provided with some perfervid diatribes in favour of liberty, but was not allowed by the police to declaim more than a few lines of an inflammatory nature. At the last performance of *Tell* the pit was composed almost exclusively of Helvetians in Paris, including the brave and devoted guard. "It is a proverb," remarked Sophie Arnould, the witty idol of opera-goers, who happened to be present, "that where there is no money we find no Swiss : here, however, we have more Swiss than money."

CHAPTER IV.

1767—1774.

For an illustration of the highest bourgeois life in Paris in the middle of the eighteenth century we could hardly do better than look in upon a family group in the Rue Saint Denis. Prominent among the overhanging houses in that ancient thoroughfare, which for a time enjoyed the honour of being the birthplace of Molière, was one occupied by a watchmaker named Caron. In his hands it had become a home of industry, of literature, of all the domestic virtues. He had succeeded in business beyond the dreams of his youth, possessed a far-reaching knowledge of science and art, and united to a fine joviality of disposition an abiding reverence for the great and the good. Of the eminence he attained we have a proof in the fact that the government of Madrid consulted him as to machines for dragging harbours and rivers. By his wife, who was not unworthy of such a husband, he had six children—Pierre Augustin, Marie Josèphe, Marie Louise (destined to be the heroine of a play), Madeleine, Julie, and Marguerite. Most of them had

rare social and musical gifts, and it must have been
a pleasant thing to join them when they came round
their parents to pass the evening together. M. Caron,
though strictly pious, did not allow Bossuet's denuncia-
tion. of the drama to interfere with a taste among them
for amateur theatricals. " On Tuesday night," writes one
of the daughters, " we played *Nanine* and the *Folies
Amoureuses.* Forty-five persons were present, and Julie
gained general admiration in all she did. Everybody declared that she was one of the best actresses
out. I do not say this for the sake of praising her—
you know how modest she is—but solely to gratify
your weakness for her. On the day after the festival
of St. Quasimodo we gave *Tartuffe* and the *Servante
Maîtresse.*"

It was in this refined home-atmosphere that Pierre
Augustin Caron passed through the period of life in
which character is most susceptible to external influences.
He came into the world at the house in the Rue St.
Denis on the 24th January 1732. Opulent as M. Caron
was, it would seem that the boy received no higher
education than could be supplied by the school at Alfort,
where his progress exceeded the calculations of his
tutors, but whence he was recalled at an early age
to learn his father's business. For two or three years
he did not prove an apt apprentice. He constantly
neglected his work for music, boyish revelry, and also,

it is said, less innocent pleasures.   M. Caron, never to
be trifled with, at length turned him out of doors,
previously making arrangements with some friends to
receive and reform the offender.   Sobered by this stroke
of paternal authority, Pierre indited models of eloquent
penitence to his father, who allowed him to return home
on the conditions that· he should devote himself to his
trade, give up the society of young people, and not
play upon his chosen musical instruments, the violin
and the flute, until after supper on all working days.
Henceforward he gave no trouble or alarm to his
parents.   He began to make watches in excellent style,
at the same time manifesting a strength of intelligence
and character which promised well for the future.   M.
Caron's former anger gave place to a sort of affectionate
enthusiasm.   " A son like yourself," he writes, " is not
made to be loved only a little by a father who thinks
and feels as I do."

Caron had scarcely come to man's estate when a
flattering prospect opened before him.   He invented
a new kind of escapement.   Mastering the secret,
Lepaute, a well-known watchmaker, claimed the merit
of the idea for himself, probably in the belief that
the word of an obscure beginner would not be taken
against his.   In a letter to the *Mercure*, however, the
obscure beginner firmly asserted his rights in the matter.
Lepaute, in reply, referred to his extensive connexion,

repeated his falsehood, and produced a certificate
signed by three Jesuits and the Chevalier de la Morlière.   Presently, at the instance of the Comte de
St. Florentin, the dispute was referred to two com-
missioners from the Academy, who decided in favour
of Caron.   As though to complete his triumph, he
then received an order to make a watch on the new
principle for the King, and had the privilege of de-
livering it to him in person at a levée. " Never," we
are assured, " did his majesty receive an artist with so
much kindness."   *Regis ad exemplar*, all the courtiers
thought it expedient to patronize Caron, each striving to
be served before the others.   Meanwhile, it seems, the
ladies at Versailles were impressed by what is described
as his lofty stature, his elegant figure, the regularity of
his features, his clear complexion, his confident look,
his commanding air, his involuntary ardour in their
presence.   Indeed, one of them, the young wife of
an old Court official, fell straightway in love with
him, called at the shop in the Rue St. Denis under
pretence of taking him a watch for repairs, and allowed
him to see that he would please her by returning it
himself.   Her husband, after complacently sanctioning
the intimacy thus begun, agreed, in consideration of
a respectable annuity, to resign his post in favour of
Caron, who, bidding a final adieu to trade, then became
" contrôleur clerc d'office de la maison du Roi," married

his benefactress as soon as she was free, and added the name of Beaumarchais (said to have been derived from a fief owned by his wife) to that of his fathers.

His position at Court showed a marked improvement in the course of two or three years. Fashion suddenly smiled upon the long-neglected harp, and Beaumarchais, who soon became a widower, acquired sufficient skill in playing it to be asked to give lessons to the King's daughters. Delighted with their tutor, the Princesses made him the manager of and chief performer in the concerts which they gave every week to their majesties and the Dauphin. This sudden stride, of course, excited much anger among the courtiers, and the harpist was beset with temptations to forget himself in such a way as to cut the ground from under his feet. But his courage and presence of mind never forsook him. One afternoon a noble boasted that he would disconcert this protégé of " Mesdames de France," and, finding him in the midst of a group at the door of their apartment, put a very handsome watch into his hands. " Monsieur," he said, " as you understand such things I beg you to examine this, which is out of order." " Monsieur," replied Beaumarchais, alive to the underlying taunt, " since I left the business I have become very clumsy at it." " Pray do not refuse me." " Be it so ; but remember the caution I have given you." He then opened the watch, held it up high as though to examine it, and let it fall upon the hard polished flooring. "Monsieur," he said, turning away with a low bow, "I had warned you of my extreme clumsiness." On another occasion the insolence to which he was exposed had a more serious result. Honour compelled him to challenge a Chevalier de C—. Unattended by seconds, they fought under the walls of Meudon, and Beaumarchais inflicted a fatal wound upon his antagonist. "Hence!" cried the dying man; "you are lost if it becomes known that you have killed me." Beaumarchais returned to Paris, but not before procuring a doctor from the village. On being taken home the Chevalier firmly refused to name his adversary. "I have only what I deserve," he moaned; "to please persons for whom I had no esteem I insulted an unoffending man." Beaumarchais, however, took the Princesses into his confidence, with the result that he was protected from the ordinary consequences to a bourgeois of killing a man of high birth. But a citizen he was not long to remain. Pâris-Duverney, out of gratitude for an important service, advanced him large sums for purposes of speculation, with sage advice as to how they should be invested. Befriended in this way, he was enabled to purchase various offices, including that of the captainry of the Warren of the Louvre, and in 1761 to give his adopted surname the coveted prefix of "de" by procuring for 85,000 francs the nominal

charge of Secrétaire du Roi.   He would also have had
a grand-mastership of Waters and Forests if his intended
colleagues, remembering that he had been a tradesman,
had not protested against his appointment—a protest
which may have led him to dwell with some bitterness
upon the peculiar prejudices inseparable from rank in
old France.

M. Caron, in order to facilitate his son's progress at
Court, had reluctantly retired from business, and was
now living at a house in the Rue de Conn.   In a few
months two lights of the household disappeared, one
of his elder daughters marrying an architect at Madrid,
and Marie Louise accompanying her thither as a sort
of companion.   Fitted to grace any society, the latter
was wooed by a government official named Clavijo,
who, however, broke off the engagement in such a way
as to leave her under a sort of stigma.   Beaumarchais,
quivering in every fibre, repaired in all haste to
Madrid, confronted the faithless lover, and, by a rare
union of firmness and tact, forced him to untarnish
her reputation in terms by no means flattering to
himself.   In revenge for this humiliation, which he
could not avoid except at the cost of meeting an
unerring swordsman, the Spaniard sought to have him
arrested on a charge of conspiracy against the government.   Hearing of the net spread for him, Beaumarchais
found access to the King himself, satisfactorily cleared

himself of the imputation, and caused Clavijo to be
dismissed from Court.   For a time, as may be supposed,
the high-spirited and resolute young Frenchman was the
observed of all observers in Madrid.   His adventures,
his wit, his musical accomplishments, and his grace of
manner made him welcome to the most exclusive salons,
especially those of the English, French, and Russian
Embassies.   But he did not give up all his time to
pleasure.   He entered into commercial speculations,
wrote memoirs on political questions, and keenly
studied the literature of the country.   Eventually he
returned to Paris, possibly a little poorer than he went,
some of his speculations having miscarried, but "richer,"
as his biographer says, "than he was aware, since he
carried in his head the lineaments of those strongly
marked and original figures which, some day or other,
were to make the glory of his name."

A contempt for the latter-day Spanish drama seems
to have fired him with a desire to show how much that
drama could be improved upon in France.   Entirely
ignoring the real bent of his talents, he wrote a
comedy after the manner of Diderot, to whose influence
he yielded in more than one respect.   A Marquis de
Rosempré, nephew of a War-Minister, contracts a sham
marriage with the daughter of a Baron de Kerbulec, a
valet in disguise taking the place of the priest.   In the
end, however, he legally marries her, though not until

he has failed to capture an heiress. For some unexplained reason the censor required the scene to be
transferred to England, at the same time striking out
a few sneers in the dialogue at the expense of social
distinctions. M. le Marquis accordingly became Lord
Clarendon, and Eugénie, the heroine, the daughter of
a Welsh nobleman. *Eugénie,* as the piece was entitled,
came forth at the Comédie Française on the 29th of
January, with Mlle. Doligny and Préville in the
principal parts. Its dramatic and literary value was
not very great, and the fact that the author aspired
to mount the ladder of Court distinction may have
done something to intensify the coolness with which
it was received. Beaumarchais, writes Grimm, "will
never do anything, even mediocre. In the whole
piece there is only one thing that pleases me. It
is in the fifth act : Eugénie, recovering from a long
fainting fit, finds Clarendon at her feet, and, throwing herself back, exclaims, 'I thought I saw him!'
This phrase is so happy, it stands out so much
from the rest, that I would bet he did not write
it." In Collé's opinion, too, the author had proved
beyond the shadow of a doubt that he had neither
genius, nor wit, nor talents. In this case the danger
of prediction was again demonstrated. Beaumarchais,
nothing daunted, made structural and other alterations
in the piece, which reappeared " with éclat" (*f*).

In the midst of the applause ultimately bestowed upon *Eugénie* we seem to hear a sigh of relief. Five months previously, after an abortive attempt to find favour in the eyes of Jeanne Vaubernier, then living with the Comte Jean, who proposed to enrich himself by means of her beauty, Molé was seized with what the doctors declared to be a dangerous pulmonary complaint. Never had the popularity of a player been more conclusively proved than it was in this instance. It is not too much to say that the news created consternation in all quarters. The street in which Molé lived was more or less blocked all day by the coaches of inquirers. Every morning a bulletin was affixed to the door of his house ; every evening the performance at the Comédie Française had to be preceded by an announcement of the progress he was making. Ladies would take boxes a week in advance to be among the first recipients of intelligence, while the lightest words of his physician were eagerly caught at. On one occasion it was whispered that the interesting patient had been ordered wine, and in less than twenty-four hours about two thousand bottles from the choicest cellars of Paris and Versailles were sent to his house. Some came from the King, who also made him two presents of fifty louis d'or each. By the 10th of February he was well enough to reappear. He did not know whether to make a speech or not, but the reception he met with was of a nature to decide the question in the affirmative, and in two or three " most modest " phrases he thanked the audience for the remarkable solicitude of which he had been the object.

One of Voltaire's amusements during the winter had been to compose in ten days a tragedy entitled *Les Scythes*, in which the interest of a pathetic story was deepened by an ever-present contrast between the manners of that people and those of the Persians, but which also showed that his old power in verse continued to decline. On being completed it was played at Ferney, with the author as a venerable old man among the characters. " I was much moved," writes a guest, Chabanon, " by his declamation, emphatic and cadenced as it might be. He made you feel harmony of verse and the interest of a situation. He had the first requisite of the stage, that of feeling strongly himself." Nevertheless, the *Scythes* did not create a very marked effect, and the author's disappointment was augmented by a request for *Adélaïde Duguesclin* when he wished to have the new tragedy given again. " I do not know," he rather quaintly said, " why they should be so fond of this *Adélaïde*." Inscribed to Choiseul and Praslin, who might induce the King to let him return to Paris, the *Scythes* was printed early in the year. Grimm saw the weakness of the style, but thought that the piece would succeed on the stage in spite of its defects.

" M. de Voltaire's old age," he writes, " is very different
from Corneille's."   In the result, the *Scythes*, though
certainly superior to *Pulchérie* in dramatic force, had
only four representations, the first of which took place
on the 26th of March.   " I am told," Voltaire writes,
" that a horde of barbarians in the pit made a nice
clamour, and had no respect for my years."   In a week
or two, however, he allowed that the *Scythes* was " un
ouvrage fort médiocre."

" Our poets," says Grimm, " seem to be desirous of
carrying the art of failing to its highest perfection."
Les Deux Sœurs, a two-act comedy by Bret, with a
moral to the effect that charms of character win more
hearts than mere personal beauty (a debatable proposi-
tion), had but one representation ; while an original
tragedy, *Amélise*, fared equally ill.   Jean François Ducis,
the future adapter of Shakspere, was responsible for the
latter piece.   Born in 1733, this enterprising poet, the
son of a haberdasher, had obtained, thanks to the
influence of the Comte de Provence and others of his
father's customers, whom he delighted in his childhood,
a lucrative appointment in the bureau of Versailles, and
was occupying his leisure in learning English, in adapting Shaksperean plays to the French stage, and hovering
about the green-room of the Comédie Française.   Meeting Garrick there in 1765, he informed him, " in confidence," that he intended to recast the divine *Hamlet*

in such a form as would make it acceptable to an audience bred up in the faith of the unities. Before doing so he wished to show that it was in his power to compose an original tragedy, and *Amélise* sprang from his active brain in the course of a few weeks. The players, with unwonted warmth, regarded it as a means of filling their exchequer for many evenings, though only to find it suffer, despite the efforts of Mlle. Doligny, the most inglorious of theatrical deaths. Fortunately for the French drama, but hardly so for an intelligent appreciation there of Shakspere, Ducis did not allow this crushing reverse to divert him from his former studies. He seemed to feel that his mission in life was to introduce the "barbarian" to Paris in a new dress.

Both the old and latter-day English drama had become an object of careful and somewhat felonious attention to French authors. *Les Fausses Infidélités*, a one-act comedy by Barthe, was really a compression, with the humour of the original ingeniously left out, of the *Merry Wives of Windsor*. It is said that the players announced the piece before sending it to the police, who vindicated their dignity by withholding a few days the indispensable permission. If Barthe's aim here was primarily to exhibit Falstaff, he ought, of course, to have adapted the first part of *Henry IV.* in preference to the *Merry Wives*. Falstaff at Windsor is scarcely the delightful old rogue of Gadshill, Eastcheap, and Shrewsbury Plain. Much of his humour and self-possession and good luck seems to have deserted him in the royal borough. Barthe was unequal to the task of reproducing the character even in its less amusing aspect, partly because such a reproduction was almost out of the question, but chiefly, it is certain, from an utter inability to catch the real significance of what he attempted to translate. Mondor, as the knight is here called, is only a faint and blurred reflection of a striking portrait. Nor was it improved in the representation. "Préville," writes Grimm, "is not suited to the part. His sharp voice, his pointed chin, and also, perhaps, his associations with the valets give him a Gascon and burlesquing air quite out of place in the impersonation of Mondor." On the whole, according to Grimm, the comedy "pleased, diverted, and was therefore accounted perfect." In regard to plays from the more recent English drama, a trifle by Rochon de Chabannes, *Les Valets Maîtres de la Maison*, was obviously derived from *High Life Below Stairs*, and an adaptation by Saurin of Moore's *Gamester*, with Molé as Beverley, Préville as Stukeley, Bellecourt as Lewson, and Mlle. Doligny as the wife, figured among the novelties in preparation for the forthcoming spring.

Before dealing with this last-named piece, the production of which promised to be an event of considerable importance, we may go into the green-room to inquire how far a remark of Grimm, to the effect that the Comédie was going from bad to worse, is borne out by facts. It is to be feared that the facts are on his side. Molé was compelled by the weakness of his chest to appear only thrice a week. Grandval, so long at the head of the company, the original representative of Nérestan and other Voltarian heroes, finally withdrew at the *clôture*. He first quitted the stage in 1762, but was prevailed upon to return shortly afterwards. Notwithstanding the weight of fifty-eight years, he was admirable to the last in high comedy, especially as Alceste and the Glorieux, and might have done much to maintain his former reputation in tragedy but for the advent of greater actors. Heaviest blow of all, Lekain found it necessary to take some months' rest, apparently in consequence of overwork. However, there was some hope for the future. Dugazon, an unsuccessful débutant in 1739, but for some years a prosperous manager in the country, was the father of three children evidently destined by nature to be players. Marie, the eldest, now appeared at the Comédie as Dorine in *Tartuffe*, and, though somewhat feeble in a physical sense, was received to double Mlles. Luzi and Fanier in the soubrettes.

Under the title of *Béverley*—for the title of *Le Joueur* was borne by Regnard's still popular masterpiece—Saurin's adaptation of the *Gamester* appeared on the

7th of May.   In point of principle it exhibited the
most daring innovation yet attempted on the French
stage.   Following the original rather closely, it was the
first example in Paris of the domestic tragedy so firmly
implanted in England, of that dramatic species in which
the play' of tragic passions is portrayed in pictures of
middle-class life.   In making this experiment, we may
presume, Saurin flattered himself that many circumstances were in his favour.   Innovation, especially when
inspired by England, now had an attractiveness of its
own.   The rising democracy would hail with delight
the severance of the long connexion between tragedy
and courts.   Domestic tragedy obviously extended the
scope of the drama, and had been advocated by so
powerful a writer as Diderot.   But the inferences which
the dramatist seems to have drawn from these incontest-
able facts were hardly borne out by the event.   Paris,
with all its love of change and growing antipathy to
courts, was not yet prepared to welcome the new school
of art.   Nothing had taken firmer possession of the
minds of the playgoing public than a conviction that
palaces and diadems were essential to the dignity of
Melpomene, and that with less exalted associations she
was wickedly vulgarized.   Accordingly, men distinguished by an eager receptivity of new ideas joined the
conservatives in deploring the " profanation " involved
in *Béverley*.   Tragedy, they insisted, ought to go on as

it had been handed down to them by Corneille, Racine, and Voltaire. Perhaps the best summary of the arguments they employed may be found in an extract from Campbell's prose. "Undoubtedly," he says, "the genuine delineation of the human heart will please us, from whatever station or circumstances in life it is derived. But something more than pathos is required in tragedy; and the very pain that attends our sympathy requires agreeable and romantic associations of the fancy to be blended with its poignancy. Whatever attaches ideas of importance, publicity, and elevation to the object of pity forms a brightening and alluring medium to the imagination." Yet, notwithstanding the prejudice it had to encounter, *Béverley* brought together many large audiences, thanks in part to the force shown by Molé as the Gamester (*g*).

By rare ill-fortune, a dramatist who at once understood the value of the exotic, and who, I think, might have done more than any of his fellows to cultivate it with success, was induced by an unexpected difference with the players to abandon them. For this untoward incident they were indebted to the old custom of giving an author a ninth of the gross receipts until the sum on two consecutive nights, or three nights separately, came to less than 500 livres, when the piece became the property of the theatre—an arrangement which, first laid down in 1653, had been acquiesced in by all writers for the stage, from Corneille to Voltaire inclusive. Sédaine, after sending to the theatre a one-act comedy in prose, the *Gageure Imprévue*, applied to the treasurer for what a revival of the *Philosophe sans le Savoir* might have placed to his account. " Monsieur," was the reply, " the piece had previously ' fallen within the rules,' so that you are no longer entitled to a share." In temporary want of money, he addressed an angry letter to the company, to the effect that they had not apprised him of this alleged falling within the rules, that his piece had been maliciously played at fruitless times, that the annual subscriptions had not been taken into calculation, and that no allowance was made to authors in consideration of the numerous free admissions to the house. The company, full of resentment at the imputation upon their " probity," then returned to him the manuscript of his comedy, remarking that they would not play the piece again. Nevertheless, the *Gageure Imprévue*, a bright little piece, apparently derived from the same source as *L'Ecole des Femmes* (a novel by Scarron), was produced in due course. Sédaine did not allow this indirect compliment to appease his disappointment. He resolved to write nothing in future except for the Opéra and the Comédie Italienne.

By this time the performances at the Comédie had derived an added charm from the frequent presence there of the King of Denmark, who was on a formal visit to the Court of France. His majesty seems to have glowed with enthusiasm over any fine piece of dramatic or histrionic work. He complimented Lekain so profusely as to his Tancrède that the great tragedian felt bound to interrupt him—"Your majesty is too good." He gave Clairon a superb ring after she had played Didon at Madame de Villeroi's for his edification. He sent Mlle. Luzi and Mlle. Doligny a gold *tabatière* each—not that either of them was a snuff-taker—and presents of money to the leading actors of the company. During a representation of the *Fausses Infidélités*, according to Grimm, Barthe was emboldened by the King's usual affability to enter the royal box uninvited. He ventured to express a hope that his majesty liked the piece. "It is very pleasing," said the King, somewhat taken aback. "Sire," continued Barthe, "permit me to offer you a copy." For this poet was not disinclined to thrust himself forward in and out of season. He rose superior to modesty. On the appearance of his *Art d'Aimer* he was saluted by a young poet as the "conqueror of Bernard and Ovid." "No, no," he affectedly said; "'conqueror' is too much." His flatterer then substituted the word "rival." "On further reflection," said Barthe, after a pause, "'conqueror' *does* seem to be the more euphonious of the two."

Lekain, it will have been seen, had returned to the Comédie, where a performance of *Sémiramis* for his

benefit was given on the 2d of December. He was
still unequal to the fatigue of playing, but had been
asked by the Duc de Duras, First Gentleman of the
Chamber, to give the advantage of his advice to a
débutante in whose success that peer evinced the liveliest
interest.   Marie Josèphe Dugazon, the second of three
youthful players recently mentioned, had begun her
career in the company collected at Stuttgart for the
amusement of the Duke of Wurtemberg, and in the
previous spring had come to Paris in the hope of
winning a position at the Comédie.   Before this she
had become the wife of Angelo Marie Gaspard Vestris,
brother of that more famous Vestris who, shining
serenely at the Opéra as ballet-master and dancer,
used to say that Europe boasted of only three really
great men—the King of Prussia, M. de Voltaire, and
himself   By way of testing her powers, the Gentlemen of the Chamber caused her to play Andromaque
and in a little comic opera at a private theatre, that of
the Menus-Plaisirs, in the Rue Bergère.   Lekain and
Molé appeared with her in the tragedy as Oreste and
Pyrrhus respectively.   Eight hundred tickets were
issued for the performance, the cost of which was
defrayed by the King.   Endowed with considerable
talent and still more striking beauty, the actress was
pronounced "divine" by the whole of her august
audience, and the Duc de Duras, enamoured of her

from the first, forthwith put her under a course of instruction by Lekain, Dumesnil, and Clairon.

Madame Vestris, as she elected to be called, opened her début at the Comédie Française on the 19th of December as Aménaïde in *Tancrède*. Her success was instant and unequivocal. In the words of Bachaumont, she "delighted every spectator by her looks, the dignity of her attitudes, her gestures, the purity of her declamation, her intelligence—to be brief, by all the qualities which form a great actress, and which are necessary to make the public forget her predecessors. She has already left Mlle. Dubois far behind, and beyond all question will be the chief player in this theatre if she goes on as she has begun. Her appearances attract a surprising number of people to the Français, making other novelties there unnecessary." And the actress did go on as she began. Bachaumont subsequently notes that the crowd in the theatre increased day by day, and that every place was occupied when the orchestra struck up. In comedy she gained a few laurels, but the public preferred to see her in characters of the sterner cast, for which she was eventually admitted to the theatre.

In the sequel, perhaps, her popularity declined rather than increased. Bachaumont may have seen cause to withdraw or modify his remark that she had all the qualities of a great actress. Her pretensions to that

rank were at best 'slight. Notwithstanding excellent
tuition, she had contracted a measured and statuesque
style, and, unlike Clairon, was without the imaginative
force and intellectual subtlety required to atone for
the disadvantage. Her sudden advancement was due
simply to an elegant figure, fine dark eyes, a musical
voice, grace of manner, and a cultivated intelligence.
In the parts which for a time she made her own—
Aménaïde, Idamé, Cléopatre, Ariane, Alzire, and Lao-
dice—she lost much by comparison with Clairon. In
pathos, as in natural truth, she was inferior to Mlle.
Sainval, of whom she felt a jealousy which imported
a new element of discord into the theatre. Nor would
it appear that she had as great an aptitude for comedy.
If the Old Amateur may be trusted, she was deficient
in ease, *abandon*, and vivacity.

Molé was to distinguish himself in other than a
histrionic way. For about seventy years, it will be
remembered, the Church had refused to let a player
marry unless he or she had sworn to abandon the stage.
In no case had the renunciation been adhered to, for
almost as soon as the ceremony was over the newly
married person or persons received an order from the
Court to reappear. Christophe de Beaumont, the Archbishop of Paris, at length exerted himself to end a
scandal which could not fail to lower the dignity of
the priesthood. By relieving players of the disability

in question he would only have acted in harmony with
the spirit of his faith, but the old jealousy and hatred
of the theatre, joined to a reluctance to admit in effect
that any of his predecessors had been in the wrong, led
him to take a different course.   He would refuse to let
an actor or actress be married unless the Gentlemen of
the Chamber formally declared that as far as they
could prevent it the oath should not be broken.   Consequently, many members of the profession were living
in open sin, Molé and a Mlle. d'Epinay being among
the number.   Before long, however, the former, by
means not explained, contrived to have an order for
his marriage sent to the Archbishop with other such
documents ; the stern prelate signed all without looking
at them, and in an hour or two Mlle. d'Epinay became
Madame Molé.   Paris, with its proverbial love of mischief and antipathy to the clergy, naturally screamed
with delight on hearing of the trick ; nothing was
talked of but this " affaire ; " and never did Molé
experience so tremendous a reception as when, the
honeymoon over, he returned to the Comédie.

The players next put in rehearsal the first of Ducis'
intended adaptations of Shaksperean tragedy. *Hamlet*
appeared on September 30, with Molé as the Prince.
Broadly considered, it offered but little resemblance to
the play which it professed to reproduce in a classical
form.   Ducis, unlike many other adapters, might fairly

have termed his work original. In rearranging the plot, for example, he took far more liberty than was necessitated by the assumed conditions with which French dramatists had to comply. His late majesty has been poisoned by the Queen and her favourite. In the spirit, unseen by the audience, he unfolds this secret to Hamlet, who undertakes to avenge him. Hereupon a storm of contending passions arises in the breast of the young Prince. Nature forbids him to lift the dagger against his mother ; the favourite is the father of a beloved mistress. In an interview with her son, the Queen, alarmed by his agitation, confesses her complicity in the crime, and is made to faint at the sight of an urn in which the ashes of the murdered King have been placed. Hamlet, melted to filial tenderness, resolves to spare her life, but not that of her partner in guilt. Finding himself branded as a murderer, the latter provokes a sort of insurrection, though only in the end to be turned upon by the people ; he then slays himself, and the Queen follows his example. It is needless to add that in all these circumstances the very essence of the English *Hamlet* is lost. In place of Shakspere's Prince we have only what Collé justly called an "infuriated maniac." Irresolute and procrastinating the hero certainly is, but without suggesting the idea of a great and highly-strung nature sinking under the weight imposed upon it by a terrible mission.

Of the far-reaching philosophy ascribed to the character in the original—a philosophy which makes it an incarnation of the intellectual agitation induced by the Reformation—there are still fewer traces. Yet, notwithstanding the abuse lavished upon the piece by Shaksperean enthusiasts, Ducis's *Hamlet* is in many respects an impressive tragedy, and the audience received it with sufficient favour to make him persevere in his design of familiarizing his fellow-countrymen with the "conceptions of the illustrious English dramatist."

Beaumarchais, who continued to make way in the world, had not yet lost faith in himself as a writer of drames. In a five-act piece, *Les Deux Amis*, he again acted upon the principle of subordinating the delineation of character to the illustration of social situation. But the plot framed for this purpose was too improbable to create the desired effect. Aurelli, a merchant, and Mélac, a tax-collector, reside under the same roof. In order to relieve the first from temporary embarrassment, the second places at his disposal a large sum received for and on account of the State, but said to have been drawn from a bank in Paris. Hardly has the money been spent when an application for it is made by the Fermier-Général. Mélac avows that he has misappropriated it—an avowal which exposes him to many reproaches from the unsuspecting Aurelli. In the end, of course, all is set right, the Fermier-Général, whose heart is not very hard, consenting to overlook the irregularity in consideration of the offender's motives. *Les Deux Amis* is as prosaic in tone as it is improbable in substance. Grimm preserves an epigram to the effect that the capital employed in the story did not produce any interest. "To-day," writes Bachaumont on the 3rd of February, "is the tenth and last representation of the *Deux Amis*, which now expires after a longer agony than usual." Beaumarchais thought that he deserved a better reward, but he accepted his failure as a proof of his incapacity to shine in serious comedy, and was disposed from that moment to cultivate a species more in harmony with his gay and satirical temperament.

Idlers in the green-room were missing an old and noting a new face. Beetle-browed, taciturn, and good-natured Paulin, who as a "tyrant" had been *élevé à la brochette* by Voltaire, but who was less well placed in tragedy than as rustics, died on the 19th of January, after nearly thirty years' service. He had been a *sous-officier* at the Invalides, and his sword might have been seen on his coffin at the funeral. Jacques Mouvel, a provincial actor's son, born at Lunéville in 1745, was then haunting the theatre in the hope of being called upon to appear there. Nature, it is clear, had not intended him for a great career on the boards.

His figure was ungainly, his voice unmusical, his countenance pinched and wan. Privation had set an ineffaceable stamp upon his exterior. During his début, which opened on the 20th of April, he injudiciously undertook young heroes, thereby courting a damaging comparison with Molé and Bellecourt. Sophie Arnould remarked that on meeting such a lover a mistress would first offer him something to eat. But in parts of a sterner type, whether in tragedy or comedy, he impressed the audience to an extent which made his admission to the Comédie a certainty. He had intelligence and sensibility in a very high degree, and it was suggested more than once that Lekain—who, by the way, was still absent on account of ill-health—would find in him a dangerous rival. His elocution was faultless, his pantomime the perfection of theatrical eloquence. Off the stage Mouvel distinguished himself by pleasant manners, appreciable literary talent, and a fanatical hatred, born in some measure of many years' misery, of existing institutions. Never did the doctrines promulgated in the *Encyclopédie* obtain a more fervent advocate than the young player now received at the theatre.

Mouvel found the Comédie Française established in new quarters. Nearly two centuries old, the house in the Rue des Fossés St. Germain had fallen into a state of hopeless dilapidation, and the players received permission to occupy the *salle des machines* at the Tuileries until another theatre was erected for their use. Few of them could have made the change without a deep sentimental regret. Henri Quatre's favourite tennis-court had gathered to itself a thousand literary and artistic memories. It had been associated for eighty-one years with the varying fortunes of the Comédiens du Roi. It had been the scene of many splendid triumphs, of many disheartening reverses. It had been the home of the players who made French acting a household word throughout civilized Europe. It had been the means of introducing to the public the most monumental of the plays written during its existence as a theatre. Its audiences had from the outset included the flower of intellect and culture and rank. It had witnessed an infusion of new warmth and colouring into tragedy, the development of pathetic comedy, and the introduction of a species of the drama which, in harmony with the altered spirit of the time, sought to promote the cause of social reform. Moreover, if walls could speak, what a bright story might those of the green-room in that theatre have told— stories of brilliant gatherings there every night since the days of Madame de Maintenon, the peer meeting the brainworker on a footing of equality, each of the company knowing everybody else, and the conversation abounding in that refined wit which forms the most

distinctive feature of the time when men wore wigs
and ruffles and swords. Racine, Lafontaine, Boileau,
Molière's wife, Lafosse, Regnard, Fontenelle, Dancourt,
Baron, Dufresny, Brueys, Palaprat, Mlle. Duclos, Le-
grand, Crébillon, Mlle. Desmares, Boursault, Lamotte,
Lesage, Destouches, the Quinaults, Adrienne Lecouvreur, Voltaire, Marivaux, Marie Dangeville, Armand,
Piron, Jeanne Gaussin, Panard, Marie Dumesnil, Lachaussée, Gresset, Clairon, Lekain, Bellecourt, Palissot,
Préville, Molé, Brizard, Diderot, Laharpe, Collé, Sédaine,
Beaumarchais,—these, among many others, had joined
the circle in the *foyer* as time passed on, the earliest
of the names taking us back to the best years of the
Golden Age. Such a link with the past was not to be
resigned without regret. But the players had a substantial recompense for their loss in being allowed to
take possession of the *salle* at the Tuileries, where they
appeared on the 24th of April. For this *salle* (lately
the seat of the Opéra) was that erected by Vigarini
in 1671 for the representation of *Psyché,* and the fact
that Molière had set foot in it did not escape the men
and women who were so proud to call themselves his
" children."

If the wedding of the Dauphin and Marie Antoinette,
which took place this spring, induced a reaction in
favour of the monarchy—a reaction at best slight and
temporary—the current of popular feeling against the

Church flowed on with accelerated strength, especially
as the clergy, with their usual indifference to the moral
sense of the community, had caused a youth to be
executed at Abbeville for having, in a post-prandial
freak, made sport of a crucifix on the high road.
Lemierre, one of the hardiest of sceptics, was encouraged
by that feeling to undertake a task from which Voltaire
would have shrunk with horror.   In a tragedy entitled
the *Veuve du Malabar* he openly assailed the very
principle of religion, notably in a discussion between
the grand Brahmin and a novice as to the propriety
of the widows being burnt. How such a production
escaped the vigilance of the censor we are not told.
Plaudits frequently rang through the theatre as the
scene referred to went on, but the piece was not strong
enough in a dramatic or literary sense to obtain more
than six representations.   It remained to be seen, however, whether the *Veuve du Malabar*, reconstructed and
revised, would not be revived with success, since its
onslaught upon priestcraft was obviously to the taste of
a large section of the audience.

No other event of importance occurred at the new
home of the Comédie until the 3rd of December, when
a youthful candidate for histrionic honours, Jean Maudit,
otherwise Larive, opened a début as Zamore.   Born at
Larochelle in 1749, he had been an actor from his boyhood, and was now fresh from a series of triumphs at

Lyons. No votary of the art had enjoyed greater physical advantages. He had a noble countenance, a finely proportioned figure, large black eyes, a sonorous and flexible voice. Another thing in his favour was that he had been prepared for the Comédie by Lekain and Clairon, the latter of whom introduced him to Madame de Villeroi. "Allons," said the retired actress, "votre extérieur est fort beau ; montrez à madame que votre intérieur ne le céde en rien à votre extérieur." Between the two, however, there was a wide difference. Larive's acting lacked the charm of inspiration, sensibility, and verisimilitude. It was studied, regular, measured, statuesque. It is said that he never drew a tear, kindled the imagination, or emitted one of those accents which go to the soul. On the other hand, he was never wanting in intelligence and refinement, while his deportment had a grace and picturesqueness always pleasing to the eye. For these reasons he was eventually admitted to the Comédie, though not before he had made a second trial.

Lekain, cured of his long illness, reappeared on the 6th of February as Néron, with a cast comprising Molé, Brizard, and Mlle. Dumesnil. Bachaumont assures us that a new piece would not have attracted a larger audience, and that it was impossible to carry histrionic art to a higher degree of perfection than it reached in the principal performance. Indeed, it seems to be a

question whether the illustrious player had ever been
so great as he was from this time. "To that illness,"
writes the author of the *Réflexions sur Lekain*, "he
owed the perfect development of his gifts. This may
appear strange, but it is literally true. Certain dis-
orders in the animal economy often give the imagination
an inconceivable impetus. If the body suffers the mind
is active. It would seem as though these shocks
purified and renewed our being. And so it was with
Lekain. The inaction to which he had been reduced
became of service to him; his rest was that of labour.
Genius does not always require exercise; like the gold-
mine, it forms and perfects itself in silence and repose.
When he returned to the stage, the audience, instead
of having to show indulgence to a man enfeebled by
suffering, saw him, as it were, rise from the tomb with
a higher intelligence, with a purer and more perfect
existence. His acting—full, profound, pathetic, and
terrible—roused and moved the most apathetic of his
hearers."

Following close upon the return of Lekain was the
arrival of one of the most amusing comedians yet
secured by the theatre. Madame Vestris's brother,
Jean Baptiste Dugazon, born at Larochelle in 1748,
appeared on the 29th of April. Handsome, elegant,
and agile, with a wealth of humour and penetration
underlying his acting, he at once ingratiated himself

with the audience, and before long was made one of the
King's players. His style, it is true, was in the spirit
of farce rather than of comedy. By the side of Préville,
so refined in all his vivacity, he must have appeared
a mere caricaturist. Between the talents of these two
players, the Old Amateur tells us, there was the same
difference as between those of Molière and Regnard.
" It was in broad comedy," he adds, " that Dugazon
had the misfortune to appear perfect. No actor has
played better in the farces of Scarron and Legrand.
He eclipsed all his predecessors as Don Japhet and the
Roi de Cocagne, in which he was more extravagant than
these *auteurs de carnaval* themselves. He was, in fact,
the carnival personified." On the same authority, however, we learn that he " often merited the praises of
the sensible, playing with an infectious *verve* certain
characters in which his defects stood for qualities."
That he should have felt particularly at home in
Don Japhet was appropriate enough. He was himself
another Scarron—eccentric, joyous in all circumstances,
totally unable to put two serious ideas together, and
disposed to regard everything in a ridiculous light.
One of many strange notions in his head was that the
nose afforded a valuable means of expression, and he
wrote an elaborate treatise to prove that there are no
fewer than twenty ways of working that organ on the
stage with variety of effect.

His majesty's players, bearing in mind that the *Père de Famille* had been revived with far more success than might have been expected, ventured to produce the earlier of Diderot's dramas, *Le Fils Naturel* (July 26). Here, working upon a story borrowed from Goldoni's *True Friend*, the editor of the *Encyclopédie* pointedly combats the common prejudice among persons born in lawful wedlock against those who are not.   Dorval, the bastard, is betrothed to Constance, but secretly yearns for Posalie.   Unknown to himself, this passion is fully reciprocated, although its object has promised her hand to Clairville.   Pained by her indifference towards him, the latter takes counsel of Dorval, who on expostulating with Rosalie discovers where her affections lie.   In the course of the play, heroically sacrificing love to friendship, he revives her old attachment to Clairville, and a new susceptibility to the charms of Constance steals into his heart as he finds that she is not moved by an avowal of his abject birth.   Rosalie eventually proves to be Dorval's sister—decidedly a repelling incident.   *Le Fils Naturel* furnished another illustration of Diderot's inaptitude for the drama, but the reverence in which he was held, joined to a few passages of high and nervous eloquence, secured for it at least a success of esteem.   Fréron, predisposed against the piece on account of its author's heterodoxy, watched the development of the plot with malicious glee.   He knew the

True Friend, and, believing that he had the infidel on the hip, accused him in the *Année Littéraire* of an unscrupulous plagiarism. Diderot could well afford to laugh at the attack; the execution of the piece was peculiarly his own, and if he did wrong in borrowing a plot it was in such excellent company as Shakspere, Calderon, Corneille, Molière, Racine, and Voltaire (*h*).

By a curious coincidence, the next play we have to consider is one direct from Goldoni himself, who, after doing much to substitute the comedy of character for idle buffoonery on the Italian stage, had settled in Paris about nine years previously, and was now writing French with a fluency and grace which many Frenchmen might have envied. Recently completed, his three-act comedy of the *Bourru Bienfaisant,* supported by Préville, Molé, Madame Bellecourt (Mlle. Beaumenard), and Mlle. Doligny, appeared at the Comedie on the 4th of November. It was represented to a running accompaniment of plaudits, the chief character, that of a surly benefactor, delighting all from the outset. Goldoni, according to his own account, marched to and fro in his box all the time, quickening his steps in the best passages, more than satisfied with the players, and echoing the plaudits bestowed upon them. "Come," said Dauberval to him at the close, "you have to show yourself." "Show myself to whom?" "Why, to the audience." "No, no, my friend, let me go." Lekain and Brizard, entering the box at this moment, good-humouredly forced him, however, to make the expected bow. Goldoni did not like the practice of calling the author of a piece. He " could not conceive why a man should, as it were, say to the spectators, ' here I am, gentlemen, ready for your applause.' "

Looking over their accepted novelties, the players might well have wished that a few more foreign dramatists would write for the Comédie, since native talent was but poorly represented in the list. A tragedy by Leblanc, the *Druides*, is chiefly remarkable as involving indirect but emphatic attacks upon Christianity —attacks which, though resented by the Archbishop of Paris, did not prevent its being represented at the Court of his most Christian majesty. Ducis's second "adaptation" from Shakspere, *Roméo et Juliette* (July 23), was, if anything, of more audacious originality than his *Hamlet*. Montague, carried away by his hatred of Capulet, requires his son to immolate the heroine under the eyes of her parents, but is met with a point-blank refusal. Juliette finally poisons herself in order to reconcile the two houses, and Roméo, unable to survive her, stabs himself to the heart. How much of the nameless spirit and beauty of Shakspere's tragedy was preserved in such a story I need not stop to say. Next came a tragedy called *Les Chérusques*, the author being

that Beauvin with whom Marmontel had lodged over
a greengrocer's shop about a quarter of a century before,
and who had been enriched by the death of a wealthy
relative. Falling again into poverty, he had recently
written and printed this piece, which met with so little
praise that the players would have broken a promise
to produce it if the Dauphiness had not been led to
take an interest in its fortunes. Mlle. Dumesnil, Molé,
Madame Vestris, and Brizard were in the cast. Convinced that the audience would not sit out the
representation, they took but little pains to learn their
parts. "Never," writes Grimm, "have I seen a piece
so badly acted." The pit testified its sense of this
neglect by affecting a lively admiration for the play.
Beauvin was called at the close with "unprecedented
warmth." He did not appear, "possibly," Grimm
thought, "for the reason that he had not a coat to
appear in." Molé and Madame Vestris were publicly
rebuked on the third night for continued carelessness,
and the fourth performance was deferred in order that
they might make themselves letter-perfect.

But if the theatre was poor in striking novelties it
became richer in the means of enrobing its repertory
with a fresh interest. Elise Sainval, a younger sister
of the Mlle. Sainval already known to us, had appeared with some success on the stage in Copenhagen.
Migrating thence to Paris, she modestly asked for

permission to play once at the Comédie Française on her way to the south, as players who had trod those classic boards, albeit without acceptance, were more followed in the provinces than those who had not. Her sister seconded her request, and it was arranged that she should come forward as Alzire on the 27th of May. According to all the authorities, she so far underacted her part at the rehearsal that most of the company, seeing in her only a mechanical actress, stayed away from the performance. By doing so they missed the pleasure of speaking from personal experience of a really important event. From the moment she came on and spoke the audience were enchanted with her, and seldom had the theatre resounded with more ringing acclamations than those lavished at the close upon the actress who a few hours before had been pronounced in the green-room to be detestable. Grimm described her as one of the most valuable acquisitions the Comédie had made for some time, while Bachaumont thought that she would even surpass the elder Sainval. Nor were these eulogies undeserved. Mlle. Gaussin, the Old Amateur assures us, seemed to live again in the new-comer—a girl of too feeble a physique, indeed, to scale the heights of tragedy, but with the charms of beautiful eyes, a musical voice, simple grace of demeanour, and, above all, the most touching sensibility.

Hardly less fruitful than this début was one that

followed. After practising as a procureur at Langres,
where he was born in 1738, Denis Duchanel became
an actor under the name of Desessarts. Soon after
that, at Marseilles, he chanced to be seen by Bellecourt, who lauded him in Paris as the best of financiers
and rustics. Invited to try his fortune at the Comédie
Française, he made his first bow there on the 4th of
October as Lisimon in the *Glorieux*, and was promptly
admitted for the types of character just mentioned. No
living actor could compete with him as George Dandin,
M. Grichard in the *Grondeur*, Orgon in *Tartuffe*, and
Arnolphe in the *Ecole des Femmes*. Barely thirty-four
years of age, he was yet corpulent enough, like Stephen
Kemble, to play a Falstaff without padding. It is said
that the table under which he concealed himself in
Tartuffe had to be made expressly for the purpose, and
roars of laughter filled the air when, as Petit-Jean in
the *Plaideurs*, he mournfully complained of being " thin."
His comrades, of course, did not forget to jest at his
affliction. " Monseigneur," said the comic Dugazon to
the Minister of Police, introducing to him the new
actor, " we hear that the elephant in the menagerie
has at length breathed its last. My friend here hopes
that you will make him its successor." Desessarts
took the pleasantry in ill-part, and a challenge was the
result. " My friend," said Dugazon on meeting him
at the ground, " we are not equally matched. It is

easier for me to hit you than you me. Now, I will chalk a circle on your huge belly "—he suited the action to the word—" and all the thrusts made outside it shall not count." In another moment, laughing outright, they were locked in as close an embrace as physical conditions would permit. Notwithstanding an occasional irritability, Desessarts was of a bright and happy nature. His heart seemed to be in proportion to his *ventre*, which attained a circumference of three yards.

Desessarts had scarcely established a footing at the Comédie when preparations were made for the first appearance there of another well-known provincial player. Françoise Marie Antoinette Raucourt, a barber's daughter, was born at Dombasles in 1753. In early life, her father having more children than he could conveniently support, she was adopted by the postmaster of the place, one Sancerotte, who presently became a strolling player. For some years the course of the pair are traceable only at intervals. First we find them at Nancy, where Françoise, liking the sports of childhood better than the study of characters, would have a game of romps with a future comrade. Hissed off the stage at Lyons, M. Raucourt, as the former postmaster called himself, adventurously went to Spain, and at Cadiz his supposed daughter undertook a leading tragedy-part for the first time. It would appear that

after this she played at St. Petersburg. In 1771, at
Rouen, she made herself famous by a performance of
Euphémie in *Gaston et Bayard*, and in a few months
was invited by the Gentlemen of the Chamber to try
her fortunes in Paris. Arriving there with M. Raucourt
in the spring of 1772, she put herself in the hands of
Brizard, who soon came to feel a parental interest in
her success.

It would not be easy to convey an adequate idea of
the excitement caused by her début, which opened with
a performance of *Didon* on the 14th of December. Her
range did not include parts requiring delicate sensibility,
but in the portraiture of the sterner passions she
displayed much of the power and art of Clairon. In
addition to this, she was inexpressibly pleasing to the
eye, having a finely-proportioned figure, a beautiful
face, and a queenly dignity of demeanour. Moved to
enthusiasm by her varied attractions, the town rated
her at a little more than her real value. It was seriously
contended that she surpassed all her predecessors.
Dumesnil, Vestris, and the Sainvals found themselves
eclipsed. Her praises were loudly sung in the periodicals and correspondence of the time. Bachaumont
hailed her as a veritable prodigy ; Grimm predicted
that she would be the " gloire immortelle " of the French
stage ; another declared that the annihilation of the
British fleet alone could have produced a deeper sensa-

tion than her acting. Nor did the Court fail to echo this verdict of Paris upon her. Louis XV., despite his indifference to tragedy, sat out her Didon to the end, presented her to the Dauphiness as the Queen of Carthage, and gave her an order for reception at the Comédie and fifty louis. Madame Dubarri was not slow to follow his majesty's example. "Permit me," she said to the actress, "to make you a present. Which would you prefer, three dresses for your private use, or a *robe de théâtre?*" "Madame," was the reply, "I will take the latter, as in that case the public will profit by your goodness as well as myself." Nothing, in a word, was wanting to the success of the new *sociétaire.* From an early hour in the morning the bureau of the Comédie was besieged, and a few enterprising persons made large profits by buying tickets at the usual price and selling them by auction from scaffolds in the streets.

Before long, however, the enthusiasm she had excited began to cool. Her popularity seems to have been enhanced at first by an unsullied reputation off the stage. "I understand," writes Grimm, "that this charming creature, so inspiring in the theatre, is very simple in private life, occupying with girlish amusements the time not set apart for study." Idolized by all, she was approached, it is almost certain, by none. M. Raucourt, an excellent swordsman, announced his

intention to challenge any spark who might make
dishonouring advances to his adopted daughter, and
the virtue thus protected became so notorious that
Bachaumont occasionally felt himself called upon to
note that it continued to hold out.   It did so only for
a short time.   Voltaire, writing to the Duc de Richelieu,
adverted to a calumnious rumour that during her stay
in Spain she had been the mistress of a grandee.
D'Alembert, the Raucourts, the Princesse de Beauvan,
and the Marquis de Ximenès were at dinner with the
Duke when the letter came to hand.   Richelieu asked
the Marquis to read it aloud.   Ximenès complied, pro-
ceeding until he had uttered the sentence in question,
and then abruptly stopping.   Much commotion ensued ;
the actress fainted, M. Raucourt swore that he would
run the patriarch through the body, and the Princesse
de Beauvan called the maladroit Marquis a fool.
D'Alembert reported the incident to Voltaire, who
handsomely expressed regret for having taken notice
of the rumour, addressed a variety of pleasing madrigals
to Raucourt, and doubtless advised Richelieu to be more
cautious in future with what were intended to be
private letters.   But the scene at the Duke's soon
came to be noised about ; the actress's many lovers
took courage ; all her protestations were discredited.
Nothing, as Fleury observes, is more dangerous to
chastity than such a want of faith, nothing more dis-

heartening than to make sacrifices in which the world does not believe. In the result, M. Raucourt notwithstanding, she recklessly formed profligate connexions, first with the Duc d'Aiguillon, and lived as an opulent lady of fashion. From that moment she had to contend with an increasing coolness on the part of the pit. Darlings of the aristocracy were not to the liking of men with whom hatred of the aristocracy was fast becoming a species of madness.

Mingled with the criticisms passed upon the acting of Mlle. Raucourt at the outset were some vague rumours as to the character and purpose of a play just accepted at the theatre. Beaumarchais, arousing himself to a perception of the actual bent of his powers, had at length abandoned the lugubrious drama for comedy of a sportively satirical kind, and the *Barbier de Séville* now awaited rehearsal. In the first instance, as a means of giving effect to his admiration of tonadillas, the piece was written as a comic opera for the Italian players, who, however, rejected it with unusual promptitude. Not only did it bear a superficial resemblance to Sédaine's *On ne s'avise jamais de tout*, produced at their theatre in 1761, but the leader of the company, Clairval, an ex-barber, was pleased to recognize in the chief personage a sarcastic reflection of himself. Rarely had the influence of Molière been more clearly proved than it was by the *Barbier de Séville* in its

ultimate form. *Le Sicilien*—described by Voltaire as
the first one-act French piece with grace and gallantry
in it—supplied him with hints for nearly all the
characters; the pretty scene between Cléante and
Angélique in the second act of the *Malade Imaginaire*
is substantially reproduced, and the style bears ample
evidence of having been modelled upon that of the
master in his lighter mood. But these borrowings,
which could scarcely escape the notice of any frequenter
of the Comédie Française, did not prove incompatible
with a really high degree of originality. Beaumarchais,
like Shakspere, could allow himself to be inspired without
sinking to the level of a plagiarist. His *Barbier de Séville*
is pervaded by an animation and brilliancy peculiar to
himself, while the principal figures it brings before us—
Figaro, Almaviva, Rosine, Bartholo, Don Bazile, and La
Jeunesse—have an individuality and colouring of their
own. Especially is this true of the ingenious barber,
who may be deemed worth all the conventional Crispins
and Merlins of the Paris stage put together. In substance, however, the piece is one of intrigue, a cleverly
woven imbroglio rather than a collection of portraits.
If the author sought to delineate Spanish character he
was signally unsuccessful, but this was at best a slight
blemish in a work which otherwise deserves classical
rank in French comedy.

Nevertheless, the players showed some courage in

resolving to produce the piece. Beaumarchais had lately incurred so large a measure of public odium that nothing from his pen was likely to obtain an unprejudiced consideration. Pâris-Duverney, it seems, died in 1770, leaving a paper to the effect that he owed the dramatist 15,000 francs, and was desirous that 75,000 francs should be lent to him for eight years without interest. But the sole legatee, a Comte de Lablache, denounced the signature as a forgery. He confessedly hated Beaumarchais as a lover loves his mistress, and that hatred was to be gratified at all hazards. Beaumarchais asked that the accusation might be stated in the regular form, but the Count, not liking to give him the chance of proving his innocence, simply called upon the tribunals to annul the statement of accounts in question. His petition being rejected, he pertinaciously appealed against their decision to the superior court, whose judgment was now being awaited. " Il faut que Beaumarchais soit payé ou pendu," said the Prince de Conti. " If I win the case," retorted the dramatist, hearing of the remark, " I think my adversary should also pay *cordialement* un peu de sa personne." Meanwhile, to further his own interests, the Count called the Grub-street of Paris to his aid; Beaumarchais found himself branded far and wide as a forger, and the death of a second wife of his —more than half of whose fortune, by the way, consisted

in a life-annuity—was generously ascribed to slow poisoning. Nor did some of this mud fail to stick. Beaumarchais, already obnoxious to the populace by reason of
his progress at Court, became what Grimm calls the horror
of all Paris—a circumstance distinctly unfavourable to
the chances of any comedy brought out under his name.

Le Barbier de Séville, however, was not to appear
as soon as the players anticipated. It had yet to
undergo a careful revision, and the author met with
misfortunes which could not but unfit him for such
a task. Mlle. Ménard, one of the opéra singers, was
living under the protection of the Duc de Chaulnes,
who laboured under a violence of temper hardly com-
patible with sanity. Finding that she had transferred
her affections to Beaumarchais, he fiercely determined
to run his rival through the body, and for this purpose
went one morning to the Louvre as the latter, by
virtue of the most important of his offices, was dealing
with cases under the game laws. " I mean to kill
you, to tear out your heart, to drink your life's blood,"
he hissed when they were alone. " What complaint,"
asked Beaumarchais, " can you have against me ? I
have not seen you for six months." " No explanations ;
come out at once." Beaumarchais saw that he was in
an awkward position. In swordsmanship and coolness
he had an immense advantage over his adversary, and
it was certain that by killing a peer, even such a peer

as the Duc de Chaulnes, he would incur all sorts of
pains and penalties. He accordingly tried the effect
of a little reasoning in the matter, although the Duke's
utterances and gesticulations left no doubt that it would
be useless. "Hold," he said, "when a man wants to
fight he does not talk so much. Come to dinner at
my house, and if you are not restored to your senses
by four o'clock our quarrel shall then be settled by
arms." Chaulnes, anxious to keep his intended victim
in sight, at once consented. But even the presence of
Beaumarchais' sisters could not induce him to smother
his rage. He suddenly attempted to stab Beaumarchais
with a sword, and, having been disarmed by the
servants, tore out a large quantity of his hair. Beau
marchais then lost his self-command; he struck his
assailant in the face with all the strength he could
summon. "What!" exclaimed Chaulnes, "strike a
duke, a peer!" In another moment they were locked
in a terrible struggle, and it is difficult to say what
might have happened if a commissaire had not come
upon the scene. In the end both men were sent to
a State prison for some weeks, though the nature of
Beaumarchais' offence is not very clear. During his
incarceration he received a piece of news which might
well have plunged him into despair. The decision of
the Court of First Instance respecting the Duverney
bequest had been reversed on the appeal. In other

words, the superior court declared him to be a forger, and everything he possessed would become the property of the Crown. He seemed to have lived in vain; obloquy and ruin stared him in the face.

From this fall he rose with "added strength and glory." Buoyant, resourceful, and tenacious of purpose, he registered a vow to re-establish his broken credit, and was not slow to perceive a means of attaining that end. The day had gone against him upon the report of a judicial functionary named Goëzman, whose wife had been heard to declare that they could not live decently on their pay if they did not contrive to "plumer la poule sans la faire crier." In an early stage of the case, apprised of this curious venality, Beaumarchais had lent her one hundred louis, a watch of equal value, and fifteen louis as a fee for her secretary, on the understanding that if he were defeated all save the fifteen louis should be returned. Returned the one hundred louis and the watch were, but Beaumarchais presently discovered that instead of giving the fifteen louis to the secretary, Madame Goëzman had put them into her own pocket. Now, the Parliament was that which, composed of Court-parasites, had been thrust into the place of the ancient Parliament three years previously by Maupeou; and the dramatist, mindful of the widespread indignation excited by that stroke of arbitrary power, saw that

by convicting Goëzman of corrupt practices he might
bring over the whole of the people to support him
in an attempt to overthrow the judgment just pronounced. It was a dangerous enterprise for anybody
to undertake, but dangers, like difficulties, served only
to confirm his resolution. He applied to Madame
Goëzman for the return of the fifteen louis. Her reply
was precisely what might have been expected. M.
de Beaumarchais had offered her presents in order
to influence her husband's report, but without effect.
Goëzman, manifestly in great alarm, applied for a
lettre de cachet against his assailant, and, failing to
procure one, denounced him as having indirectly
attempted to interfere with the course of justice.
Beaumarchais, whose life was now at stake, instantly
proceeded to state his case in those memoirs or *factums*
which are always regarded as the best proof of his
powers. No juridicial writings have ever produced so
deep an impression. In all quarters they were read
and re-read with savage joy. Goëzman and his wife
were reviled, jeered at, and accepted as types of a
species. Louis Quinze, it was remarked, had destroyed
the old Parliament ; Quinze louis would destroy the
new. No less remarkable was the effect of the memoirs
upon the current estimate of the author. Paris rang
with praises of his courage, determination, and literary gifts. It was almost forgotten that he had been

regarded as a poisoner, a forger, and a hanger-on at
Court. "What a man!" wrote Voltaire to D'Alembert;
" he unites everything—humour, seriousness, argument,
gaiety, force, pathos, every kind of eloquence." Again,
obviously in allusion to a remark that in the many-
sided author another Voltaire had arisen, he says of the
memoirs—"They abound in wit; I fancy, however,
that more was needed to produce *Zaïre* and *Mérope*."

But it remained to be seen whether the Parliament
would not punish the intrepid author by holding him
guilty of the offence of which he was accused. Pending
their decision in that matter, it appears, he did little or
nothing with the *Barbier de Séville*, although the players
had become poorer and poorer in fresh matter. Even
on the hundredth anniversary of Molière's death they
could offer no better tribute to his memory than two
of the weakest pieces of the year. *Régulus*, tragedy,
by Dorat, brought the patience of the pit to a test
it could not withstand, but the credit of the author
was redeemed by the afterpiece, *La Feinte par Amour*,
in which a mistress discovers the passion of an
apparently indifferent lover by means of a portrait,
secretly painted by him, of herself. Marie Antoinette
and the Comtesse de Provence crept incognito to the
theatre, but were soon recognized by the audience.
"Lorsque," says Dorat in some lines addressed to the
former on the incident—

Lorsque vous trompez les yeux
Le cœur des François vous devine.

Next came a tragedy, *Orphanis*, by Blin de St. Maur, afterwards censor royal. Laharpe criticized the tragedy with
considerable acrimony, probably because its author had
spoken contemptuously of his *Eloge de Racine*. St. Maur
was not to be attacked with impunity. One afternoon,
as Laharpe, dressed with scrupulous care, was strutting
along on his way to a dinner, he had the misfortune
to encounter his victim, who gave him a sound caning.
No duel between them, however, seems to have followed.

Early in 1774, according to Bachaumont, the rumour
went forth that the *Barbier de Séville* was about to
be represented. This rumour may have been well-
founded, but before it could be verified the attention
of the author was diverted to other and more important
matters. The judges were about to give their decision
on the charge brought against him by Goëzman, a
decision that would make or mar him. The anxiety
with which that decision was looked forward to can
hardly be described. Beaumarchais was still regarded
as the defender of oppressed liberty, his cause as that of
the public at large. The judges, though convinced of
the guilt of the Goëzmans, ardently wished to send
the detested memoir-writer into exile or to the pillory,
but were restrained by a fear that such a sentence
would provoke a serious disturbance. On the 26th

February, after a long sitting, they hit upon a sort
of middle course.   Goëzman was "placed out of court"
—in other words, branded with disgrace.   Madame
Goëzman and Beaumarchais were "blamed," the former
being ordered to return the fifteen louis.   The sentence
upon Beaumarchais, which declared him "infamous,"
excited general indignation.   His door was literally
besieged by sympathizing friends; his table was
covered with letters of ardent sympathy; the Prince
de Conti and the Duc de Chartres gave a brilliant fête
in his honour.   In these favourable circumstances he
was about to reply to his judges, when the king,
anxious to see the agitation at an end, ordered him
to discontinue the memoirs, but promised to rehabilitate
him if he should satisfactorily fulfil a delicate trust.
Morande, the "Journalist in Armour," was on the
point of publishing in London some libellous Memoirs
of Madame Dubarri.   The English Government had
consented to his removal by a body of French police
on the condition that it should be accomplished in
secrecy, but Morande, apprised of his danger, defeated
the plan by publicly representing himself as a political
exile.   M. de Beaumarchais should be reinstated in his
civil position if he induced the libeller to suppress the
book.   The dramatist both reluctantly and joyfully
undertook the mission, and the production of the
Barbier de Séville was again put off *sine die*.

CHAPTER V.

1774—1778.

In the spring of 1757 the theatrical company in the service of ex-King Stanislaus at Nancy gave a performance of the *Glorieux* for the début of an actor of the mature age of seven. It would seem that the announcement excited much interest; the theatre was full, and Stanislaus, accompanied by his mistress, Madame de Boufflers, appeared in his box. According to the Comte de Tressan, the débutant was the son of M. Fleury, formerly of the Comédie Française, and at present the manager of the Nancy Theatre. In his infancy the boy was confided to the care of a nurse, who, while regularly receiving a sufficient allowance for his maintenance, lodged him in the Hôpital des Enfants Trouvés. Having been restored to his parents, he began to play parts under his father's eye, and had already earned a certain reputation as Joas in *Athalie* and M. Fleurant in the *Légataire*. On the present occasion, although the performance was for his début, he was to play only the unimportant part of the *laquais mal vêtu*—had only to speak a few lines and take a pinch of snuff.

In due time he came on ;—a plump, rosy, black-eyed
boy, not quite seven years of age, but with the confidence and self-possession of a veteran.   His performance
was such as to leave a very favourable impression.   He
spoke his few lines with ease and correctness ; but the
pinch of snuff (taken in the most approved manner)
gave rise to an irrepressible fit of sneezing.   Stanislaus
graciously smiled at the mishap, audibly exclaiming,
perhaps by way of encouragement, "God bless you,
mon enfant !"   The benediction was repeated by the
pit, and the little actor, brimful of delight, made his
best bow.   To him the words "sounded like an augury
of future success."

The performance over, he was carried to the royal
box by the Comte de Tressan.   Stanislaus, speaking to
him in a reassuring tone, drew him forward, wiped away
with his handkerchief a portion of the powder on his
face, and conferred upon him a royal kiss.   Fleury was
surprised that Madame de Boufflers did not immediately
follow the example thus set.   "All the pretty ladies
behind the scenes have kissed and embraced me," he
said with a sort of pout.   "And I suppose," said
Stanislaus, "you expect all other pretty ladies to do
the same.   Well, let the young cavalier be presented."
The young cavalier, without waiting for the ceremony,
ran to and kissed her.   Madame, with a smile, took
him upon her knee.   "I think," said Gallissiére, the

chancellor, "that our young friend is likely to become
a fine actor." "At least," added the Comte de Tressan,
"he has begun well. Baron used to say, 'Tout
comédien devrait être élevé sur les genoux des reines.'"

Stanislaus took much interest in the prosperity of the
Fleurys, and the boy-actor was frequently included in
the society which the ex-King gathered around him at
Lunéville and Commercy. M. Fleury does not appear
to have had a very exalted notion of his duties as a
father. "Fully persuaded," writes the player, "that
his son would become a distinguished pupil of the
comic Muse, he very much neglected my education.
I was taught only to read and write. He maintained
that for an actor, especially a comic and provincial
actor, this was education enough." However, Fleury
was by no means incapable of self-improvement, and
the conversation of the men whom he met at Lunéville
could not have failed to help him on. But this was not
the only way in which he profited by the kindness of
Stanislaus. Endowed with considerable power of imitation, he quickly acquired the tone and manners of
aristocratic society, that elegant varnish which, as he
reminds us, was afterwards called *l'éducation de la peau*.
To render his copy complete he would steal unperceived
into his father's wardrobe, deck himself in the richest
Court dress he could find, and imagine himself to be
some exalted personage. His father once surprised

him as, personating the King of France, he said to himself in the mirror, "my dear Stanislaus."

Great was the mortification of Fleury when, on arriving at the age of fifteen, he found a set of characters consisting chiefly of valets marked out by his father for special study. "Think what a stab, crueller than daggers through one's heart" — valets! The paternal yoke began to weigh heavily upon him; he wished to be independent, to soar upon his own wings. Before long an opportunity of realizing his wishes presented itself. A sister, Félicité Fleury, had turned the heads of some officers garrisoned in Nancy, one of whom, the Vicomte Clairval de Passy, was loved by her in return. M. and Madame Fleury, believing that a marriage was out of the question, repelled his advances. He then became dangerously ill, and in the end offered Félicité his hand. Her parents, not a little flattered, gave their consent to the marriage, which was solemnized in due form. On the following day the Vicomte expressed his determination to become an actor under the name of Sainville, "the better to identify himself with his young bride." M. and Madame Fleury were both astonished and annoyed. They had hoped that M. Clairval would have made a Vicomtesse of the actress; as it was, the actress had made an actor of the Vicomte. Fleury, on the contrary, was much pleased with the turn affairs had taken. M. and Madame Sainville

secured an engagement at Geneva, and he obtained
leave to accompany them.

While at Geneva the trio were invited by Voltaire to
pay him a visit, Madame Sainville having distinguished
herself in some of his own pieces. The invitation was
gladly accepted, and during their stay at Ferney, which
lasted about a fortnight, they were "overwhelmed with
kindness" by their host. For that kindness Fleury
made a somewhat ungracious return. He ventured one
morning to make sport of "that strange sanctuary
of genius," the philosopher's voluminous wig. Voltaire turned sharply round, transfixed his little assailant with a glance, and presently said—dividing
the syllables clearly—" Per—met—tez moi, monsieur"
—a pause—" per—met—tez moi, Monsieur de Fleury,
to tell you that I am not royal enough to understand
pages' tricks. Remember that at the court of Ferney
a wig is respected in consideration of what may happen
to be in it." Fleury assumed a mortified and penitent
air. "Come," said Voltaire, taking him by the chin,
"let me look at you; if I mistake not, there is something in your face that tells me you will be an arrant
rogue but a good actor." And so the incident ended.
Voltaire attended the rehearsals as well as the performances in his theatre, repeated some of the lines allotted
to Lusignan in the grandest style, and gave Fleury
an idea of the importance of accurately conceiving a

character. " In your leisure," he said to him at parting, " study earnestly; on the stage, think only of what you are playing. An actor at your age may possess talent, but cannot possibly be a master of his art."

From Geneva the youth returned to Nancy, but the paternal yoke was now more irksome to him than ever, and at length, "furnished with a light wardrobe and a still lighter purse," he left home to turn strolling player. His first engagement was under Madame Nicetti, manageress of the Troyes theatre. Here he received an order to appear at the Comédie Française. He was then twenty-four years of age, " agreeable in his appearance without being good-looking, of middle stature, well-made, active, and slender, distinguished by an elegance of manner and an air of high life in which few could compete with him, and with a lively and intelligent countenance." Brimful of joy, he at once set out for Paris, and on arriving there went to see Lekain. The great tragedian, knowing the elder Fleury, received him as a future comrade, marked out a set of characters for him to study, and enjoined him not to be daunted by obstacles. On the 7th March *Mérope* and the *Fausses Infidélités* were announced, the characters of Egysthe and D'Ermilly by M. Fleury. "This critical event of my theatrical life," he says, "threw me into a state of excitement which I will not attempt to describe. Had it not been for shame, I really believe I should have left

the company to provide another Egysthe.   To appear
on the stage with Lekain—to play to such a Mérope
as Mlle. Dumesnil!   When I went on I was quite
bewildered ; my memory seemed to forsake me ; I could
not utter a word.   Dumesnil contrived to prompt me—

"Est-ce là cette reine auguste et malheureuse ?"

This broke the spell ; I repeated the line, and from
that instant proceeded without trepidation.   If Mlle.
Dumesnil had been my mother she could not have
shown more solicitude towards me.   In the intervals
between her tirades she reassured me by looks and
words ; the next moment, with more than the rapidity
of lightning, she was Mérope, and the audience were
stirred to enthusiasm."   In the *Fausses Infidélités* Fleury
was more at his ease, but the pit altogether thought
him "indifferent," and in a few weeks we find him
working hopefully at Lyons (*i*).

He had scarcely left Paris when the theatre was
closed on account of the death of Louis XV., which
occurred in May.   In vivid contrast with this outward
mark of respect for his memory was the fierce joy
shown by the people at large at the event, and keen
observers probably saw that the hopes centred in the
accession of Louis XVI. were all but swamped in the
feeling now spreading over the country.   His majesty's
players had no reason to feel deeply grieved by the

change.   Louis XV. had never liked the drama, and
the company rarely appeared before him at Versailles or
Fontainebleau without being chilled by the sight of the
wearied expression upon his apathetic face.   Lekain and
Mlle. Raucourt, perhaps, were the only players who had
elicited from him anything like warm praise.   On the
other hand, Louis XVI. was not indifferent to the
charms of their art, while his pleasure-loving wife would
not have been reluctant to witness a theatrical performance every day.   Nobody, in fact, regretted the death
of Louis XV. except those whose interest it injuriously
affected.   Among them was Beaumarchais, who, having
succeeded in the object of his journey to London, had
just returned to Paris.   " I reflect with astonishment,"
he writes, " on the strange fate which pursues me.   Had
the King lived eight days longer in health I should
have been restored to the rights of which I have been
so unjustly deprived."   But this proved only a passing
difficulty ; another libeller by profession, Angelucci, was
on the point of printing in London what purported to
be a biography of the Queen, and Beaumarchais received
a commission to deal with him as he had done with
Morande.

Before noting the result of his new expedition we
may glance briefly at what occurred at the theatre
during his absence.   Louis XVI., it would appear,
signalized the opening of his reign by insisting upon

greater vigilance on the part of the censorship. *Monsieur Pétau, ou le Gâteau des Rois*, a piece intended to portray the lower bourgeoisie, was followed by a more decisive illustration of the King's views as to liberty of speech. Perched upon a mock throne, the hero signs several papers, one of which, unknown to himself, is a marriage contract between his daughter and a youth whom he hates. One of the personages had to sing of him—

> Il est des sages de vingt ans,
> Et des étourdis de soixante—

and the lines were applied by most of the audience to the late king. Louis XVI. did not think it expedient to pass over the matter in silence. Crébillon, the censor, was suspended for three months; while the author, Imbert, a disciple of Dorat's, and the player who had sung the words, Mlle. Luzi, were clapped in For l'Evêque. In one respect, however, his majesty showed more good sense. Proscribed by Louis XV. out of a fear that it might suggest unwelcome comparisons, the *Partie de Chasse d'Henri Quatre* was now allowed to appear (November 6), and a characteristic impersonation by Brizard of the King at once gave it a high position in the repertory of the theatre. Michau was to have been played by Feulie, who, however, succumbed to an attack of small-pox a few weeks before the production.

Beaumarchais, having returned to Paris in triumph,

the *Barbier de Séville*, temporarily prohibited by the
censor on account of some real or supposed reflections
upon the Government, was at length put in rehearsal.
Figaro was allotted to Préville, Rosina to Mlle. Doligny,
Almaviva to Molé, Bartholo to Desessarts, and La
Jeunesse, the old steward, to Dugazon. In his anxiety
as to the result, however, the author fell into a mistake
which could not but neutralize the advantage of such a
cast. He extended the play to five acts, amplified the
dialogue, and generally outpainted his picture. In this
state the *Barbier* was acted for the first time (February
23). "Never," writes Grimm, "did a *première* bring
together a larger assemblage." Everybody was anxious
to see a comedy by the author of the eloquent *Mémoires*.
If the disappointment of the audience was in proportion
to their expectations it must have been past expression.
Brilliant in parts, the piece was found decidedly weari-
some as a whole, despite the high and varied talents
employed in its representation. Nor was this the only
mortification it brought upon Beaumarchais. Next
morning, probably armed with much-needed alterations,
he called at the theatre during a rehearsal of the *Siége
de Calais*. "Ah," he writes, "you should have seen the
Barbier's feeble supporters break up, avert their faces,
and take to flight; the women, always so brave when
they have anything to protect, smothered up in their
coqueluchons, and casting down their eyes in confusion,

BEAUMARCHAIS.

the men hastening to each other to make amends for
what they had said in favour of my piece. Some of
them looked through their glasses on the left as I passed
on the right; others, more courageous, but taking care
that nobody saw or was likely to see them, drew me
into a corner and said, ' How is it that you have deceived
us so much ? ' " For nothing fails like failure. But the
derided dramatist was not to be beaten. His buoyant
nature again asserted itself. In a few hours, alive to
his mistake, he restored the piece to its original dimen-
sions, struck out all the superfluous dialogue, and imparted additional pungency to what he retained. Represented in its amended form—that in which it has come
down to us—the *Barbier de Séville* met with a very
different fate Paris basked eagerly in the sunshine of
its unforced gaiety and wit, especially when, as in the
tirade upon "justice, reason, and authority," they were
pressed into the service of satire. Hissed at first, it
now had what Madame du Deffand calls an "extravagant
success." Beaumarchais, of course, was in the best possible spirits ; he printed the comedy as one "représentée
et tombée" at the Théâtre Français, and in the preface,
perhaps to amuse himself, affirmed "with astounding
aplomb" that he had merely reduced the piece from
five acts to four.

Much less fortunate were the players in their next
ventures. In a "moment de distraction" they accepted

a tragedy by one Beausobre, *Les Arsacides*, originally
printed in 1756 as a *Stratonice*, but hitherto rejected
at the theatre.   Molière's liveliest "farces" had never
aroused more obstreperous merriment.   It was proposed
to drop the curtain at the end of the second act, but the
audience were too much amused to let that be done.
Beausobre gravely proposed on the morrow to extend
the piece to seven acts.   In a few weeks from this the
company found themselves in another difficulty.   Having
been called upon to give a dramatic performance at
Versailles in honour of the birth of a Prince, they
decided, by a strange want of judgment, to play a
tragedy not yet produced, the *Connétable de Bourbon*, by
one Guibert.   In addition to being ill-written throughout, it illustrated a story of which the reigning dynasty,
to say nothing of the people at large, had little reason
to be proud.   Louis XVI. was visibly annoyed ; and the
august throng about him cried shame upon his own
players for favouring a piece which, if represented in
Paris, would have added fuel to the flame of anti-
monarchical feeling.

"It is whispered," Bachaumont writes, "that M.
Rousseau de Genève, tired of his repose at Ermenonville,
is about to reappear before the world, and that to do so
with greater *éclat* he has chosen the Comédie Française."
This turned out to be true, although in an *Essai sur les
Spectacles*, victoriously answered by Marmontel, he had

vehemently denounced such entertainments. Some time before this, it appears, he had embodied the story of Pygmalion and Galatea in a single prose scene, depicting with warmth of imagination and voluptuous fervour the sentiments of the sculptor for the statue. The work had been stolen from him and secretly printed, and now, thirsting for applause, he gave his consent to its being played at the Comédie Française. Its own merit, joined to the fact that he was the author of the *Contrat Social*, assured its success; but the charm which seems to have stolen over the minds of the audience as they witnessed it must have been due to the acting. "It is impossible," writes Laharpe, "to imagine a more seductive picture than Mlle. Raucourt on the pedestal at the moment when the veil fell away from her. Her head was that of Venus, and her leg, half-discovered, that of Diana." In *Pygmalion*, at any rate, the audience could not so far resist the influence of her beauty and talent as to manifest their customary ill-will towards her. Though Rousseau (who composed the overture) said he did not wish to receive anything for the piece, his share of receipts was regularly sent to him—with what result is not known.

His majesty's players here involved themselves in a controversy with a man who in one respect presented a strong resemblance to the philospher of Geneva. This was Louis Sebastien Mercier, son of a tradesman

in Paris, and formerly professor of rhetoric at the
Collége de Bordeaux. Five years previously, after
trying his hand to little purpose at héroïdes and
romances, he wrote *L'An* 2440, which speedily brought
him into notice. In addition to revealing rare literary
power, it was a book exactly suited to the temper of
the times. Its hero, a Frenchman of the eighteenth
century, goes to sleep for 670 years, and on waking up
finds himself in a state of society which he would have
thought too good to be possible. Reason and virtue and
justice hold absolute sway ; priest and nobles, with the
abuses they brought in their train, have vanished into
space. It may appear strange that such a work should
have passed the censorship, but its real tendency was
not seen until the mischief had been done. Mercier
united to his anti-religious and anti-monarchical prejudices a mania for paradox which Jean Jacques himself
could scarcely have outvied. His ideas on all subjects
were to be different from those of anybody else. For
one thing, he maintained that painting and sculpture
were useless. Did not artists petrify everything they
attempted to represent ? On their canvas the stream
had no murmur, the foliage no rustle, the breeze no
breath. "Look at those combatants in marble ; they
raise their arms, but they never strike !" Indeed, the
player's art was more estimable than that of the painter
and sculptor. But the players could not reanimate

nature without the aid of poetry. By poetry he did
not mean the stuff usually designated by that word.
Writers of poetry in prose were the only true poets.
Perrault's stories were worth more than the *Iliad* and
the *Odyssey* put together. Malherbe, Boileau, and
Racine had ruined French poetry. Molière was entitled
to more respect, since, although he wrote in measure,
he would occasionally display a contempt for rules, as
in the line,

Mais elle bat ses gens, et ne les *paie* point.

M. de Voltaire, while submitting to the fetters of rhyme,
had introduced many salutary innovations on the stage,
but had not pushed them quite far enough. Modern
history, so rich in events, contrasts, and the ideas created
by the march of civilization, should be the chief, if not
the only, quarry of the dramatist. The time was not
far distant when the players would substitute elevated
prose for alexandrines, when the statuesque figures
of antiquity would be exchanged for flesh-and-blood
personages, when the plays of Corneille and Racine
would be relegated to the nursery. Mercier had no
doubt that of this dramatic revolution he was "pre-
destined to be the Luther," and as a first blow he sent
to the Comédie Française a number of pieces written
on the English and German models. But the players,
having been educated in what he scornfully called the
"school of the versifiers," were not of the same way of

thinking, and only one of his pieces, *Natalie*, was
accepted.   Before it could be brought out he published
an *Essai sur l'Art Dramatique*, in which, not content
with expounding his theories, he glanced at the Comédie
Française in effect as an asylum of bad taste.   In reply
the players revoked his free admission and put his play
on the shelf.   Mercier's indignation at their reprisals
knew no bounds.   He brought the matter before the
Council, and, determined to plead his cause in person,
made himself an advocate at Rheims.   The actors,
however, had influence enough to put a stop to the
proceedings,—yet another proof of the corruptness of
French tribunals under the old *régime* (*j*).

This was the signal for a series of fierce attacks on
the Comédie.   Most of the dramatic authors of Paris
went over to Mercier with surprising ardour and una-
nimity.   His cause, they said, was that of every man
who had written for the Comédie Française.   The
actors, evidently labouring under the impression that
the creation of a work was of insignificant importance
as compared with the interpretation, had for some time,
it was alleged, treated the dramatists with provoking
disdain ; had cruelly sported with their feelings by
capriciously inverting the order of received pieces, and
on more than one occasion, in order to make themselves
richer, had laboured to bring a piece within the rules.
In support of these accusations Sédaine publicly related

the history of his last play, Molé found himself held
up to reprobation for his conduct in regard to the
Chérusques, and Lekain was accused of having played
his worst for the purpose of ruining a play which he
disliked.   Palissot and Louvay de Lasoussaye next
rushed into print with a detailed account of new
grievances.   In the previous March the former had
sent to the theatre *Les Courtisanes*, a comedy of
considerable literary merit.   The actors rejected it,
ostensibly on the ground that it was indelicate, but
really, the author suspected, because he was the avowed
enemy of their friends the philosophers.   In reply to
the ostensible reason he applied for and obtained the
approbation of the censor, M. de Crébillon, not, perhaps,
the person best able to discriminate between decency
and indecency.   Nevertheless, the company held to
their previous decision, at the same time addressing
to him an offensive letter.   In consideration of his
feelings, they said, the first refusal had been based
on the indecency of the piece.   But the *Courtisanes*
possessed faults of another kind.   It might be acted if
M. Palissot could throw into it—1, action ; 2, interest ;
3, taste ; 4, character."   Naturally incensed at all this,
he printed the play, first as the *Courtisanes*, and
afterwards, having regard to the charge of indelicacy,
as *L'Ecole des Mœurs*.   Such, in brief, was Palissot's
story.   Louvay de Lasoussaye's indictment was much

heavier.   For ten years the production of an *Alcidonis*
from his pen had been put off from time to time,
simply because he would not cringe to the actors.
Forced at length by the influence of others to play
it, they mutilated the piece until it looked like a
burlesque, dressed the characters in ridiculously in-
appropriate costumes, and finally sent him an account
setting forth that, instead of being indebted to him,
they had lost one hundred and one livres, eight sous,
and one denier by his play.   Cailhava, who in consequence of a quarrel with Molé had been treated like
Mercier, discharged a volley of epigrams and tirades at
the actors, crowning all by a suggestion which became
the rallying cry of the insurgents—" Let us have a
second Théâtre Français."

Before long the authors' attack upon the Comédie
narrowed itself to the most important point, the pay-
ment for dramatic work.   Beaumarchais had hitherto
been neutral in the quarrel, partly out of good-will
towards the players, who had treated him well enough,
but chiefly because he wished to give all his thoughts
to other matters.   Again in favour at Court, he saw
in the fratricidal war between England and America
an opportunity of improving his fortunes.   " If the
colonists are no match for the British troops in military
efficiency," he wrote to the King, "they will certainly
win their independence.   Now is the time for dealing

a heavy blow at our ancient enemy; the colonists should have the support of France." Louis XVI. yielded to these representations; and the author of the *Barbier de Séville*, setting up a firm under the style and title of Roderigue Hortalez and Co., became the sole or principal agent in surreptitiously providing the Americans with arms, ammunition, and ships. In the earlier stages of his new business, however, he consented, at the instance of the Duc de Richelieu, who had faith in the clearness and impartiality of his judgment, to arbitrate between the authors and the players, his decision to be binding upon both parties. His first step was to apply for the books of the theatre, but the company, at least jealous of the secrets of their house, declined to comply with his request. "Never mind," he thought; "they have yet to reckon with me for the *Barbier*, and then I shall be in a position to decide."

It was at this point that a most promising young player underwent the ordeal of a début. In or about 1770, it appears, a bright-eyed and lively little girl might frequently have been seen to steal behind the scenes of the Comédie Française, and, placing herself in some out-of-the-way corner, gaze with mingled awe and admiration upon the great players as they made their entrances and their exits. Her father seems to have had some employment in the theatre, and she

had already distinguished herself in amateur performances.   By and by she attracted the notice of Préville,
who undertook to instruct her for the stage.   " And
never," writes Fleury, " did pupil prove more worthy
of such a master.   The young actress did not master
intuitively the secrets of an art which cannot be taught ;
but the great comedian, charmed with her precocious
intelligence, facilitated her acquirement of those elements
of diction, the *solféggi* of speech, which are indispensable
to a career on the stage."

Fifteen and a half years of age, but seemingly older,
this girl, by name Louise Contat, appeared at the
Comédie as Atalide in *Bajazet* on the 3rd February.
Both her face and figure were deemed " exquisite ; " and
if her arms were not quite so fine as those of Madame
Vestris she managed them with sufficient grace to conceal the fact.   Her first début does not seem to have
created any effect.   Laharpe thought she had but little
talent ; Grimm pronounced her " mediocre."   Subsequently she played Zaïre and Junie, but with the same
result.   In truth, she had no talent for tragedy, and
it was only in compliance with the regulations of the
theatre that she undertook such parts.   In comedy of
the light and vivacious kind, however, she soon fixed
the attention of the playgoers, as nothing but experience
was needed to make her console old playgoers for the
retirement of Mlle. Dangeville.

Her rare talents being more than suspected in the theatre, a powerful little cabal was soon organized to obstruct her progress. In the first instance they pitted against her a Mlle. Vadé, who, though of prepossessing appearance, proved inferior to her even in the *jeunes princesses*. Préville took advantage of this circumstance to secure for his pupil a place in the company. In no wise discouraged by this defeat, the cabal, with Mlles. Fanier and Luzi at their head, availed themselves of their seniority to exclude her from parts which they would not have accepted themselves, but out of which she was likely to make theatrical capital. If anything, however, this continued enmity did her more good than harm. "It stimulated her," says Fleury, "to prove how much she had been wronged. She exerted herself to give importance to the insignificant parts allotted to her. She acted under a sense of the injustice with which she had been treated, and that kind of feeling is a never-failing spur to the young artist."

During Mlle. Contat's début, as though to show how much pressed they were for novelties, the company brought out two gloomy drames which they had previously rejected—*Lorédan*, by Fontanelle, and *L'Ecole des Mœurs*, by Fenouillot de Falbaire. Each of these pieces was enough to create a strong prejudice against the class they represented. *Lorédan*, which was divided

into four acts, with as many changes of decoration,
turns upon the poisoning of a youth by his father.   It
fell at the first performance, although Lekain had
charge of the principal character.   In the *Ecole des
Mœurs* we have a father and his two sons seeking
the hand of a young girl.   Simultaneously, unknown
to each other, they attempt to carry her off ; there is
a fight in the dark, and the wicked father, having
received a mortal wound, repents of his errors, gives the
girl to the more favoured of the two sons, and then
serenely expires.   In detail, it is said, this play was
more revolting than in plan.   "How is it," asked Marie
Antoinette of Lekain as he bowed her to her coach,
" that so detestable a thing should have been received ? "
" Madame," pleasantly replied the tragedian, " that is
the secret of the Comédie."

Mlle. Dumesnil, the most natural and powerful of
queens, withdrew in the following May.   In spite of
the formidable rivalry of Clairon, she had remained
unapproachable in some of the characters previously
associated with her name.   Among the best of her
" creations " were Sémiramis in Voltaire's tragedy,
Clytemnestre in *Oreste*, and Marguerite d'Anjou in
Laharpe's *Comte de Warwick*.   Now and then she made
an excursion into the domain of serious comedy, and
in parts like Lachaussée's Gouvernante was completely
at her ease.   In *Esope à la Cour*, as we learn from the

Old Amateur, she played the mother of Rhodope, a comparatively subordinate personage, with sufficient feeling and skill to step into the foreground of the picture. When, in the course of her complaint to Esope of the wretchedness of her daughter in the midst of opulence, and having said, with a *bonhomie* at once pleasing and impressive—

J'ai loué cet habit pour paraître un peu brave,

she uttered in an accent so true and pathetic the subsequent line—

Pour m'avoir méconnue en suis-je moins sa mère,

the whole of the audience was visibly moved. Unlike Clairon and Lekain, she aimed at magnificence rather than partial historical accuracy in the matter of costume, delighting to array herself in all the bravery of satin and velvet and diamonds. It is said of her dress as Athalie or Sémiramis that only a few trifling alterations were needed to make it resemble that of the Queen of France at State ceremonies. Off the stage, it is pleasant to find, Mlle. Dumesnil was distinguished by a dignified simplicity of manner, an unostentatious mode of living, a peculiar indifference to flattery, and a readiness to help less fortunate members of her profession. Her modest pension from the theatre after her retirement was stopped in 1792, but she seems to have saved enough to pass the evening of her days in

moderate comfort at Boulogne-sur-Mer, where she died
on the 20th of February, 1803, at the age of ninety.
Not long previously she had been before the public
as the authoress of a somewhat acrimonious reply to
the *Mémoires* of Mlle. Clairon. It would seem that the
"bonne Dumesnil," as Voltaire called her, remained on
the stage a little too long. "Mlle. Dumesnil's retirement," wrote one of her most fervent admirers, Grimm,
at the time of that event, "has created but a slight
impression. She is not regretted, for the reason that
she has been regretted some years. Nevertheless," he
adds, "the memory of this actress will endure as long
as the French theatre. We shall never see Mérope, or
Agrippine, or Sémiramis without recalling to mind how
admirable she was in parts of this kind. She has contributed little to the progress of art, but has cultivated
it with a *caractère original.*"

Immediately after the disappearance of Dumesnil the
Comédie Française lost the services of Mlle. Raucourt,
though in very different circumstances. For some time
past the young actress had been made painfully conscious of the laxity of her hold upon the town. Mistress
of one or more of the noblesse, living in the most extravagant style, and ostentatiously driving about Paris
and to the stage-door in a luxurious equipage, she
daily added fuel to the hatred of the populace, who
now took a malicious pleasure in assailing her with

hisses even in most striking scenes. In Hermione she
had nearly been driven from the stage, and her success
as Galatea served to protect her only for a few days.
To make matters worse, she had contracted debts
amounting to 100,000 crowns, and her titled lovers
were not so far infatuated with her as to make her
solvent. Now, persecuted by creditors, and believing
it was impossible to subdue the public opposition, she
resolved upon flight; and at the beginning of June
it was announced that the whereabouts of Mlle. Raucourt were not known. "It was reserved for our days,"
writes Bachaumont, "to see the most brilliant actress
of the Comédie Française a bankrupt"—the brilliant
actress who less than four years previously, at Versailles, had been presented by the late King to Marie
Antoinette as "Queen Dido herself."

By referring to the Dauphiness of that day I am
reminded of the marked favour which she extended to
the leading member of the company. Desirous of
husbanding his resources, anxious to visit his old master
as often as possible at Ferney, and convinced, perhaps,
that it was good policy for an actor to absent himself
at times from Paris, Lekain appeared at the Comédie
Française at longer and longer intervals. This was a
severe blow to all lovers of theatrical art, and on one
occasion, after a performance of the *Orphelin de la Chine*,
he received a public intimation that he "did not play

enough." Such, too, was the opinion of the Gentlemen
of the Chamber, for they refused him leave of absence
when, in the course of the summer, he wished to set off
for Ferney. But the Queen—"enchanted," we are told,
"by his acting in *Tancrède*"—overruled their objections
to her own loss, and Voltaire was not denied the pleasure
of having the "French Garrick" under his hospitable
roof.

It is not difficult to say what the chief subject of
their conversation was. The poet's attitude towards
Shakspere had undergone an important change. In
1745, Laplace, encouraged by the interest shown in
English literature since the appearance of the *Lettres
Philosophiques*, began to produce a series of translations
or analyses of Shaksperean plays under the title of the
Théâtre Anglais. "Let us not condemn," he said, after
a glowing panegyric of the original, "what our grand-
children may applaud." From that time, repugnant as
many features of the romantic drama were to a nation
trained from infancy to revere Corneille and Racine,
Shakspere found an extending circle of admirers in
Paris, with the Président Hénault as its most prominent
representative. Voltaire watched this rising idolatry
with profound uneasiness. He feared that it would end
in the overthrow or a modification of the dramatic
school in whose principles he had invariably held so
robust and self-denying a faith. Full of this idea, he

at length threw the weight of his influence into the
opposite scale.   Without retracting his former criticism,
he lost few opportunities of exposing what he deemed
the barbarisms, the puerilities, the indecencies, and the
extravagances of the English dramatist.   In the preface
to *Sémiramis*, as everybody knows, he said that *Hamlet*,
while abounding in traits worthy of the highest genius,
might be taken for the work of a " drunken savage."
" Long ago," he wrote to Horace Walpole in 1768, " I
said that if Shakspere had come into the world in the
time of Addison his genius would have had that elegance and purity which make Addison so worthy of
commendation.   I said that his genius was his own,
that his faults were those of his age.   He was precisely
like Lope de Vega and Calderon.   His was a fine nature,
but one utterly uncultivated.   He had no regularity, no
sense of propriety, no art.   Lowness and grandeur,
buffoonery and sublimity, are found in his works side
by side.   His tragedy is a chaos with a hundred flashes
of light."   And the fear underlying all this—a fear that
uncritical admiration for Shakspere might lead French
dramatists to adopt his method—was gathering new
force when Lekain arrived at Ferney.   With the aid
of the Comte de Catuélan and Fontaine-Malherbe,
Letourneur, the translator of Young's *Night Thoughts*
and Hervey's *Meditations among the Tombs* (both of
which works, by the way, delighted the most frivolous

of nations), had begun to produce a complete translation
of the Shaksperean drama, at the same time sneering at
the school of tragedy to which Voltaire belonged.   Few
works could have excited greater enthusiasm among
men of letters.   " It is long," wrote Grimm, " since we
have had anything which has deserved more criticism
and praise, on which discussion has been more animated,
and on which public opinion has been more divided and
uncertain."

Nearly eighty-two years of age, but with his un-
equalled power of mockery as yet unimpaired, Voltaire
resolved to split a lance in behalf of the threatened
school.   He addressed to the Academy a couple of
letters designed to expose the enormities of Shakspere.
That he was at white-heat on the subject there can be
no doubt.   "Have you read," he writes to D'Argental,
"the two volumes of this fellow Letourneur, in which
he seeks to make us regard Shakspere as the only model
of true tragedy ?   He styles him the *dieu du théâtre.*
He sacrifices all Frenchmen, without exception, to his
idol, just as of old they sacrificed pigs to Ceres.   He
does not deign even to mention Corneille or Racine.
Have you a hatred sufficiently vigorous for this impu-
dent imbecile ?   France does not contain sufficient cuffs
and dunces' caps and pillories for such a rascal.   The
blood dances in my old veins as I write of him.   The
dreadful thing is that the monster has a following in

France. Worse than all, it was I who first spoke of this Shakspere—1 who first showed to the French a few pearls which I had found in this enormous dungheap. I did not expect that I should one day be helping to tread under foot the crowns of Racine and Corneille in order to adorn the brow of a barbarian player." Again to D'Argental five days later: "The abomination of desolation is in the temple of the Lord. Lekain tells me that young Paris is in favour of Letourneur ; that English scaffolds and stews are ousting the tragedies of Racine and the noble scenes of Corneille ; that there is nothing great or decent at Paris except the Gilles (clown) of London ; that, in a word, a prose tragedy is coming in which a meeting of butchers promises to have a marvellous effect. I have seen the end of reason and taste." In his treatise to the Academy, which was delivered by D'Alembert on the 25th of August, he instituted a comparison between the French and English stages, declaring as he went that Shakspere, if a Thespis, rose at times to the level of Sophocles, but was so far insensible to the dignity of tragedy as to introduce and assign appropriate language to the dregs of the people. Never had the power of Voltaire over the minds of his countrymen been more conclusively proved than it was here. "Either Shakspere or Racine," it was said, "must remain master of the field." Victory declared itself in favour of the latter. Romanticism, though brought within measurable reach of acceptance, was put off for nearly half a century.

Following this excitement came two new candidates for histrionic honours. Eldest son of a merchant at Marseilles, Jean Albonis was born there in 1747. He was brought up at the Collége de l'Oratoire, and, having shown a remarkable talent for declamation, was selected to pronounce the discourse at the end of the collegiate year. His education completed, it was proposed that he should rejoin an elder brother in the colonies, and a M. de Lasalle, formerly French consul in the Levant, gave him valuable instruction in the principles of commerce. Unfortunately for this project, an aunt, Madame Audibert, introduced him to the Duc de Richelieu, who took him to Paris as secretary. Prominent among the private theatres in the capital was one in Rue de Popincourt, where Albonis played Crispin in the *Folies Amoureuses*. He at once fell in love with the stage, exchanged the name of Albonis for that of Dazincourt, and started for Brussels as an actor. Hannetaire, the director of the theatre in that city, tried to divert him from his resolution, but on hearing him recite was obliged to allow that he had not made a mistake. Dazincourt's first essays on a public theatre were as Iector in the *Joueur* and the Crispin already mentioned. "Never," said Hannetaire from the pit, "has a début been more promising;" and the audience in

general, with some of the players, echoed his opinion.
Five years afterwards, the Duc de Richelieu, pleasantly
saying that the talents of Dazincourt atoned for the
ingratitude of Albonis, called him to the Comédie
Française, where he appeared on the 21st of November.
By this time he had become a refined and often brilliant
comedian, and the company accepted him as the best
second to Préville then procurable. In Vanhove, too,
the company found an excellent comrade, histrionically
and socially. Born at Lille in 1744, he had played
from an early age in French Flanders, and was happy
enough in tragedy and comedy *pères* to be regarded as
the probable successor of Brizard in Paris. In parts
demanding searching intelligence and elevation of style
he was at fault, but the playgoers were delighted with
his Géronte in the *Menteur*, his Don Diègue in the *Cid*,
his old Roman in *Horace,* and his Zopire in *Mahomet.*
In all he did there was an earnestness which made them
forgive him a monotonous delivery, a Flemish accent,
and a somewhat bourgeois air.

His admission brings us to the beginning of what
may be deemed one of the most memorable incidents
in the history of the theatre. The players, meeting in
solemn conclave on the 2nd of January, unanimously
decided to accept a new tragedy, *Irène*, by Voltaire.
It was in the summer of 1776, at the ripe age of eighty-
two, that the philosopher entered upon this onerous

task.   Fixing the scene at Constantinople, he relates
the story of a woman who loves the murderer of her
husband, and who, struck by remorse, finally destroys
herself in order to escape any association with him.
For a time the author flung aside the manuscript in
despair.   His subject, he found, was not equal to the
weight of five acts.   " I was compelled," he writes, " to
reduce it to three, and then it had the appearance of
a drama by M. Mercier.   This is a great pity, for there
was something like novelty in the bagatelle, and the
passions, as I think, were rather well painted in it."
Soon afterwards, however, he returned to the play,
restored it to its original form, re-wrote it with infinite
care, and hopefully despatched it to Paris.   Meanwhile,
he had produced another tragedy, *Agathocle*.   *Irène* did
not get beyond the casting stage without some difficulty.
For reasons unexplained, Lekain manifested the strongest
disinclination to play Léonce, although well aware that
the charm of his acting was largely relied upon at Ferney
to justify the existence of the piece.   But a tenderly
reproachful letter from Voltaire probably led him to
reconsider the matter, especially as by adhering to his
refusal he would have been wanting in gratitude towards
the " cher et illustre maître " to whom he owed so much.

Irène was followed to Paris by no less a person than
its octogenarian author.   Never exiled in legal form,
he had long cherished the idea of spending a few weeks

in the city of his birth, and the representation of the
tragedy in question furnished him with a passable
pretext for converting that idea into a reality.   He did
not ask the permission of the Court to undertake the
journey, as by doing so he would have admitted in
effect that a permission was necessary.   Louis XVI.
might call upon him to return, but it was extremely
doubtful whether so timid and irresolute a ruler would
exercise his authority against a man whom nine-tenths
of the French had come to regard with a feeling closely
allied to veneration.   Nothing, perhaps, did so much to
set Voltaire under weigh for Paris as the contemplation
of a portrait in his simply furnished bedroom of the
modern Roscius.   He had not seen Lekain act except
at private theatres, and was filled with delight at the
prospect of his still-beloved pupil appearing before him
under the more favourable conditions afforded by the
resources of the Comédie Française.   So, full of glowing
anticipations, he started on his journey early in February,
assuring the inhabitants of Ferney, who came around
him with tears in their eyes to wish him God-speed,
that he would soon be among them again.

   But the expected meeting of the poet and his inter-
preter was not to take place.   Lekain, in order to win
a fresh tribute of praise from his mistress, Madame
Benoît, who had so large an influence over his mind
that on playing a lover he would place her at one of

the wings to give his utterances a more impassioned
tenderness, represented Vendôme one evening with an
energy and self-abandonment of which even his own
history had presented few examples.   He held the
audience in the hollow of his hand, bearing all ˙of them
away in a veritable chaos of emotion.   For this triumph,
however, he had to pay a formidable price.   His exertions led to a fever ; the most approved medical skill
in Paris was employed in vain to save him, and a few
days later, on the 8th of February, it was announced
from the stage of the Comédie that although only forty-
nine years of age, he had just breathed his last.
"Dead ?" the word came upon that miscellaneous throng
like a thunderclap, and, having been caught up by
stragglers outside, was mournfully repeated in all
quarters of the city.   Nothing was to be heard in the
coffee-houses but praises of his refined sensibility, his
idealized truth to nature, his exquisite force of expression, his almost undivided sway over the world of
passion, and above all, the force of imagination which
transfigured him on the stage from a "petit bourgeois
of the Rue St. Denis" into "a hero of Homer."   "It
is widely recognized," says Grimm, "that no actor has
ever realized with more depth and dignity the genius
of tragedy," Marie Antoinette taking the lead in the
general expression of regret.   Fortunately for the
Church itself, Lekain had not died without renouncing

his profession, and the funeral was worthy of him who, if we consider both his personal disadvantages and the effects he produced, must be pronounced one of the most remarkable tragedians the world has ever seen.

Five hours after Lekain's interment, on the afternoon of the 10th of February, Voltaire, unaware of the irreparable loss he had suffered, arrived in the city from which he had been an exile for a quarter of a century. " Ma foi," he briskly said at the barrier, in answer to the stereotyped question, " I believe there is nothing contraband here except myself." Enveloped in a large pelisse, with his head in a woollen peruke and a fur-edged red bonnet, he had so quaint an appearance that a swarm of urchins, mindful of the carnival, followed his coach with joyously derisive cries as he drove through the tortuous streets to the residence of the Marquis de Villette, situated on the quay subsequently named after him, at the corner of the Rue de Beaune. Here, with many other privileged persons, the members of the Comédie Française, by appointment, were assembled to receive him—strange faces all. He glanced swiftly round the room, and then, with a wistful and inquiring expression, at his noble host. The Abbé Mignot, a nephew of the latter, endeavoured to break the news to him, but could not get beyond three words —" Vous demandez Lekain." Bellecourt put an end to what must have been a painful silence. " Monsieur," he said, gravely pointing to the mourning he and his comrades were wearing, "you see before you all that remains of the Comédie Française." The old man felt his bereavement in all its weight; he staggered faintly to a chair, covered his face with his bony hands, and sobbed like a brokenhearted schoolboy.

He would have been more than human if this grief had continued long in its first intensity. The news of his arrival spread like wildfire to the remotest corners of Paris, exciting as it went a burst of enthusiasm to which no parallel of its kind can be found. Men of every sort and condition were eager to honour the writer whose many-sided genius had given a fresh lustre to the French name, whose exertions on behalf of the Calases and others appealed to all generous sympathies, who had taken the lead in arousing the nation to a sense of the degrading despotism of the present *régime*, and who, as it was thought, had dealt a death-blow at what, mainly in consequence of his own teaching, an immense majority now deemed a childish superstition. Had it not been reserved for him to open a new and greater chapter in the history of the human race? it was asked. Crowds assembled daily in the Rue de Beaune and on the quay in the hope of catching the briefest glimpse of him; his antechamber was thronged every morning by the most illustrious persons in the capital; it was impossible for him to take an airing without his coach

becoming as "the nucleus of a comet." Every other
subject of interest—intrigues at Court, the death of
Lekain, and the controversy between the Gluckists and
the Picenists—was temporarily ignored. In vain did the
clergy endeavour to stem the torrent; the blows they
aimed at the hero of the hour recoiled upon their own
heads. It is a question, indeed, whether the coming home
of a Turenne triumphant would have produced so much
agitation. According to Grimm, "the Sorbonne trembled,
the Parliament held its peace, the literary circles were
in a ferment, and Paris in general proudly did homage
to the nation's idol."

But that homage, intoxicating as it may seem to
have been, did little to divert its recipient's thoughts
from his new tragedy, which was put in rehearsal
without delay. Every morning, after an animated
conversation with his visitors, whom he received in his
dressing-gown and nightcap, he would dictate changes
in the versification to his secretary, Wagnière. On the
15th of February, a deputation from the Comédie,
headed by Bellecourt, came to report progress, to ask
for suggestions, and formally to pay their respects to the
author of *Zaïre*, *Mérope*, and *Tancrède*. His reply to
the address was marked by a "touching affability."
Having referred to his feeble health, "henceforward,"
he said, "I live only for you and by your aid." From
this it might be inferred that he intended to do nothing

but dramatic work in future. " Madame," he said to
Vestris, the elected representative of Irène, " here are
the alterations you wished me to make in your lines.
I have worked for you all night as though I had been
only twenty years of age." Most of the players then
withdrew, Fleury, it is said, lagging behind to remind
the philosopher of the disrespect shown towards his wig
by a youth at Ferney. "I cannot but think," said
Laharpe, who took care to be seen in the house as often
as possible, " that Bellecourt delivered the address in a
very pathetic fashion." "Both of us," replied Voltaire,
" played our parts in the little comedy extremely well."
Some days afterwards, being too unwell to leave the
house, he had a rehearsal of *Irène* gone through in his
salon, and was at the pains to recite the principal
speeches for the instruction of the players concerned.
His memory, as one of the group remarked, showed as
little falling off as his wit.

Irène was performed for the first time on the 16th of
March. Never had the theatre in the Tuileries presented a more brilliant appearance. Except the King,
who pointedly went to the Opéra that evening, the
whole of the royal family were in attendance—the centre
of a dense, impatient, and agitated gathering. Illness,
however, kept Voltaire himself away—an illness so
severe that, believing his end to be really at hand, he
had, in order to save his remains from the ditch, made

peace with that church which he had so long sought to
overthrow. "Yes," he said to the curé waiting upon
him, "we ought to die in the faith of our fathers.
Had I been born on the banks of the Ganges I should
believe what the people there believe." It did not occur
to the curé that this speech deprived the recantation of
nearly all its value. And the disappointment caused
by the poet's absence from the theatre must have been
deepened by the piece. Notwithstanding a few flashes
of his former might, *Irène* was, if not precisely feeble, at
least cold in its general effect—a fact which the style
of Madame Vestris must have rendered more apparent,
although Brizard and the elder Sainval were among her
supporters. However, the audience received in "respectful silence" what they could not applaud, and the
curtain descended amidst ringing cheers for the author.
Friends hurried away to communicate the good tidings
to the latter, who found no reason to doubt that he had
gained more than a *succès d'estime*. "But if my good
fortune consoles me," he mournfully ejaculated, "it
cannot make me well."

In this, perhaps, he was wrong. By the 30th of
March, when the players gave *Irène* for the sixth time,
he felt strong enough to visit the theatre. In the
afternoon of that day, dressed in a red coat lined with
ermine, a flowing waistcoat, long ruffles, and a large,
black, unpowdered wig of the Louis Quatorze pattern,

in which his head " was so much buried that you saw
only his two eyes shining like carbuncles," he drove
in an azure-coloured and star-bespangled coach—somebody called it the chariot of the empyrean—to the
home of the Academy, where, with his portrait hung
over the Director's chair, unusual honours were conferred upon him. Meanwhile it became generally
known that he was at the Louvre, and a crowd of
the most miscellaneous kind soon filled the ample
court of that edifice to its very corners. From this
sea of heads there came a roar of delight as he started
for the Comédie ; prolonged *vivats* rent the air, and the
court was surrounded by a belt of importunate admirers.
"His progress from the old Louvre to the Tuileries,"
writes Grimm, " was a sort of public triumph." He at
length reached the Comédie Française, and, having been
got to the door by the Marquis de Villette and another
friend—a feat of which they had reason to be proud—
mounted the staircase without any aid save that of a
stout cane. But to get into the *salle* was scarcely
less difficult than to get to the doors. Illustrious
Frenchmen barred his way ; ladies pressed forward to
pluck a morsel of fur from a sable cloak in which, the
evening being chilly, he had enveloped himself on the
way. Probably with a sigh of relief, he eventually
found himself installed in the box of the Gentlemen
of the Chamber, with Madame de Villette, a foster-

child of his, and Madame Denis. He took a chair behind them, but the pit—perhaps the densest and most enthusiastic that had yet been brought together— insisted upon his sitting where they could see him. Brizard then came forward to crown him with a wreath of laurel. " Ah, Dieu, vous voulez donc me faire mourir ? " he exclaimed, with tears in his eyes. He transferred the garland to the head of the Marquise de Villette, but it was promptly restored to its destined place by the Prince de Beauvan. *Irène* was then played, the company previously advancing in a body to make silent reverences to the author. During the performance, Grimm tells us, the theatre was often darkened by the dust arising from the flux and reflux of the agitated multitude. After the tragedy, which elicited uproarious applause, the curtain rose upon a rather curious scene. On a pedestal in the centre of the stage was a bust of Voltaire, the company standing behind it with palms and garlands in their hands, and the orchestra discoursing appropriate music. Madame Vestris recited some verses to the effect that the author of *Mérope* had not had to wait for the Dark River to enjoy the honours of immortality, and the players, one by one, laid their wreaths of flowers on the bust. Mlle. Fanier ecstatically kissed it ; her comrades, as though to show how contagious example may be, instantly did the same. During the afterpiece, *Nanine*, the bust stood at the side of the stage. "M. de Voltaire," notes Grimm, "seemed much moved," as well he might be, by all this homage. The performance over, he was almost carried from his box to the doors, outside which a dense mass of people could be seen. By these he was not to be let off so easily as might have been expected. He had scarcely entered his coach when a cry of "flambeaux!" was raised, and until his withered face had been lighted up by the lurid glare of a dozen torches the horses were detained. Even then a strong disinclination to let him go was apparent; some of the crowd held on to the doors until he gave them his hand to kiss. "I shall be smothered in roses," he smilingly said to some of the most persistent. But there was one plaudit by which he set much store. "Who is this great man?" somebody asked a fisherwoman. "Why, the saviour of the Calases, to be sure," was the reply, in a tone of astonishment at the other's ignorance. Voltaire was deeply impressed by the incident. "Yes," he said, "my best work is that I have done a little good." Eventually he was allowed to start homewards, a large portion of the crowd following him over the Pont Royal with cries of "Vive Voltaire!" "Vive l'auteur de *Zaïre!*" "Vive l'auteur de *l'Henriade!*" "Vive le philosophe!"

But the excitement engendered in his mind by this apotheosis proved more than his enfeebled frame could

bear. From that time, there can be no doubt, he was
slowly dying. On the 22nd of April, Bachaumont
informs us, the players were "agreeably surprised," at
one of their business meetings in the green-room, to
see the veteran totter in to thank them anew for what
they had done in *Irène*. He was on the point, he
added, of returning to Ferney, and would there revise
Agathocle and the *Droit du Seigneur*. Later, at a meeting of the Academy, he complained, as Racine had
done, of the comparative poverty of the French tongue.
He suggested that "tragédien" should be accepted to
distinguish a tragic actor from a comedian. "Our
language," he said, "is a proud beggar; we must help
it in spite of itself." From the Academy he went in
disguise to the theatre to see *Alzire*; the pit, however,
immediately recognized him, and the performance was
interrupted for three-quarters of an hour by their
acclamations. It is worthy of note that, accompanied
by Wagnière, he called upon the Marquise de Gouvernet,
the Mlle. de Livri of fifty or sixty years before. For
some time they were both silent from astonishment,
each failing to perceive in the other any traces of what
he or she had been. On the wall, as though in mockery
of life, was Largillière's portrait of the poet at the age
of about twenty-eight, in all the freshness and buoyancy
of manhood. "Ah, my friends," he said with a deep
sigh on reaching home, "I have returned from one

bank of Cocytus to the other." In another month, with
a weakness aggravated by an overdose of laudanum, he
was on his death-bed, apparently indifferent to the fate
of his remains. In reply to the exhortations of the
curé of St. Sulpice, who had been sent for by the
Villettes, he pushed him back, exclaimed "let me
die in peace," and feebly turned his face to the wall.
Yet another letter was to come from his pen. On the
26th of May, when he seemed to be in the last stage
of exhaustion, it became known to him that his pro-
tracted exertions to procure a reversal of the sentence
upon Lally had at length been crowned with success.
"The dying man," he managed to write to Lally's son,
"revives on hearing this great news ; he embraces M.
de Lally most tenderly." Four days afterwards, at
night, he quietly passed away, his last words, accompanied by a pressure of the hand, being addressed to
an old valet—"Adieu, mon cher Morand, I am going."
Many fables to the effect that he died in an agony of
terror and misery were explicitly contradicted by Madame
de Villette, who nursed him throughout. "Down to
the end," she told Lady Morgan, "all that he did and
said was of a piece with the generosity of his character ;
all indicated tranquillity and resignation save his little
gesture towards the curé of Saint Sulpice."

It was with an emotion at least commensurate with
the excitement produced by his return that Paris heard

of the death of the man who had so long wielded the
sceptre of literature. For some days the city seemed to
be in mourning, although to a large minority of the
nation his attack upon Christianity was a matter of the
deepest and bitterest abhorrence. How far that feeling
could be carried was shown many years afterwards,
when, in the dead of night, his remains, with those of
Jean Jacques Rousseau, were stolen from the vaults of
the Panthéon, conveyed in a sack to a common near
Bercy, and there reburied in quick-lime. " Would to
God," exclaimed one of a few fanatics who thought
that they were justified by the spirit and letter of their
faith in perpetrating such an outrage, and who probably
had no words strong enough to denounce the violation
of the tombs at St. Denis, "that we could put an end
to their doctrines in the same way!" It is in something of this mood that Voltaire is usually judged. No
pains have been spared to blacken his memory. His
titles to our respect and admiration are either overlooked or described as streaks of silver on a dark cloud,
and an idea spread abroad by his opponents in the hope
of diminishing his influence, that he was a prey to
vanity, envy, and other littlenesses of mind, still ob-
tains a very wide acceptance. If, however, we get rid
of a prepossession against him so far as to form an
estimate of his character exclusively from his writings,
his indisputable acts, and the testimony of the most

clear-headed of his contemporaries—a feat which I have
striven to accomplish in these pages—he presents himself to us in a very different light; doubtless over-
sensitive to attack, of irascible temper, ready to flatter
insincerely, occasionally lapsing from strict truth, and
always irreverent save when his deism was appealed
to, but at the same time humane, affectionate, generous
to self-denial, steadfast in friendship, quick to forgive a
wrong, free from unworthy jealousies, modest in a very
high degree as to his own gifts, and full of " amenity
and grace " in the commerce of life.   Little as the fact
seems to be acknowledged, Christianity does not stand
in need of a misrepresentation of its foes, even in the
case of the man who assailed it with a force of ridicule
not likely to be reached again.

Here, of course, we are concerned with but one phase
of the universal genius which enabled Voltaire to win
a world-wide fame, fill millions with his thought, and
give so powerful an impulse to the cause of humanity,
justice, and toleration.   About the value of his plays
there is a curious diversity of opinion.   Gray ranked
them next to those of Shakspere; latter-day critics,
such as Francisque Sarcey, look upon them with something like contempt.   As may be supposed, the truth
lies half-way between these extremes.   Voltaire was
neither a Corneille nor a Racine, though it may be
said that *Brutus* and *Rome Sauvée* do not fall very far

short of *Cinna,* and that *Alzire* and *Mérope,* perhaps
his best works in this way, are scarcely less impressive
in their pathos and tenderness than *Iphigénie.* In the
inspiration of a great poet he was unquestionably wanting. But in other respects he improved upon the
example of his predecessors, notably as to breadth of
treatment, vividness of colouring, force of description,
the expression of generous sentiments, the importation
of realism, and, above all, the creation of dramatic
effect. He also addressed himself to a wider sphere
of human action, varying his scenes and periods and
characters with a boldness almost startling at a time
when nine out of every ten tragedies were based upon
the history or legends of the ancients. With one single
exception, none of his plots were suggested by modern
history, although modern names are assigned to many
of his personages. He would have done well to carry
his originality to the point of repudiating the cardinal
principles of classical tragedy, but it unfortunately
happened that he had been taught from boyhood to
regard them as synonymous with good taste, and to
the end of his life they were an integral part of his
system of writing plays. For this reason he could not
read Shakspere without a shudder, and in his irritation
would call him an "intoxicated savage." Such phrases,
however, do not represent his estimate of the English
poet in its entirety. He felt and expressed as keen

an admiration of the genius revealed in *Hamlet* and
Macbeth as was possible to any one living in the
eighteenth century. His letter to the Academy in
1776 is often ascribed to jealousy of a rival light,
but a dispassionate examination of the matter will lead
to the conclusion, which even so ardent a Shaksperean
as Charles Knight has adopted, that he was guided
simply by a desire to uphold the Racinian theory of
dramatic art. One feature of his plays deserves particular consideration. His individuality was not always
sunk in the personages here set before us. He used
some of them as a means of advocating religious
toleration. He allowed many of his tirades to be
coloured by the philosophy of which he was so un-
tiring and brilliant an exponent. Of course, this
occasional substitution of the doctrinaire for the poet
was a dire mistake, interesting as such passages were
to become from an historical point of view. It violated
one of the fundamental laws of the drama, gave rise
to somewhat offensive anachronisms of thought, and,
counteracting the effect of his welcome leanings towards
realism, imparted to French tragedy a more abstract and
rhetorical character than it had previously assumed.
But the shortcomings and faults of his work for the
theatre do not strike us so forcibly as its beauties,
which are quite sufficient to account for the sovereignty
he had possessed there from youth to old age.

CHAPTER VI.

1778—1782.

No play of exceptional value marks the records of the year that witnessed the death of Voltaire. Perhaps the most ambitious of those brought out was a tragedy by Laharpe, *Les Barmécides*, with which a rather unpleasant history is bound up. In his last illness, it appears, Voltaire asked the author to read this piece to him Laharpe declined, complacently remarking that it would arouse stronger emotions than it was good for an invalid to experience. "Nay," said the veteran, "the pleasure of hearing noble poetry will soothe my closing days." Laharpe accordingly proceeded to comply with the request. Voltaire's countenance gradually fell as he listened. In his opinion, the story, which had been taken from the *Arabian Nights*, was deplorably improbable, and many fine lines scattered over it seemed to be out of place. Laharpe's self-love was so much wounded by this outspoken criticism that he temporarily forgot his obligations to the critic. "For some time, alas!" he blurted out in print after Voltaire was in the grave, "he had been dead to us. Beautiful things,"

such as the *Barmécides*, " awakened in him no sensibility.
His taste had left him.   He would have liked to persuade us that *Irène* was superior to *Zaïre*," just as
Milton accounted *Paradise Regained* superior to *Paradise Lost.*   Before long this attack was withdrawn,
though not until the irate poet found that his ingratitude had alienated from him all the friends—and their
number was legion—of his illustrious protector.   Voltaire's judgment was amply vindicated by the production
of the *Barmécides.*   It brought Laharpe only six hundred
livres, more than half of which had to be deducted- on
account of free admissions for his friends.   Due care
was taken to make this fact public, as Laharpe had not
failed to announce any fall in the receipts when pieces
by rival dramatists were in the bills.

What has been called the eternal history of the
coulisses is again forced upon our notice.   Larive,
Monvel, and Molé were fighting hard for the characters
so long held by Lekain.   Eventually the Duc de Duras
decided to divide the heritage between the three, Larive
being formally put forward as the great tragedian's
successor.

> Lekain a passé l'Achéron,
> Mais il n'a point laissé ses talents sur La Rive.

For the present, however, Larive was the best substitute
for Lekain that could be found.   Molé's new acquisitions
did not prevent him from retaining his former *emploi,*

in which Fleury, after a prosperous second début, was elected to double him. It is alleged that at first he intrigued against the new-comer, and was within an ace of being challenged for his pains. " But," expostulated Madame Campan to Fleury, who had found in her a valuable friend, " by killing Molé you would break the hearts of a dozen ladies." " In that case," was the reply, " it may have been less out of consideration for me than from a desire to preserve himself for them that he disclaimed any intention to injure me." Molé, perhaps, was constitutionally indisposed to go to extremities. Fleury from the outset had the support of the Queen, partly because his sister Félicité, abandoned by her husband at Vienna soon after their visit to Ferney, had been employed to assist in her literary education. His prospects of promotion were soon brightened by the disappearance of a well-distinguished comrade. Bellecourt's health, at no time good, had been seriously affected by grief for the loss of Lekain, to obstruct whose progress he was originally called to the theatre, but to whom, after abandoning tragedy for comedy, he became allied in a lifelong friendship. He died on the 19th of November, in his fifty-third year.

Among the plays of the following spring were Voltaire's *Agathocle*, a *Médée* by the journalist Clément, author of the *Mérope* rejected in 1743, and *L'Amour Français*, a comedy in one act, by Pochon de

Chabannes. In the second, which owed much to the
gifts of Mlle. Sainval the elder and Larive, a half-
hearted attempt was made to give us a more flesh-and-
blood personage than the potent enchantress who
vanishes in a chariot drawn by winged serpents. But,
like most compromises in matters of art, it displeased
one party without pleasing the other; and a wicked
parody by a courtier of Boileau's line as to the *Cid*—

Tout Paris pour *Médée* a les yeux de Jason—

was not far removed from the truth. *L'Amour Français*
led to a remarkable demonstration in the theatre. Paris
had watched with keen interest the struggle of the
American colonists for their independence, partly on
account of her ancient hatred of England, but chiefly,
there can be no doubt, because they were animated by
ideas with which she was in eager sympathy. Louis
XVI., attributing that interest wholly to the first-named
cause, openly extended his sympathy to the insurgents;
and Lafayette, in common with many young and ardent
spirits, crossed the Atlantic to fight under their
colours. In *L'Amour Français* a young officer is represented as failing to obtain the hand of a beauty until
he has covered himself with glory in America. No
living person had yet been directly eulogised from the
stage, but Rochon ventured to make an exception to
this rule in favour of Lafayette. By doing so he evoked

one of the most ringing bursts of enthusiasm ever heard
in the theatre.   For some minutes the acting was
reduced to dumb show by cries of "Vivent les
Américains!" and "Vive Lafayette!" Interspersed
with these, however, were cries of "Vive le Roi!"
as the encouragement indirectly afforded to the revolted
colonists by France had generated a kindlier feeling
towards the Court.   But that feeling, which speedily
passed away, was to cost the king dear.   The course he
took could not but intensify the republican spirit abroad;
he was unconsciously rushing into a powder magazine
with a spark-dropping torch in his hand.

It was amidst the shadows of an impending calamity
to the Comédie that these pieces appeared.   Beaumarchais, who must be deemed responsible in some
degree for the error of policy just spoken of, was not
allowed to devote the whole of his attention to the
business of Roderigue Hortalez and Co.   His day of
reckoning with the players as to the *Barbier de Séville*
—a day to which all the dramatists looked forward with
keen hope—had at length come.   One morning, at a
meeting of the players, he was asked whether he intended to give the comedy to the theatre or allow it to
run until it came within the rules.   "If you do not give
it to us," said a member of the company, "at least tell
us how many times you wish it to be played for your
benefit, so that it may then become our property."   In

this speech we perceive a new system of paying the authors, to be rejected or adopted at their pleasure. Most of them had taken the latter course ; the benefits brought them a goodly sum of money at once, and the loss of a further share of the receipts was partly atoned for by the gratification of seeing the play more frequently represented. " The Comédie Française," the speaker went on, "always appreciates kindness shown to it. Do you wish the *Barbier* to be played six, eight, or even ten times ? " " Since you permit it," replied Beaumarchais, mockingly, " I should like it to be played for my benefit a thousand and one evenings." " Monsieur, you are modest." "As modest as you are just. What is this madness you have for inheriting from the living ? My piece cannot belong to you until the receipts fall to a low point; you ought, therefore, to wish that it may never belong to you at all. Eight months of a hundred louis are worth more than nine months at fifty. I see, messieurs, that you like your own interests better than you understand them." This is from Beaumarchais's statement of what passed. " I bowed," he adds, " with a smile to the company, which smiled in its turn ; its mouthpiece had blushed a little."

Beaumarchais did not neglect this opportunity of settling the question referred to him by the Duc de Richelieu. He applied for a full statement of accounts respecting the *Barbier*, which had then had thirty-two

representations. Desessarts brought him 4,506 livres,
but as the money was unaccompanied by any paper he
declined to take it. Upon this he was told that there
were a great many matters as to which the players
could offer only an account badly made out. "What
I require much more than money," Beaumarchais answered, " is an exact reckoning, to serve as a model for
all future accounts, and to restore peace between the
actors and the authors." Nearly three weeks afterwards, on another application to the same effect, the
company sent him an unsigned statement. Beaumarchais returned it with a request that somebody
would certify to its accuracy. M. Desessarts, having
been a procureur, would know, he said, that the request
was reasonable. The company, in reply, said the
account could be certified only with respect to the
takings at the door. They could not give an account of
other takings except by approximation. Beaumarchais,
" quite complacently," then gave them a lesson in
book-keeping. "Believe me," he added, " there must
be no badly made out accounts with men of letters.
Too proud to accept favours, they are too badly off to
suffer losses. As long as you do not adopt the system
of exact accounts, of which you alone are ignorant,
you will always be exposed to the annoyance of having
yourselves reproached with a systematic object of de-
priving men of letters of their rights—an object which

assuredly never entered into the heart or mind of any
of you."

Further pressed, the players threw themselves upon
the protection of the Duc de Duras, who helplessly
invited Beaumarchais to discuss the subject with his
fellow-authors.   Not without considerable difficulty
could anything like a full and representative gathering
be brought together.   Many at the outset were prompted
by a false pride to hold aloof, as the point in dispute
related to money.   Collé said that he was too old to
move in the matter, was too anxious to enjoy his repose.
Like the rat in the fable, he had retired within his Dutch
cheese, and was unlikely to come out of it to make the
world go on better than it did.   His feelings on the
subject might be expressed in a line from *Callisthène*—

A force de mépris je me trouve paisible.

Diderot was also averse from disturbing the tranquillity
of his country life.   He wished all success to the enterprise, but feared that M. de Beaumarchais would find
it more difficult to deal with the players than with the
Parliament.   Poinsinet de Sivri assigned a curious
reason for non-attendance.   He was then in For l'Evêque
in respect of a debt which he had really paid.   "I have
resolved," he writes to Beaumarchais, "to remain here
until I can get my rogue of a huissier hanged.   Your
letter arrived at 10 o'clock this morning, and I have not

sufficient time between now and dinner-time to get the good man proceeded against and disposed of. These huissiers. die hard, and, it is said, take a long time to hang ; consequently, Monsieur, allow me to defer the pleasure, etcetera." Laharpe refused to come if by chance Dorat or Sauvigny, who had threatened him, should be there. Beaumarchais pointed out to him that in a common cause there should be a truce to private quarrels, but the fear of a flagellation made the poet adhere to his resolution. In order to obviate such difficulties as these, Beaumarchais had two meetings at his house, and among those present at one or both were Séduine, Marmontel, Dorat, Palissot, Sauvigny, Chabannes, Mercier, Ducis, Barthe, Lemierre, Champfort, Cailhava, Saurin, and Laharpe. In the result, after due deliberation, they resolved with one voice to "strike" against the Théâtre Français—to abstain from writing for it until the grievances of which they complained had been redressed.

It may be doubted whether a thunderbolt falling into the green-room of the Comédie would have startled the players more than the announcement of this decision. Every one could see that the authors were terribly in earnest. To obtain a remedy for their wrongs, actual or imaginary, they had deliberately cut themselves away from what to a majority of them was a partial means of livelihood, to all a coveted privilege. It was true

that they might find an outlet for their energies at the
Comédie Italienne, but the position and associations of
the Comédie Française invested a triumph there with
an importance not attainable in any other French
theatre. Did not such self-sacrifice imply a determination from which they would never be induced to
swerve?· And the prospect disclosed by the strike
might well have created a feeling of despair among the
players. Paris looked for a large measure of novelty
in its dramatic entertainments. People indeed came
in hundreds to see plays by Molière, Corneille, Racine,
Regnard, or Voltaire, especially as they were interpreted
by a company which may be said to have included the
highest of the known histrionic talents in the country.
But an old play, ably acted as it might be, did not fill
the house so well as a new one of average value for a
few nights; and there was only too much reason to
fear that unless some hitherto undiscovered dramatic
genius should arise—certainly a poor dependence—
the public would impatiently take the side of the
rebellious authors.

Gloomy as the outlook was, however, the players
decided to fight out the battle to its bitter end. Most
firmly did they believe in the righteousness of their
cause. In truth, there is more to be said for them than
might be gathered from what has been stated up to this
point. Beaumarchais would have done them only pure

justice if he had been quite serious in acquitting them
of an intention to defraud.   It was obviously in their
interest to prevent any discords between the authors
and themselves, and the amount of money in dispute
was really too small to be worth consideration apart
from the principle it involved.   As the authors must
have known, their remuneration had been reckoned
exclusively by the takings at the doors, and of these
takings only had it been usual to keep account.   Other
receipts, such as the irregularly paid subscriptions of
fine ladies and gentlemen in the boxes, were the per-
quisites of the theatre.   If these receipts were to be
shared in by the authors, the players at present could
do nothing, as Desessarts had said, but offer a statement badly made out—a statement by approximation.
On this point, however, they were not prepared to give
way, the authors already having a relatively high
emolument for their work save in the case of failure.
Moreover, the latter were suspected of being anxious
not so much to increase their earnings as to have a
voice in the management of the theatre.   Nor were the
company less in earnest than their adversaries.   Falling
back in a large measure upon their old repertory, they
instructed five advocates, headed by the skilful Gerbier,
to watch over their interests in any emergency that
might arise.

In the heat of this conflict, when the need of union

among them seemed more urgent than ever, the players
were troubled by acute dissensions.   Probably counting
upon the support of the Duc de Duras, her protector,
Madame Vestris, the *jeune princesse*, took possession of
some characters belonging to the elder Mlle. Sainval,
the *reine*. Neither being disposed to give way, the
question was laid before the Gentlemen of the Chamber,
who, at the instance of the peer just named, decided in
favour of the usurper.   But the injustice done to Mlle.
Sainval was too glaring to escape animadversion.   It
led to fierce controversies in the green-room, the cafés,
and in Paris generally.   Pamphlets *pro* and *con* appeared
by the dozen, while enthusiastic partisans of one side
or the other went into the *sociétés* to beat up supporters.
Few could remain neutral ; to have no strong opinion
on the subject was to be thought incapable of forming
an opinion at all.   Madame Vestris soon perceived that
she had gone too far.   Mlle. Sainval was the more
popular of the two, and was not, like her antagonist,
the acknowledged mistress of an aristocrat.   Her cause
was espoused by a large majority—by lovers of fair
play, by intelligent playgoers, and last, but not least,
by the terrible democracy of Paris.

Not a little alarmed by this ferment, which made it
impossible for her to reappear on the stage at present,
Madame Vestris deemed it prudent to enter into a
compromise with her stronger rival.   In a letter to the

Journal de Paris she offered to cede nine of the characters
in dispute to Mlle. Sainval, reserving to herself only the
privilege of playing them alternately with her.   From
the terms of this letter it might have been inferred that
Madame Vestris was actuated by a purely generous
impulse.   As a matter of fact, what she proposed was
that Mlle. Sainval should have no more than twenty-
nine of about a hundred and fifty popular characters,
and nine of these twenty-nine only by turns with
another actress.   In order to enlighten the public on
this point Mlle. Sainval wrote to the *Journal de Paris,*
the editor of which, however, returned her letter with
an intimation that he had been instructed to insert no
reply.

Mlle. Sainval was not of a nature to endure this
tyranny without striking a blow.   In conjunction with
a friend, Madame de Saint-Chamont, she expanded the
letter into a pamphlet, which appeared in print a few
days afterwards.   Unfortunately, not content with
setting forth her case, she indulged in some inuendoes
which the Court construed into a deliberate attack upon
itself.   "By implication," Madame Campan remarked,
"it is said that the King is led by the nose, and that
his august consort, unmindful of the dignity maintained
by Maria Leczinska, condescends to mix herself up
with players' quarrels."   Moreover, the pamphlet contained several private letters by the Duc de Duras,

who, it was then seen, did not rise superior to petty partialities, and, though a courtier and an Academician, was unable to write his mother-tongue with any approach to accuracy.

For this betrayal of confidence the actress had to pay a heavy penalty. Louis XVI. was willing to pass over the attack upon the Queen in silence, but the Duc de Duras, smarting under the jeers which assailed him from all quarters, took speedy and condign revenge. Sainval was expelled from the Comédie Française, prohibited from performing at any provincial theatre, told that if she attempted to leave the kingdom the fact would be notified to all foreign courts, and received orders to retire to Clermont in Beauvoisin, a punishment previously reserved for ministers under a cloud of royal displeasure. According to the Fleury Memoirs, " the object of the Gentlemen of the Chamber was not to honour her with the dignity of a political exile, but to cut her off from communication with her friends, and above all to prevent her from writing."

The excitement of the public was soon at a high pitch. That Sainval had no right to publish the letters of the Duc de Duras must have been generally admitted, but this could not obscure the fact that she had been unjustly treated, and the punishment inflicted upon her was regarded as an insult to the majesty of the people. Of this a proof was soon to be given. Mlle. Sainval the

younger appeared as Aménaïde in *Tancréde*. She had
determined not to play again until her sister should be
recalled, but Fleury induced her to retract the determination by pointing out that such a course would
compromise her own interests without serving those of
her sister. The burst of applause which followed her
entrance was so tremendous that she fainted, and the
performance had to be suspended. "Recovering,"
writes Fleury, "she again presented herself to the
audience. Her emotion seemed to infuse additional
warmth into her acting ; Aménaïde was never played
with more spirit. It appeared as though she were
endeavouring to compensate the public for the loss of
her sister. The enthusiasm of the parterre was at its
height; and when she pronounced the line—

L'injustice à la fin produit l'indépendance !—

the plaudits absolutely shook the theatre. Nothing
was heard but cries of 'Sainval!' 'Sainval!' 'les
deux Sainval!' The presence of the guards had no
effect ; the parterre that night would have opposed a
whole regiment."

In the face of such demonstrations it was thought advisable to mitigate the punishment inflicted upon Sainval
the elder. To replace her at the Comédie Française
would have been too large a concession to popular
clamour, and only that part of the sentence which

exiled her to Clermont and prohibited her from playing
was remitted.   Much less harm would have been done
by recalling her to Paris, for in provincial towns her
cause was espoused with as much ardour as it had been
in the capital, and whenever she appeared it was to
meet with exceptional honours.   At Bordeaux, at the
end of *Mérope*, two Cupids descended from a cloud to
crown her with a wreath of laurel, and the audience, in
addition to demanding a performance for her benefit,
pelted her with flowers until the stage resembled a
flower-garden.

The vacancy caused by the banishment of Mlle.
Sainval was to be filled by no less a person than
Mlle. Raucourt.   Since her flight from Paris, it appears, the latter had fulfilled engagements in most of
the northern capitals.   In Berlin she made a conquest
of Prince Henry of Prussia, who, with the Prince de
Ligne, wrote to the Court of Versailles in her behalf.
The result was not so unfavourable as might have been
anticipated.   Marie Antoinette showed the utmost good
feeling towards the fugitive, even hinting to Préville
that their majesties would be pleased to see her on the
stage at Fontainebleau.   Raucourt, apprised of this,
ventured to return; the Court again yielded to the
influence of her genius, and the Gentlemen of the
Chamber decreed that she should go back to the
Comédie Francaise.   Her reinstatement there, however,

was more easily proposed than accomplished. Mlle. Luzi and other actresses opposed it with all their strength, really on the ground that her misconduct reflected disgrace on the theatre, but ostensibly, in order to avoid giving offence at Versailles, because she was almost hopelessly insolvent. " Is that all ? " the Queen innocently asked. " Well, such a difficulty is soon got over. I will pay her debts myself. Let me know the amount." The required information was speedily forthcoming—"About 200,000 livres, your majesty." Marie Antoinette hereupon reconsidered her intention, but at the same time procured from the King an order for the reappearance of the actress at the Comédie. Seldom had angry passion been more active among the audience than it was on the night when this order was acted upon. Mlle. Raucourt had been thrust upon the town in defiance of feelings that ought to have been respected, and the known willingness of the Court to meet her liabilities " out of the people's money " was not lost sight of. From her first scene she was assailed with howls of execration. It was to no purpose that a party of hired applauders strove to support her, though the most prominent of the malcontents were seized and conducted to prison by alguasils posted in the theatre by the Duc de Duras. " While the Comte d'Estaing is fighting the English to make them recognize the independence of America." it was bitterly said, " Frenchmen

are thrown into a cell for refusing to applaud Raucourt." Still more violent was the hostility shown
to her on the second night, when she played Phèdre.
Many passages in the part were eagerly applied to her.
For instance, there were shouts of assent as she uttered
the line—

De l'austère pudeur les bornes sont passées—

and again—

Et moi triste rebut de la nature entière.

But the actress, shaken as she was by all this, did not
bow to the storm, and at every manifestation of ill-
will would deliberately repeat the line which had evoked
it. By degrees, it is pleasant to add, the set of the stream
changed in her favour. The spirit of chivalry had not
been wholly deadened by the sophists, economists, and
calculators. People came to think that it was really
cruel to assail her in this way, and the dauntless courage
she displayed in the theatre compelled her foes to
admire her in spite of themselves. In a short space of
time, though the mistress of the Prince d'Hénin, who
had deserted Sophie Arnould for her, she regained
much of her former ascendency—nay, could not unreasonably boast that she enjoyed on the stage as
much distinction as Catherine enjoyed on the Russian
throne.

The troubles connected with Raucourt's return had

scarcely ended when another misfortune befell the Comédie Française. Most of the playgoers deserted that theatre for the Foire Saint Laurent, where a series of "farces" or "folies" by one Dorvigny were being played. This new luminary was supposed to be an illegitimate son of Louis Quinze, from the circumstance that a man of whom he spoke as his brother, and with whom he lived, was really entitled to that somewhat equivocal distinction. Dorvigny's pieces were whimsical enough to be valued for their own sake, but the extraordinary success they gained was due in a large measure to the talents of an actor for whom they had been written, an exquisitely droll buffoon of the Foire, born Volange, but better known as "Jeannot," the name of the character in which he first won popularity. For a time the achievements of Jeannot were the principal topics of conversation in Paris; he received invitations into the best society, and portraits and busts of him were to be found in every drawing-room. Marie Antoinette, "too ready to fall into the error of following instead of leading the fashion, purchased," says Fleury, "a number of these busts to distribute among the courtiers, who regarded them as an insignia of knighthood. Recipients of busts in plaster or biscuit ranked only as knights of the order; recipients of busts in alabaster or Sévres were treated as *grands cordons,* or commanders. Fortunately, Jeannot was not cast in bronze."

In the Comédie Italienne, too, the players found themselves confronted by a vigorous competitor. It virtually became the second Théâtre Français for which a demand had lately been raised. "Thalia, who has not hitherto dared to present herself on these boards except in alliance with the muse of harmony, now asserts her right to reign independently"—such was the purport of an address it had just delivered to the public. In all probability the Italians expected the authors on strike against the Comédie Française to write for them, and were not disposed to surrender the promised advantage without a struggle. If a struggle took place they were victorious, jealous as the other house had always been of the exclusive privileges assigned to it by Louis XIV. Many dramas by Mercier, including the *Brouette du Vinaigrier* and the *Juge*, had already been produced together with scarcely a pretence of musical accessories, and there could be little doubt that attractive plays originally intended for the Comédie Française would come into their hands. Nor were they without the means of doing something like justice to the works intrusted to them. In addition to being generally efficient, they had at least one brilliant comedian in Dorgeville, of whom we hear much in the correspondence of the day, and a sympathetic *jeune amoureuse* in Madame Verteuil, who had just come to them from the country. Indeed, with the aid of the dissident authors, they really seemed to be in the way of destroying, or at least of impairing, the supremacy so long maintained by the Comédie Française in dramatic and histrionic art.

Even here, however, the rivalry encountered by that house did not end. Many of the aristocracy seemed to prefer private to public theatres. For nearly two centuries, as we have seen, a taste for amateur performances had existed among the French. It had shown itself at Court, in the châteaux, and among the bourgeoisie. It had given rise to more than one of Molière's plays, had lent a peculiar charm to the gatherings at Sceaux, and had served to unfold for the first time the genius of Adrienne Lecouvreur, Armand, and Lekain. In the closing years of Louis XV. it became nothing less than a mania. Few opulent nobles neglected to build a theatre in their houses; some knowledge of the art of acting became a necessary part of liberal education, and the performers contracted the habit of calling each other by the names of characters in which they had excelled. An exalted personage once asked Préville how he played a particular part. In reply he roughly indicated his conception and execution thereof. "Well," said the other, "I take a different view of it." "Precisely," the actor remarked; "you conceive it as it is understood by the grandson of the great Condé." Not that these distinguished amateurs were usually put to the trouble of thinking. Most of them affected a species of drama invented for their purposes by Carmontelle, the *proverbe*. Here, under the veil of illustrating some familiar apophthegm, such as "Petite pluie abat grand vent," a scandal of the day was related in more or less piquant dialogue, and little or nothing beyond clearness of elocution and ease of deportment was needed to carry the players through their ordeal. Fired by Carmontelle's success, Collé astutely revived the *parade*, in which the mediæval farce was continued without its grossness. "In brief," says Fleury, "this passion for private theatricals was a serious misfortune to the Comédie Française. Our boxes were empty; the boxes of the amateur theatres were nightly crowded with the rank and fashion of Paris."

Before long, as may be supposed, the craze extended itself to the Court. Marie Antoinette had occasionally amused herself as the Dauphiness by joining in drawing-room performances, but a fear lest Louis XV. might interdict them induced her to keep the circumstance a secret. Elevated to the throne, she determined to gratify her histrionic tastes, took lessons from Dugazon, and proposed to have a theatre fitted up in the palace. For some time this design found a stout opponent in Louis XVI. He cared little for such diversions, and was decidedly of opinion that the Queen of France could not appear on the stage without loss of dignity. By degrees, however, he waived his objections so far as to sanction performances at the Petit Trianon, where etiquette was less stringently observed than at Versailles. Comedies and light operas were then learnt, Préville being brought from Paris to supervise the preparations. "At rehearsal," we are informed, "the Queen showed much cheerfulness and good humour; she would laugh at her own mistakes, and would readily repeat a passage or a scene if it were thought advisable." Louis XVI. was generally to be seen looking on. Now and then he betrayed a little ill-humour, as when the Queen had to kiss or be kissed. "If these things are necessary in the performance," he once said, "they may be dispensed with here." Instead of kissing, therefore, the ladies simply bowed their heads, while the gentlemen lifted the lace on their shirt-frills to their lips. Her majesty was at first content with very trifling parts. "Yesterday," we read in the *Correspondance Secrète* for 1777, "the young Queen gave a fête yet more brilliant than its predecessor. The scene was at a fair; ladies of the Court represented vendors; the Queen sold coffee as a *limonadière*." Not long afterwards, as we may see

from the appended copy of a French play-bill, she took
a loftier flight :—

Le Roi et le Fermier.

Le Roi	M. le Comte d'Adhémar
Richard	M. le Comte de Vaudreuil
Un Garde	M. le Comte d'Artois
Jenny	La Reine
Betty	Madame la Duchesse de Guise
La Mère	Madame Diane de Polignac.

Sédaine's pieces, it may be remarked, seemed to have
been as much in request at Court as any others. Her
majesty did not prove too ambitious. It is true that
one of her favourite parts was said to have been "royally
ill-played." But the most impartial testimony as to her
acting shows that it had the force of ease, intelligence,
expressiveness, and personal grace. In the unsophisti-
cated coquettes of comic opera she was particularly
happy. Nothing, we are told, could be more delightful
than her way of half-singing, half-reciting the lines in
Blaize et Babet—

> Le soir on danse sur l'herbette :
> Blaize et moi nous dansions tous deux ;
> Mais il me quitta pour Lisette,
> Qui vint se mêler à nos jeux.

The dispute between the dramatists and the players
was reaching a noteworthy stage. Beaumarchais found
that he had undertaken no light task in heading their
revolt against the Comédie. He framed plan after plan

for settling the question at issue, though only to see them thwarted soon afterwards by the skilful advocates on the other side. His colleagues, it is certain, gave him but slight assistance. Most of them took advantage of his perseverance and fertility of resource to do as little as possible themselves. Marmontel's reply to a reproach on this point is worth quoting. "In my native Limousin," he wrote, "a curé extremely fond of field sports was about to say mass. On coming to 'Lavabo' he heard the barking of dogs; the hare had been started. 'Is Briffaut there?' he whispered to the clerk, referring to a particular hound. 'Yes, M. le Curé.' 'Then it is all over with the hare—*Lavabo inter inno-centos manus meas,*'" etcetera. Beaumarchais was the Briffaut. Nor could he reckon upon active and intelligent co-operation from the Gentlemen of the Chamber. The Duc de Duras, on being asked to consider any part of the subject, helplessly referred him to the Duc de Richelieu, who as helplessly referred him to the Duc de Duras. Moreover, an attempt made by the players to sow dissension among the authors had not been wholly unsuccessful, as about a third of the number were in a state of thinly veiled mutiny. In the presence of all these difficulties, however, Beaumarchais held to his resolution. He would not rest until the dispute had been more or less satisfactorily adjusted. His reward now seemed to be at hand; the actors, anxious for a

termination of the contest, subscribed to an agreement
which he had drawn up, and a meeting to confirm it
was held at his house. But it all came to nothing.
Gerbier, blindly aided by the Duc de Duras, turned the
agreement into a State decree in favour of his clients.
In this form it was decisively repudiated by Beaumarchais, who, believing that the advocate had acted
upon instructions from the theatre, held out with
increased vigour and bitterness. Even a discovery that
he had been deserted on a minor issue by seven of his
followers, including Sauvigny and Lemierre, did not
lessen his sturdy confidence in the issue.

His majesty's players had more than reason to rejoice
at this schism in the enemy's camp. *L'Orphelin de la
Chine* was in the bill, and Lemierre, after meeting them
half-way in overtures for a reconciliation, asked them in
a quatrain to reproduce the *Veuve du Malabar*. Widows,
he suggested, deserved quite as much consideration as
orphans. His request was granted, Monvel undertaking
to appear as the young Brahmin, Mlle. Sainval as the
heroine, Vanhove as the Grand Brahmin, and Larive as
Montalban. During the rehearsals the author made
several alterations in the piece, especially in the way of
emphasizing those attacks upon priestcraft to which the
few cheers it elicited in 1770 may be ascribed. Probably
to his surprise, these passages were left intact by the
censor, who had not taken the trouble to give the

manuscript more than a cursory glance. *La Veuve du Malabar* had not been appreciably improved as a play by the revision it had undergone, but its anti-religious character, which only a decade previously had been insufficient to save it from failure, now made it one of the delights of Paris. Each tirade or sneer against worship was greeted with a burst of applause, the actual meaning of the dialogue between the Grand Brahmin and the novice as to the right of the priests to burn the widows being caught at with a fierce enthusiasm. Naturally enough, the clergy were at once up in arms, and the Archbishop of Paris called upon the King to have the tragedy purged of such pernicious matter as the discussion just mentioned. Louis XVI., absorbed in international politics, deferred a consideration of the matter, but permitted the players to go on with the piece until he came to a decision. Even his unquestionable earnestness as a Christian could not brace him in this case to a show of courage and resolution. His decision, when he did come to one, was to refrain from interfering, since the expurgation of the scenes and speeches complained of might arouse a ferment in the capital. In the result, the *Veuve du Malabar*, thanks exclusively to its atheistic fervour, had the then brilliant run of thirty consecutive nights—the most eloquent proof yet given of the extent to which *encyclopédisme* had eaten its way into the national mind.

Except the author himself, no one had looked forward to this revival with keener interest than Dorat, who for some time had been confined to his room by illness. "Let me know as soon as possible," he said to a friend on the morning of the day fixed for the first representation, the 29th of April, "how the *Veuve du Malabar* goes ; the knowledge of its success would give me a good night's rest." His friends might have asked themselves whether he would live to receive the news. He was dying from an incurable chest disease, aggravated by poverty, dissipation, over sensitiveness to attack, the importunities of creditors, and a bitter consciousness that he had toiled in vain. His ambition to outvie the many-sided brilliancy of Voltaire had not been gratified.

> De nos papillons enchanteurs
>   Emule trop fidèle,
> Il caressa toutes les fleurs
>   Excepté l'immortelle.

Indeed, what he said in reference to his first tragedy might be applied to the whole of his career. For him the gardens of Armida had been turned into a desert. Yet, aided by the affection of Mlle. Fanier, to whom he had been secretly married, the unfortunate poet affected to bear his reverses with cheerfulness, if not levity. And in this spirit he continued to the end. Death had no terrors for him. In the last stage of exhaustion, just after asking that the fate of the *Veuve du Malabar* might be

reported to him, he crawled out of bed, sat down before
a glass, and dressed himself with as much care as a beau.
He was lying in his chair dead, powdered and ruffled and
perfumed, when his friends returned from the theatre.

Lemierre's sorry triumph, it may be added, was not
confined to Paris. *La Veuve du Malabar*, despite the
opposition of the clergy, met with a sympathetic reception in various parts of the country, notably at Bordeaux, where the exiled Mlle. Sainval played the heroine,
and also at Toulouse, that seemingly impregnable strong-
hold of fanaticism, the city which only eighteen years
previously had seen Calas broken alive on the wheel
amidst the bitter jeers and execrations of his fellow-
citizens. Connected with the performance here was a
very remarkable history. Prosper Dussieux, a youthful,
enthusiastic, and educated member of the Bordeaux
company, with a good prospect of being called to the
Comédie Française at no distant period, was to have
played the young Brahmin. But on his way to Toulouse
he became enamoured of a fair travelling companion,
Mariamne Crussol, daughter of a woollen-draper there.
For her sake he at once threw up his stigmatized
profession, and, believing that nobody in the town
would recognize in him a certain M. Dennery from
Bordeaux, obtained employment from her father as a
sort of clerk. His affection for her was returned; M.
and Madame Crussol saw no objection to the match, and

one morning the lovers presented themselves at the altar of the church of the Cordeliers to be married. Suddenly the service was interrupted by the entrance of an unsuccessful pretender to the lady's hand, who gave a written paper to the priest. It was with a darkening countenance that the latter scanned it. " Your name is Dennery ? " he sternly said to the bridegroom. " My name is Dussieux," was the reply. " No Christian woman's happiness," continued the priest, " can be intrusted to your hands. Imprudent parents, would you give your daughter to an actor ? " In an instant the words were being repeated in tones of horror by most of the onlookers—" an actor ! " " Yes," said the priest vehemently, " an actor ! And this man has dared to approach the altar—this child of perdition, on whom I invoke a curse instead of the intended benediction ! Mariamne Crussol, my anathema be on your head, too, if you do not renounce all thought of this impious union. Leave the church ! " he added to the player ; " cease to profane this sacred place with your presence." Dussieux, overwhelmed by the blow, fell to the ground insensible, and in this state was borne to a house well known as a resort of actors. Mariamne displayed more fortitude ; in a sort of stupor, without betraying any emotion, she went away with her parents. Her calmness seems to have masked a terrible resolution. In the dead of night she crept to Dussieux's lodging, taking with her some poisoned wine and food. Next morning, when one of Prosper's comrades entered the room, the lovers were found dead in each other's arms, Mariamne still in the bridal dress which she had donned with so light a heart twenty-four hours before.

From this outburst of clerical bitterness towards the stage—a bitterness which the appearance of such plays as the *Veuve du Malabar* could not fail to intensify, but to which, it should be borne in mind, the anti-religious spirit breathed in that production was partly, if not originally, to be ascribed—we again turn to the Comédie Française. Mlle. Hus, apparently younger than she was, retired in consequence of a marriage to one Lelièvre, who had signalized himself by an attempt, happily abortive, to continue the sort of dictatorship exercised by the Chevalier de la Morlière until the police closed the theatre against him. Probably she was missed, as for seventeen or eighteen years, ever since her judicious abandonment of tragedy, she had played youthful heroines in comedy with "purity of style and grace of coquetry." Dauberval, one of the players imprisoned in 1765 for refusing to appear with Dubois, and Madame Drouin, the Mlle. Gauthier to whom Voltaire first confided the heroine of *Mahomet*, also withdrew at this time. Fleury is not quite correct in stating that these losses were unatoned for by gains of any kind. Madame Vanhove, wife of the Comédien du Roi, came forward

on the 14th of August as Phèdre. Her acting was
marked by cultivated intelligence, but also by a certain
monotonous artificiality which excited derision.   In
the apostrophe to Minos—

> Pardonne : un Dieu cruel a perdu ta famille ;
> Reconnais sa vengeance aux fureurs de la fille—

she angrily resented this by substituting " parterre " for
the last word.   Prone to admire courage, especially in
a woman, the audience loudly applauded the violation
of metre and rhyme, and her subsequent performances
were received with increasing favour.   Moreover, a
Mlle. Olivier, sixteen years of age, both pretty and
clever, soon won a place at the Comédie as the representative of youthful heroines.

Suddenly, after months of embittered controversy,
the authors' strike was terminated by royal intervention.
Louis XVI., slight as was the interest he took in the
stage, proposed in an interval of rest to put the relations
of the two parties on a new footing.   Probably he was
quite tired of a series of marches and countermarches
executed by the resolute Beaumarchais and the skilful
Gerbier since the dispute began.   Early in December
the Council of State issued a solemn decree on the
subject.   Each side must have read the document with
alternate gratification and annoyance.   It enacted that
the players should include in the account the whole of
their receipts, annual subscriptions not excepted, and

that the author should receive a seventh instead of a ninth share of the total. On the other hand, the return below which a piece become the property of the theatre, 1200 livres in winter and 800 livres in summer, was raised to 2300 livres and 1800 livres respectively. If anything, the players gained by this modification of the old system. Substantial remuneration for the dramatist now depended upon a longer succession of good audiences. Failure to him was armed with fresh terrors ; a striking success, such as *Mérope* or the *Barbier de Séville*, would entitle him to a larger sum than the authors of those pieces had received. Yet, unsatisfactory as it was on some points, the decree temporarily put an end to the strike, though the cry often raised in the late struggle, " let us have a second Théâtre Français on new principles," continued to be raised at intervals by one or two discontented writers.

How unprepared the poets were for the royal decree may be gathered from the fact that some months elapsed before any of them had a piece ready for the consideration of the Comédie. During this time the players had something more than revivals to occupy their minds. Mlle. Luzi, the soubrette, asked for leave to retire, ostensibly because a perusal of the biography of Mlle. Gautier inspired her with a wish to pass the rest of her life in penitence, but really, it is hinted, because the heart she now devoted to religion had been neglected by the sterner sex.   In a few weeks, probably to her surprise and annoyance, the town declared that her place was already filled by a pretty girl of nineteen, Marie Elizabeth Joly, who for the last ten years had played children's parts with acceptance, and who, opening a début there in due form on the 1st of May as Dorine in *Tartuffe*, delighted old and young by acting full of life, finesse, truth, and graceful humour.   Grimm was even disposed to think that she would console many elderly playgoers for the withdrawal of Mlle. Dangeville, so admirable were her soubrettes.   In 1778 she had married Louvoy, a cavalry officer, and in all the relations of private life was the despair of Parisian scandalmongers.   Her accession came in time to compensate the players in some measure for a diminution of their strength.   Monvel, in reply to an invitation from the lettered King of Sweden, went to play at the Royal Theatre in Stockholm, leaving two or three plays to be represented for the benefit of creditors.   As Grimm reminds us, M. de l'Empyrée, in the *Métromanie*, had made a similar arrangement, which may not have been hailed with exuberant gratitude by the persons concerned.

Laharpe was the first member of the dramatic authors' league to write for the theatre after the settlement of the late dispute.   Early in the summer

he finished a long meditated tragedy, *Jeanne de Naples.*
It did not at once get into rehearsal, as the players
were then preparing a few novelties by untried dramatists.   Among this little group˙ was one Durozoi,
who, sprung from a family originally bearing the
name of Cochon, had for twenty years dabbled rather
industriously in literature.   He had recently written a
Richard III., and the players decided to give it a
hearing.   Hissed " à double carillon " on the first night,
it speedily fell within " all the rules," and was never
represented again.   Durozoi, perhaps, had proudly
relied upon his own resources instead of adapting
Shakspere's play.   The company then took up *Jeanne
de Naples*, which appeared on the 6th of December.
It is not a little surprising that a tragedy on this
subject should have been licensed, especially as the
censor, far from being asleep, had twice set his veto
upon it until passages more or less hostile to religion
and monarchy had been struck out.   In the absence
of evidence on the point, we might well refuse to
believe that at this time, when France had come to
the brink of revolution, the stage of a theatre under
the control of the Court was exhibiting a Queen dragged
before and dethroned by a tribunal of her subjects.
How such a piece was received it is needless to say.
Even Mlle. Sainval failed to win any sympathy for
the heroine, whose downfall aroused fierce exultation all

over the parterre. Louis XVI., thinking that it would be dangerous to stop the performances, contented himself with repeating that the censorship should be exercised with "more vigilance," and a play which could not have failed to intensify the subversive spirit abroad was allowed to run its course.

CHAPTER VII.

1782—1784.

His majesty's players, after appearing at the *salle des machines* at the Tuileries for about eleven years, took possession of a theatre erected for them near the Luxembourg, which was formally opened on the 9th April with a performance of *Iphigénie*. Many of the company had wished their old home in the Rue des Fossés Saint Germain to be rebuilt, but the suggestion appears to have been wholly disregarded at Court. In one sense, as they might have confessed, their new home could not have been more appropriately placed. Its site, which had formed part of the ancient Clos Bruneau, was that occupied in the previous century by the Hôtel de Condé, a favourite haunt of Corneille, Molière, and Racine. More than ever pressed for money, the Government did not allow the architects, Peyre and Wailli, to realize in full an elaborate design for the purpose. "Que diable," said a minister to them, "can we not dispense with a few of these pillars?" For this reason the façade was much less graceful and dignified than it might have been. On the other hand, the interior met with general admiration. It was circular in form, liberally ornamented with sculpture, and lighted by a lustre hung from the centre of a dome. But the most important feature of the house has yet to be noticed. Laharpe and other dramatists had long advocated a seated pit, in the main, it is to be feared, from a conviction that the discomfort of standing for three hours or more put the groundlings in an ill-humour. Provided with seats the pit now was, together with a gradient steep enough to give spectators at the rear at least a partial view of the stage. Oddly enough, the delight afforded by this reform did not save a prologue on the first night, *L'Inauguration du Théâtre Français*, by Imbert, from being ruthlessly hissed—so ruthlessly, indeed, that a little piece by Laharpe, *Molière à la Nouvelle Salle*, in which some follies of the time, such as the popularity of the farces of the Boulevards, are rather cleverly satirized, was at once put in its place.

It is sufficiently clear that the mania just mentioned was extended by an increasing poverty of the Comédie Française in mirth-provoking matter. Years had passed since a play distinguished by rich humour of conception and treatment had appeared there. Conscious that such a production was beyond their power, most of the authors at present working for the leading theatre re-treated within a comparatively narrow circle, piquing themselves upon nothing but depth of interest, impressiveness of incident, and cold elegance of style. Lachaussée and Diderot had enlarged the domain of comedy, and their influence was temporarily rivalling that of Molière and Lesage. Follies which a capable dramatist would have seized upon with avidity were indeed patent to all, but were passed over in favour of social questions fermenting in men's heads. Nor was this deficiency always made good by revivals of the joyous comedies of old. Few of them were otherwise than well known, and all were out of favour with one section of the playgoing public. Fine ladies and gentlemen, priding themselves upon extreme delicacy of taste, "affected to be shocked," we read in the Fleury Memoirs, "at the writings of the Father of French comedy. Molière was not refined enough for them. Their ears were wounded by the somewhat free expressions which he occasionally employed. The polished Court of Louis Quatorze had heard these expressions without blushing, but the purer-minded belles of the eighteenth century resented such licence. Even courtesans spread out their fans in affected alarm at the least indication of *double entente*. And the plays of the best of Molière's successors were but faintly applauded from the boxes. Regnard was listened to with indifference, Lesage condemned as gross."

In direct contrast to the serious spirit predominating

in the entertainments offered by the King's players was a work placed in their hands at this point. Beaumarchais, who in 1780 had regained all his civil rights, found time to finish a five-act comedy sketched some years previously, the *Mariage de Figaro, ou La Folle Journée.* "How, occupied as you are, did you manage to do so?" the Comte de Maurepas asked him. "Monsieur," was the arch reply, "I wrote it while the King's ministers were in a body at the Redoute." "If there are many such repartees as that in the piece," said the Count, "I will answer for its success." *Le Mariage de Figaro,* as may be gathered from its title, is a continuation of the *Barbier de Séville,* and to a certain extent had been foreshadowed in the preface to the latter. It turns in the main upon an intention of the Comte d'Almaviva to exercise the *droit du seigneur* upon his wife's waiting-maid, Suzanne, who is about to marry the barber. Perhaps this may be thought an inadequate spring of action for a full-length comedy, but the author's wit and fertility of dramatic invention are so fully laid under contribution that we are borne along under a sort of spell from the first scene to the last. Incidentally, too, the piece is marked by a force and boldness of satire almost without precedent in French literary history. Not content with making Figaro a portrait of himself, at least to the point of attributing to the character most of the experiences recounted in

the *Mémoires,* Beaumarchais, though in some sense a
courtier, assailed through him a few of the abuses that
were gradually undermining the present social system—
lettres de cachet, the powers of the police, the restraints
imposed upon freedom of discussion in any form, and,
above all, the exclusive privileges of the aristocracy.
In the words of Grimm, the play was a picture of actual
manners among the noblesse, whose ignorance and
meanness and laxity of morals it laid bare with a master
hand. Especially vigorous was a long monologue delivered by Figaro in the fifth act. "Because you are a
great lord," he says in an apostrophe to Almaviva, "you
think yourself a great genius! Nobility, wealth, rank,
places—all that makes one so proud! What have
you done to have so much? You have been at the
trouble to be born, nothing more. A man of rather
ordinary a stamp, besides. Whilst I, lost in the obscure
crowd, I have had to exercise more knowledge and wit
merely to subsist than have been employed these hundred
years to govern Spain with the Indies." Who could
doubt the effect of such a piece, particularly in
the bitter and concentrated scorn of "been at the
trouble to be born," upon the inflammable pit of the
Comédie Française? It is too much to assume, however,
that the *Mariage de Figaro* was intended to precipitate
the threatened revolution. Beaumarchais had little
taste for politics, and, despite an inclination on the

part of the victorious American colonists to repudiate
his claims upon them, was rich enough to have a strong
interest in the preservation of order. He probably
sought to promote the cause of moderate reform rather
than of radical change, to mend instead of destroy.

If the daring author expected the satirical passages
of the *Mariage de Figaro* to escape notice until it came
out, as was probably the fact, a keen disappointment
awaited him. Bearing in mind the royal behest that
the censorship should be exercised with greater vigilance,
the Lieutenant of Police, Lenoir, subjected the piece to
a sort of microscopical examination, and, satisfied that
it would have a pernicious effect upon the public mind,
declined to pass it in its present form. Beaumarchais
appealed against this decision to the King, who, alarmed
by rumours communicated to him by the Keeper of the
Seals and others, thought it prudent to go over the
manuscript himself before coming to a decision in the
matter. Madame Campan one afternoon received a
message to attend their majesties in the private apart-
ments of the Queen. On a table near them she saw
a pile of paper. "Here," said the King, pointing to it,
"is M. Lenoir's copy of M. de Beaumarchais' comedy.
I want you to read it to us. Several parts you will
find troublesome, owing to alterations and references.
I have already glanced over it, but I wish the Queen
to hear it all. Do not speak of this reading to any-

body." Madame Campan settled down to her task. Louis XVI. frequently interrupted her to praise or dispraise. " That," he said of one line, " is in bad taste ; this man is continually dragging Italian *concetti* on the stage." Figaro's soliloquy, as may be supposed, aroused in him the deepest indignation. " Detestable ! " he exclaimed, rising ; " the comedy shall never be played. Not before the Bastille is levelled to the dust would the licensing of such a thing be other than an act of dangerous folly. He scoffs at everything that ought to be respected in government "—lettres de cachet, a fettered press, the exclusive privileges of the noblesse, etcetera. " So the piece will not be played ? " asked the Queen, speaking in a tone implying that she did not approve the intended veto. " It will not," answered the King emphatically.

Beaumarchais, with characteristic irrepressibility, met the announcement of his majesty's resolution with a vow that the *Mariage de Figaro* should nevertheless be produced at the Comédie Française, cost him what it might. In this he was more likely to succeed than fail, insuperable as the obstacle placed in his way might have appeared. Fifty years of age, he had lost little or none of the buoyancy, the courage, the cleverness, and the unwavering strength of purpose displayed in his contests with the Comte de Lablache and the Goëzmans. He had many friends at Court, and would certainly take full advantage of the influence they possessed. Lastly, the public were at his back from the moment when it became generally known that the *Mariage de Figaro* satirized some of the worst features of the existing system, notably the privileges of the detested aristocracy, and that for this reason it had been suppressed by the Court. Exclamations against such an exercise of authority seem to have been neither few nor half-hearted. Beaumarchais, always a keen observer of passing phenomena, was well aware of the power given to him by this spreading intolerance of tyranny. "I have but one thing," he said, "to wish for—namely, that my comedy should be thought at Versailles to be very dangerous and very reprehensible. Most fervently do I hope that the King will continue to dislike it, as in that case it will soon find its way to the Comédie Française. If I only get enemies and obstacles enough I am certain to win."

Remembering, perhaps, the policy adopted by Molière as to *Tartuffe*, the undaunted dramatist sought at the outset to make the *Mariage de Figaro* a subject of general conversation. Parisian society, though largely composed of the class assailed in it, unconsciously helped him here by urging him to read the piece in salons. Many of the nobles must have seen that its tendency was to reform or exterminate their order, but the rage for novelty and forbidden fruit overpowered all other

considerations. Beaumarchais accepted none of these
invitations without feigned reluctance, so as to enhance
the value of the favour he conferred. " I fear," he said,
" that virtually to publish a play condemned by the
King is a mark of disrespect to his majesty, and I will not
do so unless the rank of the applicant is such as to shield
me from royal displeasure." When he did read the play
it was from a manuscript tied with rose-coloured ribbons,
and having on the cover, in fancy letters, the words
" opuscule comique." His prefatory address might be
thought indelicate if cardinals and archbishops had not
joined in laughingly applauding it. " A young author,"
he said, " was once requested at a house where he had
supped to read one of his works. He excused himself.
' Monsieur,' remarked another guest, ' you resemble an
accomplished coquette, refusing what at heart you burn
to accord.' ' Apart from the coquette,' replied the
author, ' your comparison is juster than you imagine.
The fair and ourselves have often the same fate, that
of being forgotten after the sacrifice. The curiosity
excited by the announcement of a new work resembles
somewhat the ardent impulses of affection. Be more
just,—or ask nothing. Our portion is the labour; you
have only the enjoyment, and nothing can disarm you.'
He read his work; they criticized it: I," continued
Beaumarchais, " am about to do the same—and you
also." Whatever may be thought of this, it served to

propitiate the audience, and at each reading the *Mariage de Figaro* elicited unbounded admiration. Before long the calls made for readings became too numerous to satisfy. Every day, Madame Campan tells us, votaries of fashion were saying, "I have been, or I am going, to hear Beaumarchais' play." The result was precisely as he had expected; a desire to see the *Mariage de Figaro* at the Comédie Française grew up in all quarters.

Here, for the present, we must take leave of Beaumarchais to notice two events which might have encouraged him to persevere in his opposition to the Court. In 1779, an *Agis* by Joseph Laiguelot, son of a baker at Versailles, was represented before the King and Queen at the instance of the Duc de Villequier. Interlarded with high-flown republican sentiments, it was received rather coldly by the august audience, its protector himself not excepted. Recently, however, it had attracted the attention of Larive, who induced his comrades to play it at the Comédie Française. It was then honoured with plaudits out of all proportion to its intrinsic value, as the censor, by another strange oversight, had not drawn his pen through its anti-monarchical passages. Equally significant in a different way was a scene witnessed in the theatre on the 20th of June, when the *Philosophes* again appeared. In one sense the revival may be deemed injudicious, as the doctrines of the men ridiculed in the piece were practi-

cally the religion of the day.   For a time the sarcasm
levelled at them was listened to with seeming good
temper, but the entrance of Dugazon as Crispin on
all fours in the second act put an end to this
tolerance.   To show disrespect for the memory of Jean
Jacques Rousseau was to touch the Parisian audience on
their tenderest point.   It excited furious indignation,
and some minutes elapsed before the performance could
be continued.   "Never," says Fleury, " did a standing
pit assert itself with more violence than the seated pit
that evening."

Palissot, the author of this comedy, was again on
friendly terms with the players, but could not prevail
upon them to bring out the piece which he had offered
them in vain eight years before.   They were still of
opinion that the *Courtisanes* lacked the most important
requisites for an acting play.   Believing precisely the
reverse, he sought to bring outside influence to bear
upon the company in his favour, and for this purpose
was at pains to obtain the support of the clergy.   The
Courtisanes, in which a high-spirited youth is represented
as rescued from a sort of Marguerite Gautier, could not
fail, he contended, to promote the cause of morality.
It might have been supposed that a regard for con-
sistency would lead the clergy to abstain from any
interference in a matter connected with an art under
the ban of the Church ; as it was, the Archbishop of

Paris, perhaps out of gratitude to one of the most
prominent assailants of the philosophical sect, espoused
his cause with some warmth. Presently the comedy
was asked for by Louis XVI., who, after suggesting
a few alterations in the dialogue, gave orders that the
players should put it in rehearsal at their earliest con-
venience. It appeared on the 26th of July with some
success, partly because two or three of the characters
were recognizable portraits. " I could not have believed,"
said Mlle. Guimard to Mlle. Arnould at the doors of the
theatre, " that it is so amusing to see ourselves hung
in effigy."

It was as the heroine of the *Courtisanes* that Mlle.
Contat first realized the promise which Préville had
seen in her as a child. Down to this time she had had
no opportunity of exercising her talents to the full,
but had made appreciable progress. "The conversion
of the Théâtre Italien into a succursal of the Comédie
Française," writes Fleury, "was a good thing for Mlle.
Contat and myself. When battles are to be won, commanders find it advisable to flatter their troops with the
hope of promotion. Something like this was done with
us. Consequently, Madame Verteuil helped Mlle. Contat to advance, while M. Dorgeville did no harm to
Fleury. Occasionally we had been put forward merely
as stop-gaps. That I should have been treated with ill-
humour was natural enough ; but it might have been

thought that Contat, so young and pretty and *spirituelle*,
would have fared better.   As it was, she frequently left
the stage in a passion of grief at the *accueil glacé* which
she experienced.   Each of us endeavoured to console
the other; our common misfortune gave rise to a
reciprocal friendship, and to me she took the place of
my good sister Félicité.   We comforted ourselves with
the hope of a brighter future.   She owed me a little; I
owed her much.   Simultaneously we triumphed over the
disfavour of the pit and the obstacles put in our way."
But it was not until the production of the *Courtisanes*
that she obtained the coveted chance.   "From the
performance of this comedy," continues Fleury, "we
may date the opening of her theatrical career.   The
Comédie had found another great actress.   Préville and
I were in a transport over her success."

Les Courtisanes gave place to a comedy written by
Cailhava in 1778, the *Journaliste*, and then to *Zoraï, ou
les Insulaires de la Nouvelle Zélande*, a tragedy in five
acts, by Jean de Marignié.   In the latter the French
found themselves persistently exalted at the expense of
the English, who, it was said, were writhing under a
regal despotism.   But an audience familiar with the
writings of Voltaire and Montesquieu could not be
misled on this point, and a pertinent question, "If
the English government is despotic what must the
French be called?" might have been asked more than

once that night.   Louis XVI. instantly issued an order
that the piece should not be played a second time or
printed.   *Les Amants Espagnols*, a five-act comedy in
prose, attributed to one Beaujard, proved extremely
dull, and there were shouts of assent when one of
the characters innocently remarked that they " had had
a ' cruel ' evening."

Madame Molé died as the year drew to its close, but
the loss thus inflicted upon the theatre was balanced by
the acquisition of a " pair of saints," at least in name.
Etienne St. Fal, a Paris tradesman's son, born in 1752,
had preferred acting to wigmaking, the occupation
selected for him by his parents, and had favourably
distinguished himself at Lyons, Brussels, and Versailles.
Invariably rising above mediocrity, though never to
greatness, he was speedily received at the Théâtre
Français.   His tragedy was so good that Molé gradually abandoned to him the Nérestans and the Egysthes ;
in high comedy, notably as Alceste in the *Misanthrope*,
he displayed force and finish of style.   Probably he was
at his best in the *drame*, as it blended the grave with
the gay.   Another débutant, Jean St. Prix, obtained
admission as a promising double for Larive in the leading tragedy parts.   His father, a retired bourgeois, had
wished him to be a sculptor or architect, but could not
wean him from a passion which he conceived for the
stage.   He had four qualifications for this self-chosen

profession—cultivated intelligence, sensibility, a rich voice, and a figure athletic enough to "remind spectators of the Homeric heroes." Already, at the age of twenty-four, he had mastered the secret of combining elevation with truth, which was more than could be said of his leader.

Brizard's fame, always high, rose to its culminating point on the 20th of January, when another of Ducis' pale reflections of Shakspere, *Le Roi Léar*, was brought out by the players. None of the poet's adaptations inspired him with more interest than this ; his mother had read the original to him in his boyhood, and the impression it left on his mind was never to be effaced. But an enthusiastic appreciation of its greatness did not deter him from reconstructing it on the unity system. *Le Roi Léar* gives us only a portion of the English play. It turns exclusively on the anguish caused in different ways to the child-changed old monarch by Goneril, Regan, and Cordelia, the last of whom, by the way, is here called Elmonde. Many incidents which intensify the sublimated pathos of *Lear* are perforce omitted. In at least one instance, too, there is a gratuitous departure from the text, since Ducis, evidently sharing the Johnsonian conviction that no modern audience could endure Shakspere's catastrophe, followed Tate's example in ending the piece happily for the principal characters. This species of Vandalism, however, was

not carried so far as to rob Lear's representative,
Brizard, of an opportunity which he could turn to
full account. His exquisite sensibility, his harmonious
voice, his dignified simplicity, his noble presence, his
enthusiasm as an artist,—all made his impersonation
a treasure of the memory.

Dugazon, who seldom took anything seriously, thought
fit to ridicule the custom of summoning dramatists
before the curtain at first representations. Playing
in an afterpiece, he introduced a speech as to the close
of hostilities between France and England, and some
friends in his confidence raised a cry for " the author."
He then reappeared like " a modest poet overwhelmed
by his glory "—to be more precise, leaning heavily upon
a comrade's shoulder, faint from excitement, and with an
indescribable mixture of vanity and affectation in the
expression of his countenance. Probably such a scene
was witnessed on the production of a one-act comedy
by one Vigée, the *Aveux Difficiles*. Here an affianced
pair meet after a long separation with their affections
secretly fixed upon others, and the embarrassment they
suffer is amusingly depicted. Baron d'Etat, having
written a similar piece for the Italians eighteen months
previously, accused Vigée of deliberate plagiarism,
thereby exciting a heated controversy. " If," wrote
the shade of Destouches to the *Journal de Paris*, " the
playgoers cast an eye over my *Amour Usé*,—which,

notwithstanding its merits, was hissed, the public of my time being difficult to please—this dispute will soon come to an end,"—and the prediction was verified to the letter. Lefèvre, a young poet helped on by Voltaire, wrote an *Elisabeth de France*, but the censor stopped it on account of passages open to a dangerous application. "Our spectacles," writes Grimm, "have never, perhaps, been honoured by a more severe and august attention. Nowadays a new tragedy is an affair of state, and gives rise to the gravest negotiations. Ministers and representatives of the Powers which may be interested in the matter have to be consulted, and it is only with the sanction of all these gentlemen that a poor author gets the chance of exposing his work to the plaudits or hisses of the pit."

Beaumarchais did not allow this increased firmness to relax his efforts in behalf of the *Mariage de Figaro*, especially as a friendship he had just formed gave him fresh hope of success. For that friendship he was indebted to a curious accident. In one of the Court theatres, it appears, Hue de Miromesnil, a distinguished amateur, had to represent a drunkard, and was much applauded by all his auditors save the elegant Comte de Vaudreuil. Being asked why he disliked the performance, the latter insisted that it was contrary to nature. "M. de Miromesnil," he said, "intentionally staggers; a drunkard tries to keep himself steady.

M. de Miromesnil intentionally loses his equilibrium;
a drunkard tries to preserve it. He sidles not from
weakness, for drunkenness imparts temporary strength,
but because he has forgotten how to walk. Intoxication
is in the head, and above all in the eyes. In matters
of this kind it is amusing to observe the working of
the mind in the effort to recover memory, and the
self-abandonment to despair which follows the failure
to do so. M. de Miromesnil acted upon diametrically
opposite principles. He seemed to say to himself,
'now to the right, now to the left; now forward, now
backward; now a hop, now a skip.'" Some of the
company pleasantly ascribed these remarks to personal
experience. "Nay," continued the Comte, "they are
not my own. I borrow the lesson from the great
Garrick, who gave it on the Boulevards to Préville,
who acted upon it before a few working men,
who took the mimicry for reality." Miromesnil, a
little piqued, disputed the authenticity of the anecdote, and, being assured that it was true, offered to
lay a heavy wager that a Boulevard was not the
place. Beaumarchais happened to be of the company.
"Take the wager," he whispered to the Comte; "it
is yours." Vaudreuil did so. Beaumarchais went
away, returning soon afterwards with a letter in
which Garrick himself stated that the incident occurred on the Boulevards. From that moment the

Comte evinced a warm interest in the dramatist's fortunes.

Did this grateful nobleman, perhaps the most conspicuous member of the Queen's social circle, speak to her majesty of the *Mariage de Figaro* in such terms as to revive her wish to see it acted ? However that may be, the players suddenly received orders from Versailles to rehearse it in secret for a private performance. Beaumarchais, after reading it at the theatre with the best effect, gallantly consulted Mlle. Contat as to the cast, the result being that Dazincourt was set down for Figaro, Molé for Almaviva, Mlle. Sainval for the Countess, and Mlle. Olivier for the page. Préville was asked in the first instance to be the barber, but a sense of failing memory and sprightliness led him to reject it for the comparatively ineffective Brid'oisin. More important than all, Mlle. Contat found the part of Suzanne laid at her feet, though she had not yet undertaken anything of the kind. It was in vain that Mlle. Fanier, the senior soubrette, protested against this nomination ; the waiting maid had to a large extent been created for the other actress, and by none save her could it be played. Everything being in readiness, it was decided that the performance should be given at the Théâtre des Menus Plaisirs, where the Comte de Vaudreuil exercised a paramount influence, on the 13th of June. Louis XVI. could not long be kept in

ignorance of such an intention, but his constitutional
infirmity of purpose hindered him from interfering with
it until the forenoon of the day named, when he sent to
the players, through the medium of the Minister of the
Interior, an order prohibiting the representation of the
Mariage de Figaro under pain of disobedience. In this
instance bad news did not travel fast, for as the long-
expected hour drew near the approaches to the theatre
were blocked by five or six hundred coaches.   An
announcement then posted at the doors, to the effect
that there would be no play that evening, plunged the
gaily dressed throng into a sort of stupefaction. Madame
Campan assures us that the words "oppression" and
"tyranny" were never pronounced with more bitterness.   If the King heard of this outcry it did not divert
him from his resolution. Next day the players were
summoned to appear before the Lieutenant of Police,
who reiterated the prohibition in forms employed by
the royal authority only on the gravest occasions. Even
then, however, the dramatist did not lose heart.
"Again," he said, "I restore the comedy to the portfolio, there to keep it until another event shall draw
it forth. For that event I shall not have to wait long.
The eyes of the civilized world are fixed intently upon
my *Mariage* and on me. From England, Germany,
Spain, and America, countries now witnessing other
exploits, I am receiving attention. My honour and

reputation depend upon the play being acted,—and acted it shall be."

His ingenuity was not unequal to the task of devising efficacious means to this end. Vaudreuil, apparently taking the first step in a conspiracy between them, expressed a wish at Court that the *Mariage de Figaro* should be represented in the course of a fête to be given in his country house at Gennevilliers, and the King was prevailed upon to sanction a performance of the obnoxious comedy on that occasion. "The Comte d'Artois," writes the Duc de Fronsac to Beaumarchais from that place, "is coming to hunt here about the 18th" of September, "and the Duc de Polignac, with his party, to sup. Vaudreuil has consulted me as to giving them a play, as we have a capital room. I told him that he could not find a more charming one than the *Mariage de Figaro*. The King has given his consent; have we yours?" Beaumarchais was then in London, ostensibly on commercial business, but really, no doubt, because he thought it politic to be out of the way when Vaudreuil began to move in the matter. Returning to Paris, he gave his "consent" on the condition that the piece should be re-examined. Though it had passed the censorship, the royal veto against its production had exposed it to the charge of immorality, and he would not allow it to be played anywhere until that stigma had been removed from it

by a formal " approbation." Read between the lines,
this stipulation is seen to be full of meaning. No
censor would practically forbid an entertainment sanctioned by the King, and the desired approbation,
besides stimulating the curiosity of the public, might
cover his majesty's opposition to the piece with ridicule.
The authorities, walking blindly into the trap laid for
them, sent the manuscript to a grave Academician,
Gaillard, who reported that he found nothing objection-
able in it except a few jokes susceptible of a malicious
interpretation. His suggestions—which, strange to say,
did not apply to the sarcasms levelled at the Government—were at once adopted, due care being taken by
the astute dramatist to exaggerate their importance in
the eyes of the world. Moreover, the Lieutenant of
Police, with less than his usual sagacity, gave a promise
that henceforward the comedy should be " deemed the
property of his majesty's players "—*i. e.* put in the way
of being represented at the theatre. *Le Mariage de
Figaro* was then played in the large room at Gennevilliers, apparently as a favour somewhat reluctantly
conceded by the author. It evoked unbounded applause
from the audience, which was so dense that some ladies
would have fainted if Beaumarchais had not broken
some closed windows with his cane. " Il a doublement
cassé les vitres," it was remarked. He had certainly
done much to promote his cause. The performance at

Gennevilliers, with its attendant circumstances, gave rise to a fierce demand in Paris for the immediate production of the piece.

Beaumarchais, sensible of the advantage he had gained, coolly asked that the promise made to him by the Lieutenant of Police might be redeemed; but the King, though alarmed by the ferment he had raised, virtually adhered to his decision by indefinitely postponing the consideration of the subject. In taking this course, it appeared, he was influenced mainly by the advice of his Minister of the Interior, the Baron de Breteuil. The dramatist at once sought to propitiate this new adversary, and was fortunate enough to induce the Queen herself to second the attempt. Breteuil, assured by her majesty that M. de Beaumarchais would make all needful alterations in the piece, assumed a different attitude towards it, but said that before interesting himself in its fate he must hear it read. Read it was by the author in the Baron's library, the audience consisting of Gaillard, Champfort, Rulhière the Minister's daughter (Madame de Matignon), and other ladies. " Beaumarchais," we are told in the Fleury Memoirs, "began by declaring," with his wonted astuteness, "that he would submit without reserve to any corrections and omissions that might be thought necessary. He read; somebody stopped him; a discussion arose. At every interruption he yielded the

point in question. But after the reading he retraced
his steps, defending the least details with so much
address and force and pleasantry that he completely
silenced his critics. 'Never,' said Champfort, 'have I
listened to so brilliant a magician.' His hearers laughed,
applauded, and finally declared that it was a most
unique piece. Each auditor was eager to insert a
word or two. M. de Breteuil," completely won over,
" suggested a *bon-mot*, which Beaumarchais gratefully
accepted. That, he said, would save the fourth act.
Madame de Matignon thought that a particular colour
would suit Chérubin's ribbon better than any other.
The colour was approved ; 'who would not carry the
colours of Madame de Matignon ? ' 'But M. de Breteuil's
mot would not be heard, the pretty ribbon would not
be seen, unless the second *Figaro* were permitted to
appear.' In the result, it was the unanimous opinion
that appear he must," though no one could venture
to predict when the King would give way.

Pending that event, we may speak of three players
who had just disappeared from the Comédie Française.
At the head of these is Jeanne Gaussin's successor, the
natural, sympathetic, and graceful Doligny. In *pre-
mières amoureuses* and *jeunes princesses* she lacked force
and dignity, but in parts breathing *une âme nouvelle et
passionnée*, such as Victorine in the *Philosophe sans le
Savoir*, she exerted a singular fascination. Her time

for playing youthful heroines was now coming to an
end, and she withdrew with all the honour due to a
woman of her gifts, charm of manner, and unblemished
reputation. In theatrical history she is best remembered
as the original representative of Rosine in the *Barbier
de Séville*, though her strength really lay in pathetic
comedy. Louis XVI., as if to show that "virtue under
his reign was as profitable as vice had been under that
of his predecessor," gave her a special pension. Besides
her retirement the company had to mourn the death of
Auger, who had ruined himself by commercial speculations. Since his admission to the Comédie it had been
one of the chief delights of Paris to see him in a scene
with Préville, who seemed to arouse in him a new
humour and spirit. The name of the snuffling and horn-
voiced Bouret, so admirable as Pourceaugnac, Agnelet in
L'Avocat Patelin, and Flamand in *Turcaret*, has also to
be added to the obituary of the year.

Shakspere re-entered the Comédie Française as this
trio of players passed out. Recast by Ducis, *Macbeth*
was produced there on the 12th of January, with Larive
as the Thane of Cawdor. How far it differed from the
English tragedy may be indicated in a few words.
Ducis, as might have been foreseen from the fact that
in adapting *Hamlet* he left the Ghost to the imagination,
had not ventured to introduce the Weird Sisters. He
feared that they would excite much less awe than

derision among a French audience, serious as was
the impression created by the supernatural element in
Sémiramis since spectators had been banished from the
stage.   On the other hand, he had to bear in mind that
the essence of *Macbeth* lay in a contest between destiny
and freewill, and that it was expedient to give the first
a palpable form.   In this difficulty he decided to reduce
the number to one.   Iphyctione, a Scandinavian sorceress,
finds a temporary home among the Highland crags,
where she influences the minds of men for evil.   Even
from the adapter's point of view we may doubt whether
this was a change for the better, but it is at least
grateful to find that at a time when English players
persistently treated the witches as comic characters
—dressing as Mother Hubbards, leaping over brooms
of the traditional pattern, and generally descending
to grotesque buffoonery—Iphyctione should have been
made an engine of terror instead of laughter.   In
another respect, of course, the French system operated
most injuriously upon the play.   Faithful to the time-
law, Ducis asked his audience in effect to believe that
in the space of twenty-four hours Macbeth could yield
to supernatural suggestion, wade through slaughter to a
throne, experience the keenest pulses of remorse, seek
relief in accomplishing fresh crimes, and withstand the
siege that ends in his death.   Nine out of every ten
Parisians would have fiercely resented an infringement

of the unities, but the improbability of the story in its
present shape was sufficient to neutralize the effect of
a comparatively unaltered Lady Macbeth—here named
Frédégonde (Madame Vestris)—and of many passages
echoing the weird grandeur of the original.

Macbeth was not the only means of casting doubt at
this time on the wisdom of the existing dramatic system,
which, as everybody with eyes could see, robbed the poet
of a variety of welcome subjects.   One of these subjects
was the fate of Coriolanus.   It had been repeatedly
treated for the stage, but the difficulty of preserving
its interest without a violation of the rules had always
proved insuperable.   " Do you think," the elder Crébillon
scornfully asked a young author who thought of treating
it, " that if it had been suited to the theatre the Corneilles
and Racines would have left it to you ? "   Laharpe, however, flattered himself that he could accomplish the impossible hero, and a *Coriolan* of his invention appeared
on the 3rd of March.   His failure was unequivocal ;
the *Barmécides* itself had not been pronounced more
ineffectual.   Epigrams against the vainglorious and discomfited author were written by the dozen, Champcenetz,
the would-be " gay Zoïlus of literary greatness," taking
advantage of an announcement that the performance
was for the relief of the distress in Paris to write—

> Pour les pauvres la Comédie
> Donne une pauvre tragédie ;

Nous devous tous, en vérité,
Bien l'applaudir par charité.

Other places of entertainment followed the example thus
set them.   In all about 37,000 livres was collected, and
the companies lost no time in taking the money to the
curés of the different parishes.   But the Archbishop of
Paris, though aware that hundreds of poor creatures
were literally dying of want on beds of straw, delayed
the relief by refusing to take it except through the
medium of the police.   He could not allow a direct
communication between his clergy and players in the
exercise of their profession.

For the new indignity to which their self-denying
generosity had exposed them, and which could not fail
to be remembered with some bitterness, the Comédiens
du Roi may have been partly consoled by important
news from Versailles. *Le Mariage de Figaro* was not
to be kept out of their bills much longer.   His majesty,
probably at the instance of the Baron de Breteuil,
referred " that ill-conceived piece," as Madame Campan
termed it, to five specially appointed censors, who,
not content with pronouncing it unobjectionable, went
so far as to praise it.   Bewildered by the increasing
clamour for its representation—a clamour to be heard
in the coffee-house, the cabaret, the theatre, the salon,
and the palace itself—he then withdrew his decree
against it, hoping to the last that its political satire,

which his dread of the public forbade him to expunge, would have but an ephemeral effect. " What do you think the verdict upon it will be ? " he asked the Marquis de Montesquieu. " Sire," was the somewhat fencing reply, " I hope it will fail." " And so do I," heartily rejoined the King. Beaumarchais, on his part, saw no room for fear. In a letter to Préville, who talked of leaving the stage, he says—" I now want only your co-operation, my dear friend, to make a nice disturbance when we begin." Like the other members of the cast, the player responded with alacrity to the call, and the 27th of April was fixed upon for the first performance of the long suppressed comedy.

Except when Voltaire went to see *Irène* at the Tuileries, no such crowd as that which assembled before the theatre on the morning of that day had been seen in Paris. " Ten hours before the opening of the doors," says one description of the event, " the whole population of the capital seemed to be there. What a triumph for Beaumarchais ! If he loved fame he had it now. Even princes of the blood besieged him with requests for ' author's tickets.' The Duchesse de Bourbon sent her valet to the office at 11 o'clock to wait for the distribution of tickets four hours later ; at 2 p.m. the Comtesse d'Ossun did sufficient violence to the hauteur of her character as humbly to ask the crowd to allow her to pass ; Madame de Talleyrand, usually so parsimonious,

paid triple price for a box, and *cordons bleus* had
to elbow their way to the theatre through a swarm
of Savoyards." Eventually the eagerness to secure
places broke through all restraint; "the guards were
dispersed, the iron bars broken down, and the doors
forced open. Most of the people had not been able to
procure tickets, and threw their admission money to the
doorkeepers as they passed along." Quite unprecedented was the spectacle that met the eyes of those
who were fortunate enough to obtain a seat or standing room in the theatre. No fewer than three hundred
persons were dining in the boxes. They had procured
tickets privately, and to be sure of their places had
entered by the stage door. "Our theatre," writes
Fleury, "might have been taken for a tavern; nothing
was heard but the clattering of plates and the popping
of corks." Even the *loges* of the players were invaded.
Fat Marquise de Montmorin was the guest of pretty
Mlle. Olivier, and pretty Madame de Sénectère of fat
Desessarts. Mlle. Sainval, too, offered acceptable
hospitality to the Princesse de Chimai and Madame
de Matignon. Elsewhere could be seen the Princesse
de Lamballe, the Duchesse de Polignac, the Marquise
d'Andlau, the Duchesse de Lauzun, Madame de Simiane,
Madame de Châlons, and other representatives of the
proudest aristocracy in Europe. Behind or among these,
on tip-toe to have a better view of the house, were

no less distinguished men—princes of the blood, peers, ministers, ambassadors, poets.   Beaumarchais himself was seated in the author's box, two abbés with whom he had dined being there "to comfort him in the event of death—*i. e.*, of failure."   Their services were not to be needed.   From the opening scene the piece carried the audience with it, and each of the pointed allusions to State abuses, but more especially the monologue in the fifth act, evoked tremendous and long-continued bursts of applause from the parterre and even other parts of the house.   Now and then a spectator looked at another in silent astonishment, first that any one should have dared to introduce such passages, and secondly that they should have been allowed to be repeated in a theatre.   Meanwhile, however, the excellence of the acting created a perceptible effect.   Dazincourt was full of spirit and intelligence ; the Almaviva of Molé was pronounced perfect in principle and detail ; Préville came to the front as the comparatively unimportant Brid'oisin ; Mlle. Sainval was an excellent Countess, and Mlle. Olivier gave an indescribable charm to the character of Chérubin.   Desessarts was the Bartholo, Vanhove the Basil, Bellemont the Antonio, and Larive —the great Larive—the Grippe-Soleil.   As for Mlle. Contat, the Susanne, she more than justified the author's confidence in her versatility.   Her most devout ad-mirers, it seems, were unprepared for the gaiety and *entrain* with which she, hitherto a dignified and expressive *amoureuse*, sustained the part. From that night she stood forward as one of the brightest ornaments of the Comédie Française, as a truly great actress. Préville, her old instructor, was in tears of delight at her success. "This," he said, as he embraced her, "is my first infidelity to Mlle. Dangeville."

For seventy-five nights was the *Mariage de Figaro* played at the Comédie, persons coming from distant parts of the country to refresh themselves with its vivacious satire. Louis XVI., of course, regarded its success with a feeling of the deepest annoyance. He wisely declined to have any of the obnoxious passages removed, but was at no pains to conceal his ill-will towards those who had helped the author to attain his ends. Did his majesty instigate some attacks that were made at this time upon Beaumarchais in the *Journal de Paris?* Certain it is that these attacks, though in the handwriting of Suard, were really the work of the Comte de Provence. Predisposed to follow such an example, the *gredins d'auteurs* fell foul of the successful author, whom they termed a "scélérat" and an "intrigant." Beaumarchais at first treated these libels with prudent silence. He knew that without them his victory would be incomplete; indeed, he secretly threw off an epigram against himself. Presently, however, an article in the *Journal de Paris* made him lose all patience. "Do you think," he asked Suard in print, not knowing who the wirepuller in the case was, "that now, after having to overcome lions and tigers to get my piece produced, I am to be reduced to the level of a Dutch maidservant hunting for the vile insect of the night?" The Comte de Provence at once jumped to the conclusion that he was the vile insect in question. He asked the King to visit the dramatist with exemplary punishment. No one could doubt, his royal highness artfully urged, that the expression "lions and tigers" was intended for his majesty. Louis XVI. was at the card-table when he heard of the matter. Irritated by the advantage gained over him by the author of *Figaro*, he did not stay to consider the absurdity of the construction placed upon the metaphor, but forthwith wrote on a seven of spades an order for his incarceration at St. Lazare. To that dirty prison, which had been set apart for juvenile offenders, Beaumarchais was conducted on the following day. His majesty then found himself in an awkward position. The news of the dramatist's arrest necessarily led to intense commotion in Paris, and to state that his offence lay in comparing his sovereign to lions and tigers would have been to excite a shout of derision from one end of the capital to the other. In these circumstances, about five days afterwards, the King ordered the prisoner to be set at liberty, and then, probably as a sop to the Cerberus of public opinion, paid him the complimen of having *Figaro* performed at Court by a company including the Queen as Susanne, the Comte d'Artois as the barber, and the Comte de Vaudreuil as Almaviva. "Printed follies are of no importance save where their circulation is checked;" "it is only little men that dread little writings;" "ne pouvant avilir l'esprit on se venge en le maltraitant;"—such were some of the passages to which the King had to listen on that occasion. "If there is anything odder than my piece itself," said Beaumarchais, who was invited to be present, "it is its success." To us, with subsequent history before our eyes, it may seem odder still that the honour of being acted at Court should have been conferred upon a piece which the King had long prohibited, and which, as even he was able to perceive, gave an enormous impetus to the forces arrayed against existing institutions.

CHAPTER VIII.

1784—1789.

COMPARED with other pieces in preparation at the theatre, the *Mariage de Figaro* seems like an oasis in a broad expanse of dulness. In regard to débuts, however, the players were more fortunate. Three aspirants, Jean Naudet, Emilie Contat, and Jeanne Devienne, established more or less irrefragable claims to places in the company. Forty-two years of age, the first, a native of Franche Comté, gave up a good position in the army to act *rois* and *pères nobles*, which he did with excellent effect. Emilie Contat, a sister of Louise Contat, was in no sense a genius, but found acceptance as a lively coquette. More important was the coming of Mlle. Devienne, in whom the town promptly saw a soubrette not inferior to Mlle. Joly. Born at Lyons in 1763, the new actress, a silk-weaver's daughter, left home in her teens to go on the stage, and had already made a name at Brussels. Criticism could find nothing to complain of in her style save that it wanted some of the truth needed for Molière's immortal servants. Fleury says that she evinced all the quickness and delicate tact which make a player independent of the author. She could impart spirit and effect to a dialogue in itself dull and pointless. By a look or a gesture she made a *bon-mot ;* by a pause or an inflexion of the voice she gave meaning to the obscure. She understood Marivaux; she made Molière understood. In all the relations of private life, it is pleasing to add, she was above reproach. " Her manner out of the theatre," continues Fleury, " was simple, unaffected, modest. Unlike Contat, she never reigned the queen of drawing-room conversation, or, as it may be called, conversation in full dress."

In striking contrast to the reception accorded to Mlle. Devienne was a scene that occurred at the theatre on the 6th of May, when a comedy by Madame de Montesson, the wife of the Duc d'Orléans, came forth under the title of the *Comtesse de Chazelles.* Every precaution had been taken to keep the authorship of the piece a secret, partly because the writer had many enemies at Court, and also, perhaps, from a conviction that anything by an " aristocrat" would not be judged on its merits by the pit. By this time, however, the truth was known far and wide, and most of the audience assembled in a hostile mood. Keenly anxious as to the issue, but indisposed to witness it for himself, the Duc d'Orléans took refuge in a house near the theatre, there to receive reports at short intervals of the progress made by the comedy. His feelings as the performance went on were scarcely to be envied. *La Comtesse de Chazelles* had little of the strength required to overcome the twofold prejudice against it. Except as to its plot, which seems to have been suggested by *Clarissa* and the *Liaisons Dangereuses*, it was cold, invertebrate, and colourless. The result need hardly be stated. Even the first scene evoked derision, and the performance ended amidst a volley of hisses. Fleury was reminded by the tumult of Jean Jacques' description of the fate of his first symphony. And that tumult was largely increased by several fine gentlemen in a box, who, while ostensibly applauding the piece, sounded the "shrillest notes of discord" by means of game-keepers' whistles under their feet. Madame de Montesson, learning that rumour ascribed the authorship to Madame de Balby and others, publicly took the whole responsibility of the disaster upon herself. " Had the *Comtesse de Chazelles* succeeded," she remarked, " I should have preserved its anonymity ; as it has failed, I will not suffer it to discredit any one but the real culprit." In like case, it must be confessed, more than one dramatist had shown less courage.

No such failure as the *Comtesse de Chazelles* was to happen again for some time. Fifteen years previously a *Roxelane et Mustapha* had been left at the theatre by one Maisonneuve. Nothing had since been heard of

him, and in default of anything better his play was
now put in rehearsal. On the eve of its production,
the author, who had been induced by the non-appearance
of the piece to abandon literature in disgust, and who,
having married the widow of a rich linendraper, had
given himself up to trade, ventured, in utter ignorance
of what was passing behind the scenes, to ask that the
manuscript might be returned. By the irony of fate
Roxelane et Mustapha was rapturously applauded, and
at one of the performances the author was summoned
to the royal box to receive the congratulations of the
Queen herself. The players next produced a trifle
called *Melcour et Verseuil*, by André de Murville, a
name already known in the playgoing world. Its
plot was suggested by an incident in the life of Sophie
Arnould, the author's step-mother. That volatile lady
once lived with Belanger, secretary to the Comte
d'Artois, but did not turn a deaf ear to soft nothings
breathed into her ear by an actor named Florence.
Fatigued with reproaches from Belanger as to her
infidelity, she told him in writing that she did not
wish to see him again. No name being mentioned,
the disappointed lover had the letter redirected to
Florence, who, persuaded that his mistress had been
prevailed upon to discard him, could never be persuaded
to meet her again.

Engrossed as it seemed to be with rehearsals, the

Comédie was as alive as ever to the policy of maintaining its strength, and in the autumn two débutantes of
promise came up for judgment.   Marie Candeille, the
elder, was a daughter of a chorister of the Opéra, who
had composed the music of *Pizarre.*   Educated for the
musical profession, she distinguished herself in childhood as a singer and pianist, and in 1782 appeared
with some success at the Opéra.   Now, at the instance
of Molé, she came forward at the Théâtre Français as
grandes princesses.   Mlle. Candeille was well formed,
with blue eyes, fair hair, and a pretty face.   The *emploi*
she selected was above her reach, but Louis XVI.,
charmed by one of her performances at Court, ordered
her to be received.   Préville thereupon induced her to
exchange tragedy for comedy, to which she was much
better suited.   Unlike her, the other débutante, Cécile
Vanhove, daughter of the actor of that name, was a
plant to flower late.   Down to the age of six, far from
being a juvenile wonder, she could neither read nor
write.   Her father, then on the point of leaving the
theatre at the Hague for the Comédie Française, thought
it necessary to inform her that unless she redeemed
these shortcomings she would have to be sent back,
as ignoramuses were not allowed to remain in Paris.
Distressed at the prospect of being separated from her
parents, the poor child strove bravely to master the two
R's, with the result that soon after Vanhove became a

Comédien du Roi she was able to play Joas and other child-parts with the requisite accuracy. Her intelligence soon outstripped her years ; but her parents, who frequently predicted that she would become the pearl of the French stage, wisely refrained from forcing her gifts into a premature development. In her fifteenth year, carefully prepared for the ordeal, with the advantages of personal beauty, a musical voice, and remarkable rapidity of apprehension, she challenged the verdict of the town as a *jeune princesse*. Her success was immediate and decisive. "The whole of Paris," we are told, "flocked to see and hear her, and the applause she brought down could be heard in the Faubourg Saint Germain." In "la petite Vanhove," as she used to be called, another Gaussin or Doligny had come to light.

While Paris was ringing with praises of Cécile Vanhove, a clever dramatist took the first step in what proved to be an eventful career. In or about 1750, be it premised, an energetic young Frenchman, Louis Chénier, went to Constantinople, where he became the head of a commercial house, French Consul-General, and the husband of a beautiful Greek. In 1773, the appointment of the Comte de Vergennes as ambassador to the Porte having led to the abolition of the office of Consul-General, M. and Madame Chénier, now blessed with four sons, set out for Paris to spend the remainder

of their lives in retirement.   Two of their sons—André
and Marie Joseph, born in 1762 and 1764 respectively—
were destined to hold conspicuous places in the world
of letters.   No pair could have differed more in character : André was of a studious and thoughtful turn ;
the other was impetuous, ungovernable, wild.   In
1784, having completed his education at the Collége
de Navarre, the latter joined a regiment of dragoons,
but returned to Paris in a fit of disgust with military
life.   This disgust may have been strengthened by
literary ambition, for soon afterwards, at the instance
of Palissot and Lebrun, the company of the Comédie
Française produced a little piece from his pen, *Edgar,
ou le Page Supposé.*

Easter brought with it a heavy loss to the Comédie
Française.   Préville, Brizard, Madame Préville (*k*), and
Mlle. Fanier withdrew from the stage on the same
night, the 1st of April.   The pieces represented were
Horace and the *Partie de Chasse d'Henri IV.,* the
latter because the scene in Michaud's cottage allowed
the four retiring players to be on the stage at once in
characters associated with their names.   Brizard, as old
Horace, one of his happiest assumptions, rose superior
to himself, though his fortitude manifestly forsook him
when, in leaving his son, he had to deliver the
appropriate line—

Moi-même en ce moment j'ai les larmes aux yeux.

Naturally enough, the cottage scene in the *Partie de Chasse* aroused extraordinary enthusiasm, mingled with more or less visible grief. For one thing it seemed too much to hope that a Préville would grace the stage again. His humour, his truth, his grace, his force of colouring, his quick perception of character, his ready assimilation with almost every variety of comedy,—all gave him an individuality not previously acquired on the French stage in his own walks of art. His departure might have been thought to close a gallery of striking portraits, the most important of which, perhaps, were Sosie in *Amphitryon*, Larissolle in the *Mercure Galant*, Crispin in the *Légataire*, Freeport in *L'Ecossaise*, Antoine in the *Philosophe sans le Savoir*, and Figaro in the *Barbier de Séville*. Brizard, too, with his fine presence, his simple dignity, his searching pathos and humour, was a *roi* and *père noble* whom the town could ill afford to lose. How well he had always painted the rude courage of old Horace, " the sensibility of Don Diègue, the lofty energy of Zopire, the generous tolerance of Alvarez, the grief and madness of Léar, the grave eloquence of the father in the *Menteur*, the dissembled hatred of Mithridate, the patriotism and paternal tenderness of Brutus, the religious enthusiasm of Lusignan, the Gascon *verve*, the *bonhomie*, the chivalrous air of Henri Quatre ! " In the presence of such players Mlle. Fanier and Madame Préville were in the

shade, but it was not to be forgotten that the former
had long lighted up the stage with her soubrettes, and
that the latter, without being a great actress, had
efficiently represented characters of which the Prési-
dente in the *Mariage Fait et Rompu* may be taken as an
example. It must have been with a feeling of profound
sadness, relieved by a thousand grateful memories, that
the audience on that April evening saw the curtain fall.

Each of the retired players hastened from the gay
and busy capital, the Prévilles settling at Senlis, Mlle.
Fanier at Saint Mandé, and Brizard at Gros-Caillou.
Both the "Molière of the scene" and his wife will come
under our notice again, but we may here take leave of
the sprightly soubrette, who, holding Dorat in affectionate remembrance to the last, lived for thirty five
years more, and of the venerable "father," who died
rather prematurely in 1791. "Embrace Monsieur
Brizard," once said a magistrate to his son ; "his talents,
if it is possible, are exceeded by his virtues." Few
eulogies have been more fully justified. Brizard possessed in himself the elevation and sweetness of character
which he had so finely illustrated on the stage. Charity,
for instance, never appealed to him in vain. His income
not being large enough to let him gratify all his generous impulses, he increased it by painting pictures and
binding books—in early life, as we have seen, he had
been a pupil of Vanloo's—and scrupulously reserved the

proceeds for the benefit of the necessitous. He also rebound a goodly library of his own, but the money thus saved was applied to the same object. Many pleasing incidents of his career as a player forbade him to regret that he had abandoned his palette and brushes. Louis XVI. and Marie Antoinette had invariably taken delight in his acting. One evening, after playing Henri IV. at Fontainebleau, he had to light their majesties to their coach. "Monsieur," said the Queen, "to-night you have made quite a conversion." "Yes," the King broke in with unwonted emphasis, "you have even made *me* take a liking for the throne." Probably this compliment had less value for the old man than one paid to him by Voltaire during the poet's last visit to Paris—"Monsieur, you make me cling to life; you have revealed to me beauties in the part of Brutus which I did not perceive in creating it."

But the gloom cast over the Comédie by this fourfold loss was not wholly unrelieved by hopes as to the immediate future. Frequenters of the green-room had lately become conscious of an addition to their number in the person of a modest, self-possessed, and urbane advocate of thirty-one, Colin d'Harleville, a clever comedy from whose pen, *L'Inconstant*, was set down for early production. Eldest son of a procureur, he had come from Mévoisin, near Chartres, and was dividing his attention between law and literature with a decided leaning to the latter. For many trifles which lessened the heaviness of the periodicals, especially the *Almanach des Muses*, the public were indebted to him. He at first tried his hand at satire, but was without the sportive or serious malice, if not the wit, to make his arrows felt. Nevertheless, he addressed his devotions to Thalia, who smiled upon him in return. *L'Inconstant*, as may be gathered from its title, belongs in the main to the comedy of character, which, despite the success of the *Barbier de Séville* and the *Mariage de Figaro*, continued to find many disciples in the country of Molière, Regnard, and Lesage. Harleville could not infuse a high degree of *vis comica* into his work, but did something to atone for this weakness by ingenuity of treatment, delicacy of humour, and, above all, a characteristic grace of style. Marked by such qualities, the *Inconstant*, which appeared on the 13th of June, with Molé as the fickle hero, at once brought the author into notice, although it was sufficiently overlong to be reduced with advantage from five to three acts.

Laharpe was to find himself in what to so vain a person must have been the irritating position of a poet compelled to remain incognito in the hour of success. He had secretly composed a *Virginie*, hoping throughout that Mlle. Raucourt would undertake a character expressly designed for her. But this accomplished actress, offended by some slight, had declared that she would

never again play in a piece of his—a vow which,
suicidal as he may have thought it, she was more likely
to keep than break. In this strait he sent her the
piece anonymously, with a request that she would
represent Plautie. Much gratified by the letter, she
unsuspiciously took the piece to the theatre, where it
was given for the first time on the 11th of July. Everybody thought that so fine a *Virginie* had not yet been
written, and when the curtain fell the author was
summoned to appear. In reply a player stated that
the author had elected to be unknown. "It must be
Laharpe," cried a voice in the pit ; "one line, at any
rate, is from his *Pharamond!*" Laharpe, fearing that
Raucourt would throw up her part if the secret were
disclosed, publicly disavowed any connexion with the
piece, but was entrapped by his self-love into a virtual
confession of the truth. "*Virginie*," Sédaine remarked
to him at a sitting of the Academy, "contains some
scenes of which you might be proud." "Some ?" the
poet echoed, with a flush of angry surprise on his
countenance—"*some ?*"

La Fausse Inconstance, a prose comedy in five acts,
by the Comtesse Fanny de Beauharnais, who had been
allowed by Dorat to pass off some poems of his as her
own, and who, it was piquantly remarked, took his
death so much to heart that she at once lost the wit
revealed in them, went before a piece markedly free from

a certain leaning to licentiousness now apparent in
productions of the kind. *L'Ecole des Pères* was the
maiden effort of Pierre Pièyre, born at Nîmes in 1752,
educated in Paris, and at present acting as a merchant
in his native place. Previously applauded in the
country, it soon found its way to the Théâtre Français,
where it had no fewer than forty representations. Louis
XVI., delighted with the purity of the piece, asked the
author, through the Duc de Duras, what form he would
like a token of royal approbation to take. Pièyre chose
a plain sword ; and an elaborate Damascus blade, with
the arms of France engraved thereon, was sent to him.
" I too," said Marie Antoinette, " must give our young
poet some encouragement. No doubt a sword is a
right present for the King to make, but something
different must come from me." Pièyre, in reply to her
message, simply asked that his name might be placed
on the list of authors whose plays were acted at Court
in her presence. *L'Ecole des Pères* was accordingly
given at Versailles, Fleury impersonating the chief
character. In accordance with custom, the King presented him with a superb coat, whereas a very plain
one was required. The actor, as became the artist,
excused himself from wearing it on the occasion.
" Well," said his majesty, " it is my wish that he should
choose for the next Court performance a character to
which it is suitable, as I shall be pleased to see him

in it." Overjoyed by the compliment, Fleury appeared as the Marquis du Lauret in *Turcaret*, in which he delineated drunkenness with the best effect. "In this part," said the Comte d'Artois, "Molé seems to get drunk only in piquette; Fleury's drunkenness is that of champagne."

Voltaire used to say that he never heard of the young dying without feeling tempted to blame nature. Probably such a feeling was experienced by many in Paris on the 21st of September, when, at the age of twenty-three, pretty Mlle. Olivier, the original representative of Chérubin in the *Mariage de Figaro*, fell a victim to malignant fever. It was as though a beautiful flower had been crushed as it began to unfold its petals. Her gifts were beginning to find high expression, and a position scarcely inferior to that of Gaussin or Doligny seemed to await her. Even Mlle. Contat could not rival the effect of her grace and tenderness as Alcmène in *Amphitryon*. In her last hours, after forswearing the stage in due form, she asked that her funeral might be of the simplest kind, and that the sum which might have been spent in doing ostentatious honour to her remains should be distributed among the poor. The curé of St. Sulpice, holding that she had not prepared herself for death by any act of religion, refused at first to bury her, but eventually consented to do so on the understanding that fewer priests than usual should be

in attendance.   Mlle. Olivier, though sometimes thought
unintelligent off the stage, was not without a sharp
tongue. " How ? " said the stupid Chevalier de Cubières
to her one evening in the green-room, after a conversation in which she had fitfully shone ; "you are often
described as a fool ? "   "And why not ?" she answered ;
" you are often described as a wit."

New plays were appearing at rather short intervals,
but few of them call for special notice. One, an
Antigone, had nothing to commend it except the following lines, all the more remarkable in view of the fact
that the author, Duponceau, was a Gentilhomme
Ordinare du Roi :—

> Les grands l'ont approuvé : pourrait-il vous déplaire ?
> Vous avez vu le peuple obéir et se taire, , , .
> La voix du courtisan soutient d'injustes lois ;
> Quand le peuple se tait il condamne ses rois—

lines which the pit applauded with "indecent affect-
ation," and which, as may be supposed, were promptly
suppressed. Mercier, after giving his best work to the
Italians, seems to have been fully reconciled with the
Comédie Française, where an adaptation by him of
Goldoni's *Il Moliere* was produced on the 20th of
October under the title of the *Maison de Molière.* It
represented the illustrious dramatist in the midst of his
comrades, the honour of impersonating him, as of a
Tartuffe included in the *dramatis personae,* falling to the

lot of Fleury. Mlle. Vanhove, as young Béjart, is said to have been like Petitot's miniature of Ninon de Lenclos. Manifestly inspired by the *Ménechmes*, a three-act comedy by Forgeot, the *Ressemblance*, did not equal its original, but was saved by the acting of Contat in the two characters. Of much higher value was Colin d'Harleville's second piece, the *Optimiste*, in which Molé appeared as the hero. Its plot may have been sadly defective, but the man satisfied with everything is ridiculed with all or more of the point and easy grace of style attained in the *Inconstant*.

Mlle. Olivier's place at the theatre was fully taken by two young actresses who now made their first bows there. In 1786 the Duc de Duras established an Ecole de Déclamation in the interests of the Comédie Française, with Molé, Fleury, and Dugazon as professors. One of its earliest pupils was Mlle. Desgarcins, daughter of Louis Desgarcins, by birth a gentleman. Carefully prepared for the stage by Molé, she came forward on the 24th of May, at the age of seventeen, as Atalide in *Bajazet*, and, after a début extending to the unusually long period of four months, was received with acclamation. Like Gaussin and Doligny, she was unequal to tragedy in its sterner aspects, but brought to all her work the charms of sympathy, grace of movement, personal beauty, and a musical voice. No less fitted for the stage was the other débutante, Anne Françoise

Elizabeth Lange, born at Gênes in 1772, and even younger, therefore, than Mlle. Desgarcins. Daughter of a clever violinist, Charles Lange, she appeared at the Tours theatre in her fifteenth year, and was successful enough from the outset to be included soon afterwards in one of four companies organized by Mlle. Montausier. Lindane in the *Ecossaise* and Lucinde in the *Oracle* were the characters in which she first faced a Paris audience. Barely above the middle height, but pretty, well made, and sufficiently versatile to illustrate sentiment and *espiègleric* with the happiest effect, she was at once made a *pensionnaire.*

Larive was here impelled in a fit of dudgeon to go into private life. It appears that while playing Orosmane he was soundly hissed, probably because the impassioned beauty of Lekain's acting in the part was still vividly remembered. "Ungrateful wretches!" exclaimed the discomfited actor; "they shall never see me again." "Do not be so hasty," said a comrade who was on the stage with him at the moment; "they are hissing me." Larive, however, was not to be reassured, and the efforts of the company to divert him from his resolution proved fruitless. Some nights later a party of friends in the pit raised a call for him, but this was met by angry cries of "nous n'en voulons plus," to be crowned towards the end of the performance by a malicious application to him of a hemistich in the piece then being performed, *Iphigénie en Aulide*. His intention to retire, it seems, had become known in the interim, and was resented as a mark of disrespect to the public. Whether he adhered to it long the sequel will show.

Le Présomptueux, the first comedy of the new year, introduces us to a writer of high literary gifts, passionately eager for literary fame, but destined to win his principal distinction in other than literary ways. Philippe François Nazaire Fabre, born at Carcassonne in 1758, lisped in numbers at an early age, bore off a prize at the Floral Games, and, in commemoration of the form it took, thenceforward called himself Fabre d'Eglantine. In or about 1787, after passing some years in the country as an actor, he went to Paris in the hope of becoming a Comédien du Roi, but seems to have been found wanting. He then gave himself up to literature, and was now toiling for his bread in an obscure garret. It is a wonder that he did not find himself in the Bastille, as no fiercer or more outspoken opponent of the existing political system was to be met with in the capital. *Le Présomptueux* failed in spite of rare merits, at the head of which we may place a characteristically impetuous force of expression. Fabre's first impulse was to abandon the drama in despair, but a jealousy of Harleville, who soon afterwards achieved a striking success with a comedy entitled *Les Châteaux*

en Espagne—a success due in the main to an almost
entire reconstruction of the piece after the first performance—induced him to remain in the field.

Fleury, writing of this particular time, relates a story
which again proves that great effects may spring from
very minor causes. Mlle. Contat was one afternoon
driving across the Pont Neuf in a whisky, the sort of
vehicle then most favoured by ladies of fashion. In
front of the Rue Dauphine she almost knocked down a
middle-aged gentleman crossing the road. "Monsieur,"
she exclaimed, pulling up sharply, "what on earth do
you mean by running against my horse in that fashion?"
"Madame," he replied, "I really think that the horse
ran against me." "Impossible, Monsieur." "Perhaps,
Madame, you will admit that we were both in fault."
"No, Monsieur, I will admit nothing of the kind. My
horse is quite under control. Besides, I called out
'gare!' and you never looked up." "Madame," said
the gentleman with Voltairian grace as he made his
bow of adieu, "you have more reason to cry 'gare!'
now, when I do look up. It is very dangerous to look
at you."

In about a month, after tormenting herself with vain
guesses as to the identity of the gallant stranger, Mlle.
Contat received a note to the effect that the gentleman
who had lately had the privilege of a few moments'
conversation with her on the Pont Neuf wished to know

whether she would devote a leisure hour to a rehearsal
at the Comédie Italienne of a two-act piece in which he
took great interest. "Henri" was the signature. Mlle.
instantly repaired to the theatre mentioned, but found
that the author of the only play in preparation there
was a comparatively young man. "Ma foi," she said to
Dezède, who introduced her to him, "I must explain my
conduct in coming hither on such an errand;" and the
letter was produced. The stranger, who was manifestly
a man of high breeding, manifested some emotion on
seeing it. "Henri!" he exclaimed, "ever noble, generous, and true!" "And to me unknown," said Contat
archly. "Unknown, Mlle.? why, all the world knows
him!" "Nay, Monsieur, there is at least one person in
the world who is not in the secret, and that person is
myself." "Can you possibly be unaware, Mlle., that he
is Prince Henry of Prussia?" "Frederick the Great's
brother?" "The same." "I breathe again," said
Contat. "Brother of a king, a hero into the bargain!
I pardon him for the sake of the *coup de théâtre.*"
"And for the sake of his recommendation," the author
continued, "I hope you will befriend me." It appeared
that he was in a difficult position. The success of his
first act depended upon the character of a tavern
hostess. Madame Dugazon had declined it as beneath
her talents; the actress about to play it was unequal to
her task. Would Mlle. Contat, after hearing a rehearsal,

try to induce Madame Dugazon to reconsider her intention ? " What ! " exclaimed Susanne, " take a part
from an actress in possession of it and force it upon
an actress who has rejected it ? No, no ; impossible."
However, she expressed a willingness to know something
of the piece, which was accordingly rehearsed. " When
you next see Prince Henri," she said at the end, " tell
him that his wish shall be gratified."

It was to a very graceful little piece that the actress
had listened. *Les Deux Pages*, to use the title usually
bestowed upon it, had been written as a tribute of
respect to the memory of the late King of Prussia,
and, like the *Partie de Chasse d'Henri Quatre*, was of
the anecdotical order. Its chief incident had foundation
in fact. Frederick one day rang his bell, but could
make nobody hear. Opening the door of the apartment,
he saw a page asleep in an arm-chair, with the corner of
a note protruding from his pocket. His majesty softly
drew out and read the paper. It was from the youth's
mother, acknowledging the receipt of a portion of his
salary, regularly sent to relieve her necessities, and
invoking a blessing upon his head. Frederick put back
the letter with a purse of ducats, returned to his room,
and rang the bell sharply. In another moment the page
presented himself. " You have been sleeping," said
the King sternly ; " I have rung twice." The page tried
to excuse himself, and, chancing in his embarrassment

to put his hand into his pocket, amazedly drew out
the purse. "What have you there?" asked Frederick.
"Ah, Sire," moaned the page, dropping on his knees,
"somebody is endeavouring to ruin me: I know nothing of this purse." "No matter, my good lad," said
the King; "Heaven sometimes sends us good luck
in our sleep. Forward the money to your mother
with my regards, and tell her that I will provide for
her as well as for you." Upon this incident—one not
uncharacteristic of Frederick—the play mainly rested.
The other page was a light-hearted youth, introduced
for the sake of contrast. *Les Deux Pages*, as has been
said, was in two acts, the first turning upon a persecu-
tion to which the mother and a daughter are subjected
at an inn near Berlin by an unfeeling creditor. It was
the character of the hostess here that Madame Dugazon
had deemed unworthy of her talents.

Mlle. Contat was so much delighted with the play
that she induced Prince Henri's friend to transfer it to
the Comédie Française, the more easily because she
promised to take up the rejected part herself. Dugazon
was nominated by the author for the King, but the
actress, apparently out of personal affection as well as
clear judgment, secretly resolved that this honour should
go to Fleury. Soon afterwards the latter might have
been found speaking to her in the green-room of his
professional prospects, which had been largely improved

of late by a few "creations," as in the *Ecole des Pères*
and the *Maison de Molière*, and by his acting at Court
in *Turcaret*.   He had reached the point when the public
expected him to become great.   If a fine character could
only be invented for him; a character demanding
neither the depth of Monvel nor the brilliancy of Molé;
a character that might be for him what Susanne had
been for his fair interlocutor!   "But remember," she
said, "that I had no objection to a cap and apron; a
livery would displease you."   "I confess," he answered,
"that I hate a livery."   "Shall I propose a character
for you ?"   "By all means."   "Would you like to act
a prince ?"   "I have never occupied so high a rank;
still—"   "Could you command 100,000 men ?"   "I fear
there would be many refractory subjects among them;
still, with Mlle. Contat's recommendation—"   "Fleury,
I suspect you have an idea of what I am going to tell
you ?"   He smilingly admitted that he had.   "And now
that all is decided," he said, "I must embrace you in
my character of King to express my gratitude as a
friend."   "Then," she laughed, "you know that I am
to be your humble subject the hostess ?"   Fleury kissed
her so hard that Dugazon, who was gossiping in a
corner, looked round.   "Did anything fall ?" he asked.
"Aye," was the jubilant reply; "a bolt on your head,
a crown on mine."

Of this crown he spared no pains to make himself

worthy. He made the character a subject of close and
unintermittent study. He caught eagerly at details furnished to him by the author and others of Frederick's
idiosyncracies. He sought to imbue himself with the
idea that he was at Potsdam instead of Paris. For two
months he went to bed and rose, ate and drank, moved
and spoke, in the full persuasion that he was the
Prussian King. Every morning he equipped himself
in a military dress ordered for the part, sat down before
his glass, and painted his face to a more or less striking
resemblance to a copy—kindly procured for him by St.
Fal—of Romberg's portrait of the man to be represented.
For he was fully sensible of the value of the opportunity
here given him. "No such part," he writes, "had
previously been attempted; it was quite original. I
had to impersonate one who had just closed a wonderful
career, and on whom the eyes of Europe had been fixed
to the last. Nothing serves an actor so much as to
bear an historic name of recent date. If he succeeds
in arriving at only a fair likeness of his model, he
establishes in the mind of every spectator a sort of
association between himself and the eminent personage
in question. It is a resurrection which cannot fail to
arouse interest. The appearance on the stage of a hero
lately taken from us is more impressive because he has
lately been taken from us. It is better than a book or
a picture; the creation is palpable, sentient, entrancing.

By producing belief out of illusion the actor at once makes a name; he engrafts one great reputation upon another."

Early in March, under the name of *Auguste et Théodore,* the comedy was produced to a brilliant audience, including Prince Henri of Prussia, the Dukes of Orleans and Nivernois, and last, but hardly least, the Comte de Mirabeau.   Never had a two-act piece been more strongly cast; some of the most distinguished members of the company had loyally rallied round their comrade in what they seemed to have felt was an important trial to him.   Dazincourt and Mlle. Contat quickly made the fortune of the first act.   "The latter," we are assured, "was irresistible.   Her beauty and frank gaiety carried all before them; while her singing—and sing she really could—gave full effect to the airs left in the piece." When Frederick appeared, as he did for the first time in the second act, a dead silence fell over the theatre. No movement among that dense mass could be detected. "Frederick," writes his representative, "was not much afraid, though he had to face an auditory difficult to please.   The sentinels presented arms at me.   I cast a critical glance at their martial attitude: to the sentinel on the left I gave a shrug of dissatisfaction; to the sentinel on the right I directed one of those smiles which a true soldier is delighted to receive.   The pit remained unmoved; whereupon I said to myself—my thoughts still with the sentinel on the right—'Thou shalt have the cross of merit!' Instantly, as though the idea had been a signal, a torrent of applause came from every part of the house, to cease only when I turned to speak." It was repeated at short intervals during the rest of the piece, the impersonation being accepted by all as one of the most vivid examples of comedy-art yet witnessed in Paris. Prince Henri, hardly able to believe that his brother had not risen from the grave, presented to the actor, henceforward one of the most shining lights of the theatre, a snuff-box formerly in the possession of Frederick himself, and bearing on the lid a miniature of that personage in a circlet of diamonds. "Nobody," the grateful recipient was assured, "knows better how to use it than yourself."

For some time the authorship of the *Deux Pages* was a secret save to Fleury, Mlle. Contat, and one or two others. In the bills it was ascribed to Dezède, although he was responsible for the music only. Knowing as much, but otherwise ill-informed, Grimm surmised that Sauvigny had written the piece, and Etienne was equally wide of the mark in accepting it as the work of Faure. In point of fact, if we may trust the memoirs in which the whole story is related, the mysterious dramatist was a relative of the last Grand Duke of Courland, Baron Ernest de Manteufel, who for many years had found an asylum at Frederick's Court, and since the death of his benefactor had been one of the pets of Parisian society. Of an "ancient and illustrious race," he weakly allowed himself to be led by family reasons to disguise his connexion with a piece hardly less honourable to his head than to his heart. On the morning of the first performance, one of his closest friends, the beautiful Comtesse de Lamark, expressed regret that he was not in a position to enjoy the success he would certainly meet with, to hear his name pronounced with acclamations by a delighted audience. "I shall be 'named' before the first scene is over," he said. "Your hand will not be recognized so easily," she rejoined. "Will you lay a wager about it?" "Certainly : are you going to risk much?" "Will *you* risk a kiss?" he asked; "it is only fair to tell you that I am sure of winning." "Be it so, then; a kiss." "I shall be in your box, Madame, and shall expect to be paid, if I win, before all your friends." "Very well." Just before the curtain rose he joined her in the theatre; the performance began, and the master of the hostelry near Berlin, wanting a waiter, came on crying "Ernest, Ernest!" "That is my name," said the Baron to the Comtesse; "have I not won?" Madame might have pleaded that he had won not quite fairly. But she preferred to capitulate; her debt was paid upon the spot.

CHAPTER IX.

THE REVOLUTION.

Les Deux Pages came out on the eve of the most momentous event in the history of France, if not of the whole human race for nearly eighteen centuries. The storm which had been coming over the country since the appearance of Voltaire's *Lettres sur les Anglais*, and of which, as we have seen, the annals of the theatre contain many significant forewarnings, now broke with almost appalling fury. For some time the political atmosphere had been so deeply charged with electricity that any unpopular act on the part of the Court would have precipitated the impending crash. National bankruptcy, with the additional burdens it entailed, had brought to a white heat the vengeful passions aroused by centuries of despotic rule, class privilege, and widespread misery among the masses. Louis XVI., as a means of extricating himself from his difficulties, at length convoked the States-General, which met at Versailles in May. Conscious of the strength given to them by the confusion of the finances, the Tiers Etat, with Mirabeau at their head, resolutely assumed full

legislative power, and the capital soon afterwards rose
in its might to support their ascendency. Nothing
seemed able to withstand the revolutionary torrent
thus let loose. It must have been difficult to contemplate the work of the next few months without
distrusting the evidence of the senses :—the authority
of the throne reduced to a shadow, the privileges of the
nobility ended, the Church despoiled, the immunities of
great corporations abolished, the principle of universal
equality laid down, the sovereignty of the people
asserted, the right of insurrection declared to be a
sacred one, the capital in anarchy, the Bastille stormed
and captured by the citizens, the municipality reorganized on a popular basis, the proud aristocracy taking
to flight, and the royal family, humbled and terrified,
dragged by a mob from Versailles to undergo a sort of
captivity in the Tuileries. By the autumn, in fine,
absolute monarchy had been transformed into a democracy predisposed to violence, animated by a bitter
hatred of the system just overthrown, rejecting Christianity with the contempt to be looked for in disciples
of the Encyclopædists, and burning to realize those
ideals of a virtuous republic which the classic drama
had done so much to spread abroad. Necessary as a
radical change in the old system might be, it could not
be accomplished with safety under such conditions as
these, and incidental acts of ferocity inspired a further

doubt as to the fitness of the people for the self-government at which they aimed. How the convulsion would end none could venture to foretell. In the words of Mirabeau, a bull which had been cruelly baited to madness in bondage might be expected to make use of its horns when it became free.

Naturally enough, the Revolution split the distracted nation into two parties, one opposing it from either a love of monarchy or a distrust of the people, and the other, which generally outnumbered the first, hailing it with the wildest enthusiasm. In no quarter was this divergence of opinion more manifest that at the Comédie Française. "Even our literary green-room," writes Fleury, "was not exempt from the invasions of the moment. Melpomene and Thalia had the mortification to see their sacred altars profaned by the party pamphlets of the day, their venerable sanctuary turned into a political club." It is true that on one point the company were in complete unison. Whatever may have been thought of the inexpediency of disregarding the rights of property, the downfall of the Church could have aroused little pity among the members of a profession which it had consistently persecuted for nearly two hundred and fifty years, even to the point of denying a Christian burial to Molière—the first ascertainable cause of the anti-clerical spirit which made itself felt towards the end of the seventeenth

century, and which, fomented by Voltaire and his followers, was at present sweeping all before it. But the
virtual overthrow of the throne was viewed with very
different feelings by the Comédiens du Roi, as they
were still allowed to style themselves. In politics the
House of Molière was divided against itself. Molé,
Mlle. Raucourt, Fleury, and Mlle. Contat, to mention
only four names, had tasted too many of the sweets of
Court favour not to deplore the fall of the old *régime* ;
others, like Madame Vestris, Dugazon, and Mlle. Desgarcins, espoused the popular side with the energy of
rooted conviction. Cool observers must have feared
that if the Comédie Française escaped the hands of
the powers that now were—and as a creation of Louis
XIV. it was likely to invite their hostility—it would be
rent asunder, at least for a time, by internal dissension.

In the midst of this general ferment, with the rising
tide of democracy gradually submerging the last remaining traces of the old system, the players received
a tragedy which nothing but the helplessness of the
King could have encouraged its author to write. "Some
day," Voltaire wrote to Saurin from Ferney in 1764, "we
shall introduce Popes on the stage, as the Greeks represented their Atreus and Thyestes, to render them
odious. The time will come when the massacre of St
Bartholomew will be made the subject of a tragedy." His
prediction was to be verified a little sooner than he may

have anticipated.   Early in the summer, as the ascendency of the Tiers-Etat became manifest, Marie Joseph
Chénier dramatized this dark history in order to expose
the crown and the mitre to additional odium.   His
Charles IX., if composed too hurriedly to have much
excellence of construction or style, presents us with a few
vivid and finished portraits.   Pre-eminent among these,
as may be supposed, is that of the well-meaning but
fanatical and irresolute young King.   His better in-
stincts, though sharpened by intercourse with Coligni
and L'Hôpital, do not save him from becoming a blind
instrument in the hands of the enemies of the Protes-
tants ; he sanctions and takes part in the massacre, and
a few eloquent reproaches addressed to him by Henri
de Navarre suffice to overwhelm him with a fatal
remorse.   Neither Catherine de Médicis nor the Duc de
Guise has so large an influence for evil with him as the
Cardinal de Lorraine, who in point of fact was in Rome
at the time in question, but who, as the principal mover
in the conspiracy, is here seen doing what the clergy
on the steps of the throne really did—namely, urging
the necessity of a wholesale effusion of blood, consecrat-
ing the arms taken up for the purpose, and promising
the rewards of Heaven to the assassins who should fall
in the impending struggle.   Nothing, perhaps, was more
likely to accomplish the author's aims than this picture
of a weak-minded monarch employing his absolute

power to butcher a section of the people in the assumed interests of religion, and Paris awaited its appearance with an eagerness which only an abiding hatred of absolute power and of religion could have inspired.

Nevertheless, it was long doubtful whether *Charles IX.* would see the light. Louis XVI., still possessed of the necessary power, declined to pass the piece, and the players as a body were not disposed to ignore his wishes unless compelled to do so. Chénier was fully alive to the signs of the times. He made it known far and wide that his tragedy had been arbitrarily suppressed. Forthwith a band of fiery revolutionists repaired to the Comédie Française, scattered themselves over the pit, and interrupted the performance with calls for " *Charles IX.*" Fleury at length came forward. "M. Chénier's play," said one, "has been put in rehearsal: why is it not given?" "Messieurs," was the reply, " *Charles IX.* has not been put in rehearsal, but as soon as we obtain permission——" It was an unfortunate word. "Do not talk to us of permission," said his interlocutor, mounting on a form; "the public has already suffered too much from the despotism of the censorship, and will have what it wishes to have." Loud applause followed this speech, at which Louis XIV. might have turned in his grave. "Monsieur," Fleury continued, "the laws which have governed the Comédie Française for a hundred years are still binding upon it,

and we cannot break them." "You are right," rejoined
the other; "consult the municipality on the subject."
Fleury undertaking to do so, peace was at once restored.
On the same evening there was affixed to the walls of
the theatre a handbill setting forth that dramatic genius
was succumbing under the last efforts of despotism ;
that *Charles IX.* and other pieces had been prohibited,
and that the hour for throwing off so odious a yoke had
at length come.   Next day, according to Fleury's promise, a deputation from the Comédie attended the meeting of the representatives of the Commune of Paris, who
referred the question at issue to their general assembly.
With unlooked-for sobriety of thought, the latter body
hesitated to give orders for the representation of the
piece, on the ground that it might compromise the public tranquillity.   Four or five days afterwards, however,
they found themselves constrained by popular clamour
to ask "MM. les Comédiens Français " to represent the
piece immediately, the King's veto notwithstanding.

Bowing to the force of circumstances, but not without
a feeling of sorrow for the further humiliation thus
brought upon the chief occupant of the Tuileries, now
a gilded cage, the players prepared themselves to add
Charles IX. to their repertory.   It is to their credit in
one way that they had not done so long previously, as
the agitation in favour of the tragedy, which could not
fail to be remunerative, was strong enough to excuse

such a step. Subsequent events invested the gathering
for the distribution of the characters with exceptional
interest. Little difficulty was experienced by the author
in securing Naudet for the virtuous Coligni, St. Prix for
the gloomily fanatical Cardinal, Vanhove for the tolerant
L'Hôpital, or Madame Vestris for the vindictive, astute,
and self-concealing Catherine. " Really," said the last-
mentioned of this group to the author, " I am running
some risk on your account; this queen-mother is so
hateful that I am sure to be shot at ! "   But who was
to play the " terrible arquebusier of the Louvre
balcony," Charles IX. himself?   Chénier offered the
part to St. Fal. He, fearing that his abilities were
unequal thereto, showed a preference for that of Henri
de Navarre, which was then assigned to him. Had
the fate-driven monarch, so eminently dramatic in his
oscillation between good and evil impulses, with those
splendid bursts of remorse at the end, to go begging
for a representative ? It was a great moment in the
history of the theatre, though none of those present
knew it. Modestly standing on the outskirts of the
group, probably in conversation with Dugazon, was a
promising tragedian recently brought into the company
—in appearance hardly more than a youth, slightly
above middle stature, with a quiet dignity of manner,
a round but mobile countenance, and a somewhat sleepy
expression (when he was off the stage) in the eyes.

Might he not be asked to fill the vacant character ?
St. Fal, ever ready to help forward a comrade, himself
put this question to the author. Eventually, amidst
general acclamations, Charles IX. was offered to and
ardently accepted by the new-comer, of whose previous
life, with the aid of a presumably accurate autobio-
graphy, I must now give some account.

François Joseph Talma—that being his name—was
born in Paris, Rue des Menétriers, on the 15th of
January 1766. It was once supposed that this event
took place in London—to be more precise, in Frith-
street, near Soho-square, in the house occupied for
many years by John Bannister, and afterwards, on his
removal to Gower-street, by the comedian Wathen.
How this misapprehension arose is obvious enough.
When François Joseph was about four years of age, his
father, a successful dentist, at that time living in the Rue
Mauconseil, opposite the Comédie Italienne (the ancient
Hôtel de Bourgogne), allowed himself to be persuaded
by a grateful patient, Lord Harcourt, to settle in the
English capital. Possibly he may have begun in Frith-
street, but the influence of his titled friend brought him
so large a practice that he took the house 13, Old
Cavendish-street, Cavendish-square, and there he was
consulted by no less a person than the Prince of Wales.
It remains to be said that to the cleverness indicated by
this progress he did not unite a due sense of what he

owed to his family, which consisted of three daughters and two sons. " My father," writes Talma, " was my first instructor. Fanatically attached to the ideas of the philosophical sect, he educated me according to the method," so eloquently expounded in *Emile*, " of Rousseau. Hundreds of times did I hear him utter the maxims of Voltaire on priests and royalty. It was in the *Origine des Cultes* that I learned to read ; from an early age, therefore, I had within me all the germs of atheism."

In his tenth year the boy was placed in a boarding-school on the outskirts of Paris, possibly in order that he might not be wholly denationalized. Hitherto he had not been inside a regular theatre, but a dramatic performance given at the next speech-day served to reveal in him an inherent turn for acting. In this performance he had to narrate the death of a friend in very tragic circumstances. Both imagination and sensibility were kindled in the little player as he went on ; to him the scene became a pathetic reality ; his voice altered, sobs choked his utterance, and he fainted outright. It is significant that before long he knew no pleasure equal to that of going to the Comédie Française, whither he was frequently taken by an uncle in return for being a studious scholar. He heard the announcement from the stage of Lekain's death, and was among the enthusiasts who followed Voltaire from the theatre

to the Rue de Beaune on the following 30th of March.
His passion for the " new ideas " soon broke through
all restraint.   One day a priest came to the school to
prepare the pupils for their first communion.   He had
scarcely gone when Talma sprang on to a form, ridiculed
all religious doctrines, and warmly espoused, if he did
not go beyond, the theories of Diderot, Holbach, and
D'Alembert.   " I thought myself," he says, "the apostle
of tolerance and philosophy."   Fortunately for his
audience, a portion of his discourse had been over-
heard by the master, who at once expelled him from
the establishment.

Proudly regarding himself as a martyr in the cause
of philosophy, Talma returned to the house in Old
Cavendish-street, and his interrupted education was
finished at a school near Manchester-square.   Next, at
the pressing instance of his father, he dived into the
mysteries of dentistry, apparently with a determination
to make it his calling.   In reality, however, his heart
was still with the drama, of which he soon became
an unprofessional votary.   Jean Monnet, erstwhile of
the Foires in Paris, was then attempting, not for the
first time, to found a French theatre in London, where
he had lived many years.   Though practically supported
by the aristocracy, the project exposed him to the
patriotic resentment of other classes, and only a
miracle saved him from being hanged by an angry mob

in front of his own house. He at length confessed
that the old hatred of the English for his countrymen
was too strong for such an enterprise. Piqued by this
circumstance, a club of young Frenchmen in London,
headed by Talma, got up a series of performances at the
Hanover-square Rooms, with the speculative Monnet as
their manager. Fashion took them up, the audiences
from the outset including the flower of the aristocracy.
Much of this success was due to Talma, who, among
other characters, played Polainville in the *Français à
Londres*, Almaviva in the *Mariage de Figaro*, and
Shakspere's Hamlet (in English). The Prince of Wales
came to see him, while persons of high standing—
Burke, Fox, Sheridan, Mansfield, Miss Burney, Hayley,
Swinburne, and the Duchess of Devonshire— urged him
to make the stage his profession. M. Talma senior,
though proud of his clever son, seems to have begrudged
him the time occupied in preparing himself for these
amusements. " Mon Dieu ! " he said one morning to
Lord Harcourt, " there he is up in his room, his nose
in a Shakspere or a Corneille, and studying Othello, or
Falstaff, or Rodrigue, or, it may be, L'Intimé in the
Plaideurs."

In the midst of these studies he was sent over to
manage his father's business in the Rue Mauconseil,
which had never been given up. Lord Harcourt here
introduced him to Molé, then in the first flush of his

success as Almaviva in the *Mariage de Figaro*. After
a long conversation, the player, perceiving in his new
acquaintance the "soul of an artist," procured for him
a free admission to the Comédie Française, took him
into the green-room, and finally made him a pupil
at the Ecole de Déclamation. Having undergone the
usual course of instruction there, he presented himself to
the playgoers on the 21st of October 1787 as Séide in
Mahomet. "In spite of defective elocution," Fleury
writes, "the performance indicated that command of
varied emotion which is the best proof of an actor's
capabilities." Dugazon was still louder in praise of
the débutant, especially on seeing him act Argatiphon-
tidas in *Amphitryon*. His period of trial over, he was
provisionally reduced to the ranks, but invested the
slightest characters with an interest of which they might
not have been thought susceptible. Even at this period,
it is certain, he had determined to promote the reform
begun by Clairon and Lekain in the way of stage costume. If he had to be a Roman he resembled a
Roman. For instance, in a representation at Court of
Voltaire's *Brutus*, while the other actors were arrayed in
wigs and rich silks, he played a subordinate part not only
with his hair cut short—in itself a striking innovation—
but in a cloth mantle without any embellishment save
a classic disposition of the folds. "Mon Dieu !" exclaimed Louise Contat, "il a l'air d'une statue ! " Most

of his comrades, after advising him in vain not to make
a fool of himself, had predicted that he would excite
ridicule ; as it was, the simple dignity of his attire and
utterance made him talked of more that night than his
superiors in histrionic rank.   His success in this case
accelerated his progress ; the Comédie Française admitted him early in 1789, and seven or eight months
later the ball was placed at his foot by the representation
of Charles IX. being confided to his care.

November 4 was the day set apart for the first performance of Chénier's tragedy.   The announcement, of
course, brought together a large and heated audience,
both royalists and anti-royalists having an interest in
what was known to be an onslaught upon the oldest
institutions of the country.   In the middle of the pit,
with a fierce joy lighting up their countenances, were
Camille Desmoulins and Danton, the former of whom
declared that the work would do more to promote
their cause than the transference of the Assembly and
Court from Versailles to Paris.   In the course of the
evening, however, this bitter party spirit was often
absorbed in a common feeling of wonderment and
admiration.   Talma came on the stage a living portrait
of Charles IX.   Every record of the latter had been
laboriously looked up : the identity was complete on all
points.   But that identity, rare as it might be, was
much less remarkable than the power revealed by the

actor as he warmed to his task.   His impersonation was
a triumph of art, with the inspiration of genius to give
it an enduring charm.   "It must be confessed," writes
Fleury, "that we did not expect him to produce the
effect he did here.   When, after being bowed down by
remorse, with his face hidden in the folds of his royal
mantle, he suddenly raised himself at the anathema
upon him, and, shuddering under the look of the man
who pronounced it, shrank back convulsively, as if to
shake off the drops of blood which had fallen upon him
from his victims,—the sublimity of his conception of
this scene filled us with amazement."   As may be
supposed, the general enthusiasm evoked by the acting
was followed by a keen contest as to the play itself.
The supporters of the old order of things in State and
Church hissed with right good will, though only to find
themselves outnumbered by the revolutionists. " *Charles
IX.*," said Danton, hazarding a suggestion which, coming to the author's ears, was forthwith adopted, " ought
to have ' L'Ecole des Rois' as a second title.   Beaumarchais killed the noblesse ; Chénier has cut the throat
of royalty in France."

Except in the arena of politics, no figure of the time
will impress itself more deeply on the mind than that of
the young tragedian who bore the chief burden in this
tragedy.   Talma must be classed with the greatest of
French actors.   In warmth of sensibility, perhaps, he

was inferior to Lekain.   His strength lay chiefly in an
appeal to the understanding.   He would have given
ten of Racine's plays for one of Corneille's.   But in no
other respect could he have fallen short of his predecessors.   Imaginative power, energy of thought, fertility
of resource, eloquence of gesture, clearness of elocution,
a keen sense of the picturesque,--all this was to be
found in his acting as he threw off the trammels of
inexperience.   Madame de Staël says that in him the
varied charms of music and painting and sculpture and
poetry were allied to produce every illusion, since he
possessed the secrets of these different arts.   In scenes
of high-wrought passion he underwent a sort of transformation; his stature increased, his somewhat hard
voice became grandly sonorous, his flat face acquired
a peculiar force of expression, and his eyes, ordinarily
half covered by their lids, seemed to emit flashes of
lightning.   Described in a sentence, his style was a
superb union of dignity and natural truth, whether in
utterance, gesture, or demeanour.   In private life, as
all testimony shows, he was gay, playful, warm-hearted,
and inoffensively conscious of his own gifts, with a
simplicity and indecision of character in curious contrast
to the intellectual vigour he displayed on the stage.
He could arouse the strongest emotions in others, but
was easily influenced himself.   As for the Revolution,
he hailed it with all the ardour to be expected from a

man of generous sympathies, utopian ideas, and a poetic
rather than practical mind. "He believed in the resurrection of the Forum and its Ciceros," writes Fleury,
"as he might have believed in that of Roscius. He
imagined that antiquity had poured out its spirit upon
France, and that if our gold-laced coats and point
ruffles were pounded together in a mortar they would
re-issue as Roman togas and Greek mantles. Besides
that, he saw the value of the Revolution as a means of
assisting his genius, which inclined to the sombre and
terrible."

Unfortunately, the coming of this illustrious player
was not to be without a serious drawback in the eyes
of a majority of his comrades. He brought discord as
well as money to the theatre. When *Charles IX.* was
in the full tide of its success, the clergy, assured that it
had deepened the widespread prejudice against them,
asked the King to suppress it. His majesty, perhaps
doubting whether he had the power to do so, sent the
required order to the company through the Gentlemen
of the Chamber, and had the satisfaction to find that it
was obeyed. For the present, therefore, Talma lost the
only fine character that had fallen to his lot. Naturally
anxious to extend his fame, he sought to console himself for this check by undertaking even more onerous
tasks, but was foiled on all points by the privileges
of seniority. Indeed, conformably with the customs of

the theatre, he again found himself in trifling parts, such as Proculus in *Brutus*.   Impulsive, ambitious, and predisposed to innovation, he could not imitate the patience with which his predecessors had passed through a similar ordeal.   He contended that the "rights" exercised by his elders originated in a sort of "theatrical feudalism," and ought at once to be abolished.   No member of the Comédie was entitled to exclusive possession of particular characters ; they should be open to all.   Madame Vestris and Dugazon, among others, hastened to advocate the views of their new colleague, who, however, was overpowered by numbers.   Henceforward, with characteristic irreverence for existing institutions, he sought to bring about a rupture between the revolutionists and the monarchists at the Comédie, in the hope that the former might obtain leave to start a second Théâtre Français on sounder principles than the first.

But this increasing disunion among the players was not permitted to interfere with the work of producing new plays, some of which are of value as reflecting the spirit of the hour.   *Le Paysan Magistrat*, a modification of Calderon's *Alcalde de Zalamea*, met with loud applause for fifteen nights, chiefly because it flattered the passion for equality by presenting the spectacle of a well-born man sentenced to death for carrying off the daughter of a rustic, who, elevated to the magistracy, acts as his judge.   The adapter was no other than Collot d'Herbois,

until recently a comedian in the country, but now
roaming about Paris in search of different employment.
He had been hissed from the stage at Lyons, and at
Bordeaux, it is said, would have been hanged for felony
if Fleury's sister had not prevailed upon the *échevin*
of the district to connive at his escape.   Another drama
came from Jean Louis Laya, by descent a Spaniard,
born in Paris in 1761, and known at the theatre as the
author of a pamphlet vindicating the actor's rights to
the civil state.   *Les Dangers de l'Opinion,* as the play
was called, amounted to a protest against the practice,
already assailed with so much vigour by Voltaire, of
visiting the sins of a criminal upon his family.   So the
dramatist puts a Romeo under such a ban, and the
consequent sorrows of the Juliet—acted with exquisite
art and tenderness by Madame Petit (Mlle. Vanhove)—
created an impression which many defects in the piece
could not appreciably mar.   Fabre d'Eglantine was
audacious enough to pen what proved to be a clever
continuation of the *Misanthrope;* a little comedy, *Le
Couvent,* by one Lanjon, had no man among its personages, and Lemierre, with his powers prematurely
enfeebled, figured in the bills as the author of the
Barneveldt suppressed many years before.

By this time, perhaps more tardily than might have
been anticipated, the zeal of the National Assembly
had extended itself to the theatre.   In the first instance,

as a matter of bare justice, the players were restored to
the rights so long denied to them by the Church. In
the future there was to be no obstacle in the way of
their marrying, presenting themselves at the altar,
or being buried with the usual rites. It was in vain
that the clergy sought to prevent the humiliation to
which their own intolerance had exposed them; the
legislature, shocked by the scandal of an actor or actress
being obliged to commit perjury in order to lead chaste
lives, adhered firmly to its resolution. Nor was this
the only decree that claims our attention. Few means
of appealing to the masses had had so much influence
as the drama. Might not that influence be rendered
wholly subservient to the interests of democracy? It
was accordingly determined that the theatres of Paris
should be under the control of the municipality instead
of the Gentlemen of the Chamber, who, of course, were
" reactionaries" of the most uncompromising type. But
this was more easily proposed than accomplished; the
companies, grateful as they may have been for the
repeal of their disabilities, persistently ignored all
orders save those which emanated from the Court, and
the unhappy King showed no inclination to surrender
the authority thus respected. Last, but not least, the
Assembly established a sort of free trade in matters
theatrical, thereby enabling any body of players to
represent new tragedies or comedies in Paris.

Fresh energy was given to the Comédie Française by this radical change in the conditions of its existence, this partial breaking down of the monopoly conferred upon it by Louis XIV. In order to be prepared for the additional competition awaiting it, and also to withstand the extravagant claims, as they were deemed, of the too-impatient Talma, the dominant party in the theatre besought the co-operation of Larive, who, after a good deal of hesitation, due in some measure to religious scruples, was prevailed upon by a clerical friend, the Abbé Gouttes, President of the Assembly, to accede to their wishes. He reappeared on the 4th of May as Œdipe, and was cordially welcomed by an overflowing audience. In one sense, however, he had lost touch of the town. His style was not precisely to the taste of what the Revolution had made the most turbulent pit in Europe. " In getting Larive to oppose the despotism of old rules to the new tyranny with which we were threatened," Fleury says, " we ignored the fact that as the nation had undergone a second birth another order of things in the theatre must come. He returned with his regular and harmonious method ; what the public wanted was a method marked by fire and fitful passion. In every walk of life the spirit of innovation reigned supreme, and the theatre could not be expected to escape its contagion. Consequently, the step we had just taken was one in a backward direction.

Larive, a histrionic Montmorenci, was an actor for the aristocracy ; Talma, first revealed to the world as the hero of *Charles IX.*, became the actor of a people in the throes of revolution."

Events soon gave additional prominence to the young player just named.   Mirabeau, the all-powerful Mirabeau, appeared in the green-room one evening to ask the players to act Chénier's tragedy for the delectation of the Provençal deputies after the approaching fête in the Champ de Mars.   Fearing that the piece might provoke an outburst of party feeling on what was intended to be an occasion for the interchange of brotherly feeling, the company firmly declined to comply with his request unless the public should endorse it.   "Do you think," he said, "that you have the right to refuse ? "   " M. le Comte," replied Dazincourt, " that right is recognized by your coming here on the subject." On the eve of the fête the deputies themselves applied for a performance of *Charles IX.*, but with the same result.   The piece given on the anniversary of the fall of the Bastille was one entitled *Momus aux Champs Elysées*, in which Talma impersonated Rousseau with striking fidelity.   Irritated by their failure, the deputies went to the Comédie on the 21st of July, when *Epiménide* was in the bills, and raised what became a general cry for the forbidden tragedy.   Mlle. Lange, Talma, and Naudet were then on the stage.   Presently the last addressed the angry audience, stating that Madame Vestris and St. Prix were too ill to appear. But this was disbelieved; the tumult increased, and some of the company were charged with using the repertory as an instrument for the gratification of unpatriotic caprice. Talma at length came forward. "Messieurs," he said, "Madame Vestris is really ill. I have no doubt, however, that she will give a proof of her zeal and patriotism by reappearing as Catherine de Médicis at the first opportunity. As for M. St. Prix's part, that can be read." The performance was then allowed to go on. Finding it necessary to submit, the company revived *Charles IX.* on the 27th, and Talma acquitted himself of his task with the most powerful effect. Many passages were hissed by the monarchists, but the evening would have passed in comparative tranquillity if Danton and others in the pit had not created a disturbance by defiantly keeping on their hats—an offence for which the burly and fierce-looking advocate was punished by a temporary confinement at the Hôtel de Ville.

New troubles for the Comédie Française arose from this revival. Chénier, unaware of the real state of the case, loudly reproached the players for the injustice they had done him by giving his tragedy in the height of summer. In reply he was told to blame only those who had got up the scene in the theatre on the 21st of July. Talma gratuitously assumed, as a few

royalist writers did, that he was glanced at in this
remark.   In self-defence he wrote to Mirabeau for
permission to announce the fact that he had asked for
the representation of *Charles IX.*   "Certainly," the
orator replied; "that is the truth, and it is a circumstance of which I am proud."   Messieurs the comedians,
he added, told him that they could not grant his
request unless it were decisively supported by opinion
out of doors.   He therefore thought it necessary to
make known their reply; the public voice made itself
heard on the subject, and its behest was reluctantly
obeyed.   "It was not for players to decide whether a
work legitimately produced had an inflammatory tendency."   Soon after the appearance of this letter, Camille
Desmoulins' *Révolutions de France et de Brabant,* one
of many new-fangled sheets, printed an article in which
Naudet was accused of interfering with the liberty of
the stage, of aiming a blow at the young tragedian,
and of other grave misdemeanours.   It excited a warm
controversy, and Talma, in a letter to the same paper,
supported the allegations against his comrade by describing incidents that had occurred behind the scenes about
six months previously.   Such a revelation was contrary
to the usages of the Comédie Française, which wisely
kept its internal dissensions a secret.   Few of the
players read the letter without indignation or sorrow.
Indignation prevailed; and at a general meeting of the

company, on the motion of Fleury, it was almost unanimously resolved that the offender, great as he promised to be, should be expelled from the theatre.

It is not too much to say that this decision caused intense excitement throughout Paris. The populace came to the aid of so ardent a patriot as Talma was known to be. Fierce harangues against the players in general as aristocrats and *inciviques* were to be heard in the coffee-houses, the taverns, and the Place de la Comédie. "Hatred of despotism," writes one of the denounced, "was the dominant principle of the moment, and nothing less than despotism was laid to our charge." Nor did this resentment fail to declare itself at the next performance. Every part of the house was crowded to suffocation. Had that audience come together simply to witness the *Ecole des Maris?* the players apprehensively asked themselves. Down to the end of the overture there was no hostile demonstration, though a murmur "like the moaning of the wind among the leaves before it uproots the tree" occasionally made itself heard above the music. But as soon as the curtain rose the theatre rang with shouts of "Talma." Fleury acted as spokesman in the matter. "Messieurs," he said, when silence had been restored, "the *sociétaires*, satisfied that M. Talma has injured their interests and compromised public tranquillity, have unanimously resolved to sever their association with him until the question at issue shall be determined by the competent authority." How this statement was received need hardly be added. The plaudits of a few friends were drowned in a burst of execration. For a moment the uproar was stopped by the appearance of Dugazon. "Are we to have Talma?" somebody asked. "No, messieurs," he replied; "and I wish you to know that the company are likely to do with me as they have done with him. It is false to say that M. Talma has injured their interests and compromised public peace. He merely declared that *Charles IX.* might be performed —that is all." Here the spirit of tumult again broke loose; women thought it discreet to leave; malcontents began to tear up the seats in the pit to hurl at royalist players, and only the arrival of the military saved the theatre from being wrecked.

Of popular origin, the new municipality hastened to give effect to the popular will. Bailly, the mayor, sent to the players a message advising them to reinstate Talma, but had the mortification to find it unheeded. He then requested them to appear before him at the Hôtel de Ville, which they did. "It must be confessed," Fleury writes, "that we comedians in ordinary to the King felt deeply humiliated at being thus summoned to the municipal bar. When the chief magistrate expressed his surprise that we had disregarded his orders as to Talma, all of us, I really believe, were

tempted to repeat the words of the Doge of Venice
to Louis Quatorze—'what surprises us is to find ourselves here.'   We could not reconcile our minds to this
mixture of the stage, the mayoralty, and the science
of astronomy."   Before long, however, they were more
at their ease.   "Bailly's manner to us," continues
Fleury, "was full of urbanity.   I still remember his
study-worn countenance, which, when he lowered his
eyebrows (apparently a habit of his), presented a most
grave and dignified expression.   He seemed annoyed
when we spoke of the authority of the Gentlemen of the
Chamber, but this instantly passed away.   He sought
to make us understand that we had done with the
dynasty of Richelieu and Duras, that he himself
was the arbiter of the discipline of the theatre, and
that we must yield the point with regard to Talma."
Desessarts argued that their regulations would not
allow this to be done, but the mayor was immovable.
"The Comédie Française," he said, "is a national
institution ; and your regulations—which I advise you
to regulate—cannot entitle you to interfere with the
gratification of the public and the prosperity of art."
Nevertheless, the interview ended without a decision
being come to.   In a few hours an order for the rein-
station of Talma was issued from the Hôtel de Ville,
sent in form to the theatre, and placarded all over
Paris.   The players, still adhering to what they thought

their rights, denied the power of the municipal council to interfere in the matter, but were soon overawed into submission.   Talma accordingly reappeared, and was received, of course, with bursts of applause by an audience composed chiefly of patriots.   His triumph, however, was a source of loss rather than gain to the treasury, since Raucourt and Contat, at the risk of exposing themselves to public odium, showed their sense of his recent indiscretion by withdrawing for a brief period from the company.

But this contest with the municipality was not so important to the Comédie Française as another now forced upon it.   Most of the dramatic authors took advantage of its weakness to promote their own interests. Beaumarchais, Laharpe, Chénier, Sédaine, Mercier, Ducis, Palissot, Fabre d'Eglantine, Lemierre, Champfort, Bret, Cailhava, and Collot d'Herbois, with others, united in signing a petition to the Assembly in favour of theatrical reform.   Laharpe, as the oldest of all, was charged with the duty of presenting the document; and one afternoon, with pride in his port and defiance in his eye, he set out in a carriage for the legislature. Intense curiosity, we are told, was evinced by all the deputies as he advanced to the bar.   Mirabeau "was all attention; Barnave bent forward; Robespierre resembled a schoolboy about to have a lesson in rhetoric; the Abbé Maury raised a laugh among his neighbours

at the expense of the Academician." Did not M. de
Laharpe's look prove that he had come on urgent business ? Presently, after one or two preliminary coughs,
the self-sufficient poet broke silence. It was his proud
privilege, he said, to represent on that occasion the great
body of French dramatists. Everybody knew that they
had done much to bring about the present emancipation of
the human mind. For proofs of this, if he might speak
of himself, the most august Assembly in the universe had
only to remember his *Warwick, Jeanne de Naples,* and
Coriolan, in all of which (as in his private correspondence with the Grand Duke of Russia), he had given
the rein to a love of freedom. It was only right,
therefore, that these writers should be on a better
footing as to remuneration than their predecessors had
been. He "had the honour to present a petition that
any theatre might have the power to represent the
works of dead authors, which ought to be regarded as
national property, and that living authors might be
free to make their own terms with the players." Against
this petition, of course, a memorial was promptly drawn
up by the members of the Comédie Française. Had
they not legally acquired an exclusive possession of
their repertory ? Would not the works of the great
dramatists be degraded in the hands of ill-educated and
inexperienced troupes ? Fervently anxious to increase
the means of accelerating the Revolution, the Con-

stitution Committee, to whom the question was referred,
paid little or no heed to these arguments.   It was
gravely decided that the prayer of the authors should
be granted, and all that remained of the monopoly
which the Comédie Française had enjoyed for a hundred
and ten years was consequently swept away.

More than one brilliant success came to console the
players for the blow thus inflicted upon them.   Laya
appealed to the prevailing hatred of bigotry by drama-
tizing the story of Calas, while the enthusiasm for
freedom was gratified by a piece illustrating the triumph
of the revolutionary spirit in the country.   *Le Fou par
Amour*, a one-act drama in verse, by the younger Ségur,
relied exclusively upon a well-painted picture of passion
in several of its manifestations.   Dorval, a young officer,
is taken to a hospital to be treated for a wound he
has received in a duel.   He is nursed by Sister Adélaïde,
for whom he conceives an enduring attachment, but
who soon afterwards dies.   He then goes mad with
grief, and in this state is cared for by the father of a
girl in love with him.   It is believed that he may be
cured by the sudden appearance of this girl before him
as Adélaïde herself, but when the idea is acted upon
he gives way to a paroxysm of terror, cries " Ciel ! j'en
vois deux ! " and suddenly dies.   Fleury represented
the hero, and, though essentially a light comedian, seems
to have given powerful expression to the many varieties

of feeling of which the part is composed.   St. Prix
and Mlle. Sainval could not save a *Rienzi* by Laiguelot
from summary condemnation, but a trifle by Harleville,
M. de Crac dans son Petit Castel, with a mendacious
Gascon hobbledehoy (brightly played by Dugazon)
as its central figure, kept the audience in a continual
ripple of merriment.   Monvel, returning from Stockholm,
offered his old comrades a four-act drame, the *Victimes
Cloîtrées*, which was produced on the 29th of March.
From one point of view he had been well advised in his
choice of a subject.   The public liked to see holy men on
the stage, though only to jeer at and hiss them.   None
of the small theatres which the decree of the Assembly
had called into existence could afford to be without
a variety of sacerdotal vestments in their wardrobes.
Les Victimes Cloîtrées exposed the possible abuses of the
convent with the zeal to be looked for in so fanatical
an enemy of religion as the author.   Its most strongly
marked personage, a Père Laurent, immures one Eugénie
de St. Alban in a dungeon for a purpose which need
not be specified.   In order to enrich himself, he next
induces her lover, who believes that she is dead, to take
the frock, and consigns him to a dungeon adjoining
hers.   Breaking through the intervening wall in an
effort to escape, the youth finds himself face to face
with the heroine—a striking scene—and they are
eventually rescued by the National Guard.   Such a

piece could hardly fail to arouse enthusiasm at the time
in question, the more so as Fleury, affording another
proof of his versatility, rose to greatness in the part
of the half-distraught hero.

Les Victimes Cloîtrées brings us to the Easter recess,
when the schism exhibited at the Comédie since the
beginning of the Revolution, but more especially since
the appearance of *Charles IX.*, at length came to a
crisis. By the last decree of the Assembly as to the
theatres, it will have been seen, Talma was enabled to
appear at another house without losing the chance of
impersonating the characters drawn by Corneille,
Racine, and Voltaire Chafing against the regulations
which compelled him to wait for the means of developing his genius, and embittered against most of his
comrades on account of his expulsion in the previous
year, he now determined to make full use of the freedom
so conceded.   For some months there had been a
Théâtre des Variétés Amusantes at the corner of the
Rue de Richelieu, adjoining the Palais Royal.   Gaillard
and Dorfeuille, its managers, offered the young tragedian
a lucrative engagement, which he readily accepted.   In
his retirement from the Comédie Française he was
followed by Dugazon, Madame Vestris, Mlle. Desgarcins,
and Grandménil, the last of whom, a grandson of
Duchemin, had just completed a successful début in
parts *à manteaux*.   Monvel might have returned to the

Comédie Française, but he preferred to throw in his lot
with that of the seceders, as did a comedian of rich
humour, Michot, " the Polichinelle of the revolutionary
era." " Henceforward," said an actor of the new theatre
in an address to the audience, " a great future lies before
us. The masterpieces of the great dramatists, these truly
national possessions, have become a common patrimony,
and to us shall be a heritage worthy of all care."

If anything, this long-deferred triumph of free-trade
principles in the theatrical world was a fortunate event
for the Comédie Française, though it may not have been
regarded in that light at the time. It caused the
remaining members of the company to hold up their
banner with additional zeal, firmness, and intrepidity.
Most of them were inspired by a premonition of coming
danger with a " chivalric devotion " to the old house.
Fleury expressed a general sentiment in saying that he
had for the Maison de Molière " an attachment akin to
that of a true gentleman for the manorial halls of his
ancestors, where each escutcheon records a gallant deed
and prescribes the observance of a virtue." Looking
round upon themselves, too, they were not disposed
to take a pessimist view of their prospects. No competition could annihilate such a body of players as
Molé, Mlle. Contat, Larive, Mlle. Raucourt, Fleury,
Mlle. Devienne, St. Fal, Madame Petit, St. Prix, Mlle.
Joly, Desessarts, Dazincourt, and Vanhove. A débutant

under trial, Dupont, had achieved a marked success, while another beginner of rare promise was at hand in the person of a Mlle. Mezerai.   If, as was to be expected, a large majority of the dramatic authors went in the first instance to that second Théâtre Français for which they had so strenuously contended, their example would not be followed by Colin d'Harleville, and it was to be remembered that one or two fine plays by new hands were in preparation.   In such circumstances the company awaited the formidable rivalry in store for them with unfaltering hope.   As Fleury put it, they might not increase the prestige of the old house, but might at least contrive to preserve that prestige unimpaired.

Easter over, the two companies fell to work in good earnest.   That of the " Théâtre Français de la Rue de Richelieu" began on the 27th of April with a *Henri VIII.* by Chénier, Talma appearing as the King, Madame Vestris as Anne Boleyn, and Mlle. Desgarcins as Jane Seymour.   Partly to gratify his anti-monarchical zeal, the author had exposed in all its deformity, though not without some touches of humanity, the character of the ruler who took unto himself a third wife within a few hours of executing the second.   The tragedy was finely played, and except in the third act, which had glaring defects, was received with the favour due to one of no inconsiderable force in construction, portrait-painting, and versification.   However, the evening ended badly

for the seceders, as the afterpiece, in which Dugazon
and Grandménil had parts, was so vigorously hissed
that the performance could not be finished.   Palissot
published a letter attributing these hostile demonstrations to a cabal formed at the Comédie Française, but
the accusation seems to have been quite groundless.
Talma followed up his triumph as Henry VIII. by
another as the Cid, Monvel being the Don Diègue.
His majesty's players, on their part, brought out a
tragedy without female characters, *Marius à Minturnes,*
which met with loud applause.   It was by Arnault, at
present only twenty-one years of age, but already
known to be a poet.   Of good new plays, however, the
Théâtre de la Rue de Richelieu had a sort of monopoly.
Fabre d'Eglantine sent it a five-act comedy, the *Intrigue
Epistolaire,* which afforded a further proof that variety
and attractiveness of detail could atone for thinness of
plot.   This was succeeded by Ducis' fifth adaptation
from Shakspere, *Jean Sans Terre.*   Talma, as may be
supposed, played the King with the finest effect, notably
in the scene with Hubert (Monvel).   Arthur found a
graceful and pathetic representative in Mlle. Simon,
until recently employed to fill child parts at the Comédie
Française.   Mlle. Desgarcins falling ill on the eve of a
performance of the *Cid,* her place as Chimène had been
taken at an hour's notice by this young actress, who at
once captivated the town.   At both the theatres there

were pieces of a patriotic order, the Comédie Française decorating its bills with such titles as *Washington, ou la Liberté du Nouveau Monde*, and the other producing a dramatic illustration of the *Prise de la Bastille*.

His majesty's players, or, as the municipality preferred to style them, the Comédiens du Théâtre de la Nation, found their outlook less and less encouraging. In tragedy, to which the Revolution gave a new strength, they suffered by comparison with their rivals in the Rue de Richelieu, while an unshaken superiority in comedy did not suffice to dissipate the prejudice created against them by their sympathy with the still falling *régime*. In this strait they looked about them for exceptional means of filling the theatre, especially as Mlle. Sainval the younger, after a meritorious career of nearly twenty years, was compelled by ill-health to retire. Might not Préville be induced to come back for a short time? Fleury, who made the suggestion, set out for Senlis to determine the point. It might well have been supposed that the old comedian would decline to exchange his tranquil retirement for the fatigues and excitement and possible disgusts of a player in Paris, and that, too, at the risk of impairing his traditional fame. But on learning that the Comédie Française was in difficulties he at once complied with its wish, as did his devoted wife. "I have never," he said, "separated my fate from that of my comrades.

If they are not prospering I will go to their aid." In a few weeks, on the 26th of November, he reappeared as Michaud in the *Partie de Chasse*. Even "the hatred now pursuing the Comédie with an incredible bitterness" was not proof against the interest excited by the announcement. He faced a full audience, who saluted him with transports of delight. "For a moment," writes a contemporary, "he seemed embarrassed; then, recovering his presence of mind, he acted with that fine sensibility, that frank gaiety, and above all, that natural truth, which always characterized this inimitable artist." Some of those present may have remarked a change in his personal appearance. During a fête of the ancient Société de l'Arquebuse at Senlis, it seems, one of many shots murderously fired at the group by an expelled member of that body had grazed his left eye, wholly destroying the sight. But this disadvantage was unnoticed in the delight afforded by his acting; and after a dozen performances in plays still associated with his name, such as *Amphitryon* and the *Mercure Galant*, he returned to rural Senlis with the pleasing consciousness that he had done the Comédie a service without being accounted inferior to his former self.

Brief as it was, this resurrection seemed to infuse a new spirit into the competition between the two companies. *Mélanie*, a drama by Laharpe, with Talma and Mlle. Desgarcins at the head of the cast, was pro-

duced in the Rue de Richelieu on the 7th of December.
It had been written about twenty years before, though
only to be kept off the stage by the censorship as a
dangerous attack upon religious institutions.   Curiously
enough, it was privately listened to with delight by the
ministers, one of whom, the Duc de Choiseul, little
dreaming that he was to be lampooned by the author,
had it printed at his own expense.   " Europe," slily wrote
Voltaire, " is looking forward to *Mélanie.*"   Yet, predisposed as the audience may have been to applaud a
piece of the kind, it fell almost at the first representation,
its value being very slight.   The Comédie Française
brought forth several attractive novelties in rapid succession—among others the *Vieux Célibataire*, a comedy,
by Colin d'Harleville ; the *Mort d'Abel*, a tragedy in
three acts, after Gessner, by Gabriel Legouvé, born at
Paris in 1764 ; *Lovelace*, a five-act drama in verse,
by Népomucène Lemercier, and *Lucrèce*, a tragedy, by
Arnault.   Of these, there can be no doubt, Harleville's
play, which exhibits a fine-natured old bachelor in
exceptional circumstances, was by far the best, and
Molé's impersonation of the hero increased its inevitable
popularity.   *Lucrèce* was disfigured by a singular mistake,
that of representing Lucretia as enamoured of Sextus.
La Mort d'Abel, supported by St. Prix as Cain, proved
extremely successful.   Besides a weak and noisy *Caïus
Gracchus* by Chénier, Talma had two pieces from Fabre

d'Eglantine, the *Sot Orgueilleux* and *L'Amour et l'Intérét*
—in the second of which, by the way, Baptiste the
younger, a most original and amusing comedian in
overcharged parts, appeared for the first time in the
company—and a version by Ducis of *Othello* (November
26). It would have been better for the ingenious
adapter of Shaksperean drama to the French stage
if he had let this tragedy alone. His distortions of
Hamlet and *Macbeth* and *Lear* might be excused in
some measure by the impossibility of reconciling them
as they stood to the unities of time and place. *Othello*
lent itself much more readily to these laws, but the poet,
evidently thinking that he could improve upon its
matter, subjected it to equally sweeping changes.
Iago's villainy was thought too deep and patent,
especially for a Parisian audience. Pesare, as the
ancient is called here, is accordingly transformed into
something like an ordinary confidant, to all appearance
full of sincere *bonhomie*, and with his devilish purpose
hidden until after he has been seen for the last time.
"Ducis," it has been well remarked, "was extremely
afraid of arousing too much emotion among his auditors."
Another essential difference lies in Cassio being really
in love with Desdemona (renamed Hédelmone). It is
surprising that Talma—who, by the way, electrified his
audience in all the Moor's bursts of passion and pathos—
should have tolerated any deviation from the original

except in such concessions to the dignity of tragedy as the substitution of a letter for the handkerchief and of a poniard for the pillow. He knew *Othello* by heart, and the fear of arousing "too much emotion" in the spectator could hardly have commended itself to so profound a student and observer.

Many of the conditions under which the theatres existed had been largely altered by the course of public events. France was now beginning to experience the full fury of the revolutionary tempest. Not long previously there had seemed to be a break in the deepening gloom. Had not a new constitution come into force, and had not the King, going to the Comédie Française with the Queen and their children to see the *Gouvernante*, been received with an enthusiasm apparently undiminished by the memory of his attempted flight? But this ray of light disappeared when it became known that the armies of the allied sovereigns, aided by the French emigrants massed on the frontiers, were marching towards Paris for the purpose of undoing by military force the work of the Revolution. Naturally enough, the news aroused all the patriotism of the populace, together with a new burst of fury against the institutions intended to be reimposed upon them. The Extremist party, including Robespierre, Danton, Fabre d'Eglantine, Chénier, Collot d'Herbois, and Camille Desmoulins, were not slow to make use of their opportunity. Rising in

their might, they led an attack upon the Tuileries,
finally overthrew the monarchy, cast the royal family
for death into the Temple, established a National Convention in place of the Assembly, transformed the
municipality into the most democratic of communes,
massacred the royalists already in the prisons, and then
instituted the Revolutionary Tribunal, with the guillotine
as its special instrument, to overawe the enemies of the
new Republic. "It is only on waves of blood," said
Barère, "that we can safely complete our voyage."
Mob law reigned supreme; chaos returned to earth
the dark days of the Terror had come. In these
circumstances, of course, there was even less freedom
of thought and discussion than Louis Quatorze had
permitted. Like the press, the drama was brought
under the most rigid supervision. "No piece," writes
Fleury, "could be hazarded unless it had been repub-
licanized by the new censors. In place of M. Suard,
with his elaborate ruffles, we had the Chaumettes and
the Héberts." And the troubles of the players did
not end here. Every night the pits of the theatres
were occupied· by throngs composed of the dregs of the
people, all predisposed to turbulence, keenly alive to
anything inconsistent with the new ideas, and often
tormented by a very demon of capriciousness. Sometimes a player was called upon to sing; anon a singer
found himself obliged to recite.

Famed for a patriotism above suspicion, the company of the Rue de Richelieu met with greater consideration than that of the Comédie Française, whose anti-revolutionary views hourly became more notorious. " How often in those days," says Fleury, " did I bewail my lot in life ! Evening after evening we were racked by the sarcasms of the *beaux* and the vociferations of the *tapes-dur*. In rubbing on the rouge my hand trembled at the thought of what I had to undergo. The *beaux* were the precursors of the *muscadins*, with the difference that the latter were subsequently opposed to the *tapes-dur*. In the theatre these ephemeral figures of the Revolution played the part of fuglemen to the *tapes-dur*, hastening to point out any passage or gesture of what they deemed a reprehensible nature. More keen-sighted than Lynceus himself, they saw things which really had no existence. As for the *tapes-dur*, they sang or roared patriotic songs, to the annoyance of all respectable persons. They had not received their title before the 10th of August, but had long striven to deserve it. These janissaries of the Revolution had a livery— wide pantaloons, short waistcoats, and caps of fox-skin (the last falling over the shoulders of the wearer), with a large knotted stick, derisively called a 'constitution,' as an auxiliary to this peculiar costume. In tattered garments, half-naked, unshaven, and often smeared with mud, if not with blood, they presented an appearance of

almost savage wildness.   Shakspere might have looked
among them for a Caliban in masquerade.   They were
like colonies of strangers suddenly transported on to
French soil, with no knowledge of the language except
in the way of blasphemy, threats, and the hideous
Carmagnole.   Going about in bands, they were usually
accompanied by their women, who were, if possible,
more ferocious than themselves.   These harpics surrounded the scaffolds to excite the passions of the
spectators, and at the theatres would be as noisy as
they could.   If old, they were termed *tricoteuses;* if
young, the *furies de guillotine.*   When I first saw these
tapes-dur coming together, going through a rude dance,
and howling at somebody marked out for attack, they
reminded me of Rubens' legion of the damned."

But even the terrible spectre now brooding over the
country was powerless to daunt the Comédie Française.
In quiet defiance of the Commune, the players there
lost no chance of creating or fanning a reaction in
favour of order, security, and peace.   In December,
during the King's trial, they turned their attention to
a play which could not fail to promote this object,
and the nature of which, strangely enough, had
escaped the notice of the republican censors.   Laya, as
became a lover of liberty, had been a supporter of the
Revolution at the outset, but not in its recent develop-
ments.   Feeling that something should be done to avert

further anarchy and murder, he sat down to write the piece in question, the *Ami des Lois*. His boldness in this instance is described by one who knew him well as " not the mere enthusiasm of youth, an ardour influenced by obstacles, but as the result of calm reflection and deep feeling." In a series of eloquent invectives he inculcated the necessity of orderly freedom.

> Royalistes tyrants, tyrants républicains,
> Tombez devant les lois, voilà vos souverains !
> Honteux d'avoir été, plus honteux encore d'être,
> Brigands, l'ombre a passé, songez à disparaître !

Moreover, Robespierre and Marat, in common with other members of the Mountain party, were pointedly held up to ridicule, the first under the name of Nomophage. Obviously at the risk of their heads, the players produced the *Ami des Lois* on the 3rd of January, and the howls raised against it by the *tapes-durs* were drowned in volleys of applause from the royalists and moderate reformers among the audience.

The Jacobins, scarcely able to credit the evidence of their senses, at once resented the blow they had received. In the first instance they brought the piece under the notice of the Convention, which, instead of ordering it to be withdrawn, referred it to a Commission d'Instruction. But the plaintiffs were not prepared to await the decision of this body, as in the meantime their leaders and their cause would be nightly exposed to

derision.   After a hurried deliberation, they suppressed
the *Ami des Lois* on their own authority.   The decree
reached the players while a large crowd was filling the
theatre to witness the second performance.   Intense
indignation was excited by the announcement then
made from the stage.   Nothing could be heard but
fierce cries of "Tyranny!"   "*L'Ami des Lois!*"   "La
pièce."   The commandant of the National Guard
endeavoured to restore silence, but without effect.   Presently a drum was beaten outside ; soldiers surrounded
the house, and the Mayor of Paris, Chambon, entered
in some state.   Madame de Staël said of this functionary
that, like the rainbow, he never appeared until the
storm was over : on this occasion, as Fleury says, the
storm was at its height when he interposed.   He
might have spared himself the trouble.   Nobody would
listen for a moment to the reasons he was prepared
to give for the prohibition of the piece demanded.
He at length proposed to go to the General Council
of the Commune for orders.   "No, no," cried some ;
"not to that den ; go to the Convention!"   He
did so ; and Laya answered his representations in a
memoir laughing at the Commune as would-be Gentlemen of the Chamber.   The Convention, holding that
the municipality had no right to interfere with the
theatres, passed to the order of the day ; but the Jacobins,
after a hard struggle with the Conseil Executif Pro-

visoire, eventually procured the suppression of the
piece.

From this moment the doings of the Comédie
Française were closely watched by the insolent and
sanguinary faction against whom the tirades of the *Ami
des Lois* had been levelled, and who were fast rising
to supremacy in the State.   For some time, however, they saw nothing to call for direct interference,
although the players, with unabated courage, made the
most of any passage in their expurgated plays that
might promote what a Girondist called " le retour à
la paix après une agitation nécessaire."   One of the
novelties they produced was by a writer destined to
achieve no ordinary fame.   Louis Benoît Picard, born
at Paris in 1769, might have been either a doctor or
a lawyer, as he was a nephew of Gastelier, the famous
leech, and the son of a procureur.   But a friendship
with Colin d'Harleville inspired him with literary
ambition, and at the age of twenty he figured in the
private theatre of the Tuileries as part author of a
one-act comedy entitled the *Badinage Dangereux.*   " It
is dangerous for young beginners," said one, " to risk
such badinage."   He next contributed to the minor
theatres, and a three-act comedy in prose, the *Conteur,
ou les Deux Postes*, was the first in a long list of bright
and clever though rather superficial pieces which he
sent to the Théâtre Français.   By some he was hailed

as a Molière on a small scale. In addition to this genial
dramatist, the company discovered a valuable actor in
Baptiste the elder, at present in his thirty-second year.
In early life, while his parents, provincial players both,
were on a visit to Voltaire at Ferney, he acted in the
little theatre there with Lekain, who urged him to make
the stage his profession. He took the tragedian's
advice, made a name in the north of France, and in 1791
appeared in Paris at a resuscitated Théâtre du Marais.
His début at the Comédie Française was brilliantly successful. " Baptiste," we are told, " was an actor as soon
as he stepped upon the boards. No other actor could
give equal effect to Tartuffe or the Glorieux. He caught
the points of the latter character with admirable nicety
and discrimination. Pride, spleen, insolence, embarrassment and humiliation were illustrated with a skill
which few players possessed." It was not only in the
Glorieux that the players returned to the " starched
style and perfumed phrase " of the past, however counter-
revolutionary such things might appear to the Commune. Probably at the instance of Mlle. Contat,
Marivaux's *Fausses Confidences*, originally brought out
at the Théâtre Italien in 1736, was played in the
Faubourg St. Germain. " To praters about equality,"
writes Fleury, " we showed the manners of the Court ;
to fanatical atheists we preached toleration ; to assassins we made an appeal to humanity ; to the ragged

tapes-dur we appeared in all the pride of spotless linen."

In their continued opposition to the Jacobins the players were supported by a man long known to them as one of the most distinguished visitors to their green-room. Something like a halo of romance surrounds the name of François de Neufchâteau, who, contrary to nearly all precedents, deliberately sacrificed rare talents for literature to a love of the law. Eldest son of a poor schoolmaster, he came into the world at Saffais, in the Vosges, in 1750, and was educated at the expense of the bailly of Alsace. How well he profited by this kindness may be gathered from the fact that in his youth the doors of three Academies were opened to him as the author of a few gracefully-worded poems. Voltaire, acknowledging the receipt of a copy of the little volume, characteristically wrote to the author—

J'aime en vous mon héritier.

Even such flattery as this, however, did not turn him into a poet by profession. He aspired to forensic honours, and, after occupying a chair of eloquence at Toul for some months, was called to the bar in Paris. Before long his prospects were darkly overclouded. He married a player's daughter; and the Corporation of Advocates, holding that by doing so he had brought discredit upon them, erased his name from their roll. Half-stunned by the blow, he left Paris with his wife,

bought a magisterial appointment in Lorraine, and
resigned himself to a comparatively hum-drum life.
Madame de Neufchâteau, taking to heart the misfortunes she had innocently brought upon him, soon fell
into a *maladie de langueur*, which carried her off
about a year after their luckless union.   The Corporation of Advocates then restored him to his former
place amongst them, and he set out for Paris with his
father.   But the stars in their courses were still fighting
against him.   He was about to marry again, and the
intended bride, with her friends, met him at a notary's
for the arrangement of the settlements.   Pale and
agitated, his father, to whom he was deeply attached, led
him into a secluded part of the garden.   " François,"
said the old man, producing a pistol, " I have to tell
you that I shall destroy myself to-day."   In an instant
the son possessed himself of the weapon.   He glanced
keenly at his father, but saw no trace of madness in his
face.   " What can you mean ? " he asked.   His father fell
at his feet in abject distress.   " François," he at length
moaned, " I love her myself, and should be unable
to outlive your marriage to her.   I know that she loves
you, but by taking her you would kill me."   Neufchâteau, beside himself with grief, immediately rushed
out of the house.   Months elapsed without anything
being heard of him ; he was believed to be dead, the
cognoscenti deplored the loss of one who bade fair to

heighten the glory of the French name, and a collective
edition of his works was announced.   Hopelessly seared
in heart, but amused to find himself so famous, he presently reappeared in the world, chiefly as a reforming
member of the Legislative Assembly.   His sympathy with
the Revolution came to an end on the 10th of August.
In a new adaptation of *Pamela,* perhaps the best known
story in France, he incidentally repeated the lessons
conveyed in the *Ami des Lois.*   It is curious to find that
he should have fallen into such an error as that of
making the heroine of high birth, for this necessarily
impairs Bonfil's claims to our respect.   Carelessly passed
by the censor, who never dreamt that the source of
Nanine would lend itself to political purposes, this play,
with Mlle. Lange as the gentlest and most winning of
Pamelas, came forth on the 1st of August, and was
received with transports of delight.   In vain did the
players refrain from appearing to endorse the author's
sentiments; every allusion in the dialogue was seized
upon with startling avidity.

Exasperated by these demonstrations, which could
not but tend to undermine their power, the Terrorists
now resolved to rid themselves of so formidable an
enemy as the Comédie Française had proved.   In
order to prevent an explosion of public indignation,
however, they thought it expedient to allow four weeks
to pass without taking steps in the matter, however

much they may have winced at the enthusiasm evoked
by the passages in favour of order, humanity, and
tolerance.   On the 29th of August *Paméla* was suspended in due form, on the ground that it tended to
re-establish, or at least awaken regret for the abolition
of, the scattered order of the nobility.   Neufchâteau
then expurgated some of the most obnoxious speeches,
and the players had the hardihood to announce a ninth
performance of the piece for the 2nd of September.   If
appearances may be trusted, the Commune sought to
excite a tumult in the theatre on that occasion, so as to
provide themselves with an additional excuse for the
blow they intended to strike.   " In conformity with
the orders of the municipality," ran a notice at the
foot of the bills, " the public is required to enter without canes, sticks, swords, or other offensive weapons."
Such a warning, as Fleury remarks, was more like an
incitement to than a precaution against disturbance.
But the apprehensions it aroused among the players
were dissipated when the time of performance arrived
by a glance at the audience, which consisted mainly of
the respectable bourgeoisie so long familiar to them.
In due time the curtain rose, and the company went to
work in good spirits.   Apart from one or two grunts
of dissatisfaction, nothing but applause came from the
salle until, in reply to two lines in the mouth of
Andrews—

Ah! les pérsecuteurs sont les seuls condamnables,
Et les plus tolérants sont les plus raisonnables—

Lord Bonfils (Fleury) warmly said—

Tous les honnêtes gens sont d'accord là-dessus.

Here an interruption occurred. "No, no," exclaimed
a fierce-looking man in the balcony near the stage;
"this is insupportable; you are reciting passages which
have been struck out and prohibited!" "On the contrary, Monsieur," said Fleury quietly, "I am playing
my part as it has been passed by the Committee of
Public Safety. Messieurs," he continued, turning to
the audience, "are we to go on or stop?" "Go on,"
was a general cry; "turn out the disturber." "You
are favouring the Moderates," howled the latter; "the
piece is counter-revolutionary." "Out with him!"—the
injunction was too peremptory to be resisted; and the
performance was completed in peace. While preparing
for the after-play, *L'École des Bourgeois*, the company
heard that the fierce-looking person had just denounced
the Comédie Française to the Jacobins as a den of
aristocráts, where public opinion was poisoned by the
production of reactionary matter. "Save yourself,"
whispered somebody to Dazincourt. "Well, Fleury,
shall we be off?" calmly asked the hero of the *Mariage
de Figaro*. "No," was the answer; "it would be of
no use. Let us stay where we are; this is our 10th of

August." It then became known that the military were
surrounding the theatre. Nevertheless, the *Ecole des
Bourgeois* was represented in .the usual way, Fleury
being the Marquis de Moncade. Each of the players
expected to be arrested on leaving the theatre. In this
expectation they were disappointed. But arrested they
all were a few hours later; and the Maison de Molière,
after an existence of a hundred and thirteen years,
seemed to become a thing of the past.

Forthwith, amidst shrieks of execration from the
furies of the guillotine, but also carrying with them
the regrets of those who could appreciate culture and
bravery in circumstances little favourable to the display
of such qualities, the captured comedians found themselves on the way to one or another of the religious
houses which had been converted into succursals of
the overflowing gaols of the Republic,—the men to
the Madelonnettes, in the Quartier St. Martin des
Champs, and the women to St. Pélagie, in the Rue
de la Clef. Two prominent members of the company
were conspicuous by their absence from the group;
Molé had escaped, and fat Desessarts was drinking
the waters at Barèges. The news of his comrades'
incarceration preyed so deeply upon the mind of the
latter that he died shortly afterwards. Experiences
similar to those of Charles Darnay at La Force fell
to the lot of the players as the doors closed behind

them. " It was not as unknown persons," writes
Fleury, "that we arrived at our destination. We were
a sort of literary corporation, bringing with us into
exile all the past graces and accomplishments of France.
We were thought to represent in miniature all that
sweetens existence, and we were honoured as a number
of men who had shown courage at a time when, apart
from the trivial courage of dying, all courage had disappeared. We awakened a thousand pleasant recol-
lections, of which our removal to gaol seemed the
funeral procession. It was a fine sight! I still see
the long file of prisoners drawn up in a double row
and uncovered; I still hear the repeated *vivats;* I still
think myself passing with my companions between men
who had been ministers, generals, magistrates, and even
sans-culottes. There, too, we found wealthy protectors
of the arts, whom 200,000 livres of income had exposed
to the suspicion of being counter-revolutionists, and
also abbés and venerable pastors. All that remained
of the old society of France seemed to have come
together to receive its last stage representatives."

Reluctantly leaving the arrested players to await
their trial, with its almost inevitable sequel, we must
now inquire into the doings of the Théâtre de la
République since the production of *Othello.* By turns
worthy and unworthy of the traditions of the French
stage were the pieces that invite notice. In the former

category may be placed two written for Talma—a
drama by Chénier, *Fénélon*, in which the great Arch-
bishop's benignity is illustrated by means of a story
told of Fléchier, and a *Mutius Scaevola* by Luce de
Lancival, a youthful professor of rhetoric at the Collége
de Navarre, who had received a guerdon from Frederick
of Prussia in return for a Latin poem on the death of
Maria Theresa. Of a very different character were *Robert
Chef de Brigands*, a drama in three acts, and *Le Général
Dumouriez à Bruxelles*, a four-act drama in prose, by
Madame Degouges. The former (brought from the
Théâtre du Marais) abounded in coarse clap-trap, and,
further aided by the elder Baptiste's acting as the
hero, of whom he was the first representative, obtained
an enormous success. *Le Général Dumouriez*, however,
failed to please. The first performance ended amidst
derisive calls for the name of the author. Mlle.
Candeille came forward to announce it, but an erratic
old blue-stocking, showing her wrinkled face in a box,
took that office upon herself. "Citizens," she said,
"the piece is by me, Olympe Degouges. You must
admit that it has been villanously acted." At this
Mlle. Candeille showed signs of irritation. "No, no,"
cried several voices in chorus; "the piece is execrably
bad, and no acting could have saved it." Madame
Degouges was by no means in good odour with the
populace. During the trial of Louis XVI., she, in her

proverbial eccentricity, wrote to the Convention for permission to defend him. Her letter, though passed over in silence, nearly brought her to a violent death within a few hours; an angry mob surrounded her in the street, and one ruffian, snatching off the cap which covered her gray hairs, invited bids for her head. "Four-and-twenty sous for this wonderful head!" he cried; "once, twice, three times!" "My good friend," she said coolly, "I offer thirty sous for the lot, and I think I am fairly entitled to the preference." Everybody laughed; and she was allowed to go. After the performance of *Le Général Dumouriez* another horde followed her from the theatre, some facetiously asking for their money back. It would have been better for her if she had not written the piece. The Jacobins, who had already declared her to be suspected, saw in it a proof of complicity with the treason of her hero, but offered to spare her if she furnished evidence against him. In the event of her death, they added, she would leave her son destitute. "No," she replied, "I will not purchase life with a lie. I am a woman; I fear death; I dread the punishment you may award me. But I have no confession to make, and the love I have for my son will give me strength in my extremity. To die from a sense of duty is to prolong my maternity beyond the tomb."

It is not a pleasant task to describe the work of the

actors in the Rue de Richelieu after the suppression of
the Comédie Française. Far from emulating the artistic
enthusiasm and refinement of their imprisoned rivals,
they produced pieces in which the worst passions and
tastes of the mob were deliberately appealed to. Of
this, perhaps, the most vivid illustration is to be found
in the *Dernier Jugement des Rois*, a drama in three acts,
by Sylvain Maréchal. It exhibits the sovereigns of
Europe, with the Pope (Dugazon), on a desert island,
whither they have been transported by their incensed
peoples, and where, shorn of any claim to respect, they
are swallowed up by an earthquake.   Louis XVI. is not
among the group, for to him the French had " already
done justice." It is humiliating to think that such a
spectacle should have been received with shouts of
delight, as it actually was.   Picard raised the standard
of pure comedy in the *Moitié du Chemin*, but failed to
win anything like the applause bestowed upon four
plays akin in spirit to Maréchal's—the *Modéré*, *Arétaphile*,
Les Contres-Révolutionnaires Jugés par Eux-mémes, and
L'Expulsion des Tarquins, ou la Royauté Abolie, by Leblanc—all of which were plentifully besprinkled with
horrors. For *Arétaphile* the public were indebted to
General Ronsin, the associate of Danton, Hébert, and
Clootz.   In the midst of these atrocities, however, the
lettered playgoer saw reason for hope.   Mlle. Joly,
Dupont, Vanhove, and Madame Petit were released

from durance on the condition that they played at
the Théâtre de la République, which they did.   Mlle.
Devienne also recovered her liberty, but obtained permission to accompany Molé, who had made his peace
with the authorities, to the Théâtre de Montausier.   It
is worthy of note that a tragedy brought out here, *Les
Catilinas Modernes*, by Feru the younger, with the
brilliant comedian just named representing Marat, was
long the rage of the town, chiefly because it abounded
in hideous charges against the fallen Girondists.   But
the additions made to the company in the Rue de
Richelieu did not effect a change in the character of
the entertainments there.   Comedy was temporarily out
of fashion, and with the exception of a tragedy by
Legouvé, *Epicharsis et Néron*, no serious piece met with
unqualified favour unless it had features akin to those
of the *Dernier Jugement des Rois*.

For this revolting degradation of the stage, it must be
added, Talma's company were not primarily to blame.
Bred as they had been in the highest and purest
school of art, even the revolutionists among them
must have experienced an acute though veiled sense
of shame on appearing in such productions.   But they
were not free to consult their real inclinations in the
matter.   In one way they had ceased to be their own
masters.   They were in the toils of the serpent which
they had helped to create.   In common with all others,

their theatre was kept under the strictest supervision
by the government, and to incur the suspicion of
moderatism, as they would have done by rejecting or
modifying a piece of the class I have described, was
generally equivalent to being sent to the scaffold.   For
the triumphant Jacobins allowed no consideration of
humanity or former zeal in their cause to interfere
with the work of consolidating their power, of obliter-
ating all traces of the past, and of realizing the glowing
ideals that filled their minds.   " In the interests of
virtue," they said, " Terror is irrevocably the order of
the day."   And behind them, vengeful and resolute,
stood the multitudinous dregs of the populace, of whom
the audiences at the theatres were now for the most
part composed, and who, we may be sure, would have
made things decidedly unpleasant for any actor of
doubtful patriotism.   For these reasons, therefore, we
need not deem Talma and his associates responsible
for the abominations which flooded the stage under
their auspices.   Monvel might carry his unbelief to
the point of defying the Deity in public, but even with
him the artist was stronger than the blasphemer.

Of the subjection in which the theatre was held we
have some striking proofs.   No new play, it has been
seen, could be hazarded until it had been revised by
the Jacobin censors.   Many of the masterpieces of the
drama were now brought under the same process.   Each

had to receive a certificate of "civism" before it could
be represented. Republican sentiments were inserted
in *Athalie;* the catastrophe of the *Mort de César* underwent an alteration ; two lines in *Mahomet*—

> Exterminez, grands dieux, de la terre où nous sommes
> Quiconque avec plaisir répand le sang des hommes,—

were carefully struck out. Nobles, too, could not be
allowed to sully the stage with their presence. They
became "citizens," however much the measure and
rhyme of a line might suffer by the transformation.
If a game of chess had to be played, as in the *Bourru
Bienfaisant,* "check to the tyrant" was substituted
for "check to the king." Fleury says that the literati
of the Commune would have wished to decorate
Mahomet with the tri-coloured cockade. In such
enterprises as this, indeed, they were often successful,
a representative of Phèdre appearing in the most
approved Republican costume. One incident has a
special significance. Chénier, whose tragedies had
materially aided the Revolution, had a *Timoléon* on the
point of production. Several friends of Robespierre,
remembering that the *dramatis personae* would include
an usurper and tyrant, attended the last rehearsal.
"Infamous!" exclaimed one of the party, Julien de
Toulouse, in the middle of a scene; "it is a sign of
revolt. But that was only to be expected; Chénier
has always been a counter-revolutionist at heart." He

then hurried away to denounce the piece; and the dramatist, dreading the worst, soon afterwards burnt the manuscript in the presence of the Decemvirs themselves.

It may be thought surprising that just now any theatres should have been open at all. Society was in a state of apparently hopeless disintegration, in the throes of the most fearful convulsion yet experienced. Men and women of every grade daily thrown into prison, put through a mockery of trial before the Revolutionary Tribunal, and hurried under the knife of the guillotine; religious services prohibited, churches despoiled of their riches, harlots installed on the altars as Goddesses of Reason, prelates compelled to revile their faith, atheism preached from pulpits, and the ashes of illustrious dead scattered to the winds; statues pulled down, monumental paintings shot at by the soldiery, and venerable châteaux razed to the ground; commerce almost at a standstill, innumerable houses empty, poverty hourly increasing, food stores besieged, and a swarm of mendicants let loose by an unscrupulous confiscation of the revenues of charities; persons liable to be regarded as reactionaries venturing forth only at night, effecting their escape from the city in various disguises, or preferring death by their own hands to a continuation of painful suspense; the so-called leaders of the democracy panting to fly at each other's throats, unalterable in their murderous fanaticism, and, mindful of the fate of Marat, going about armed to the teeth against possible Charlotte Cordays; the streets virtually in the hands of the ragged sans-culottes, who, as though to show that the old ferocity of the French character had not disappeared under the influence of a refined civilization, used to hang respectable looking citizens from *la lanterne*, outrage defenceless women with impunity, and dance round the scaffold as heads fell upon it;—these were a few of the most salient features of the picture presented by Paris during the Terror. "Every heart," says the Republican writer, "was frozen by fear; a general torpor overspread the country;" intelligence and manliness were alike silenced. How dangerous it was to stir abroad two incidents will clearly show. Michot, mistaken by a crowd in the Place de Grève for some obnoxious person, was incontinently seized, gagged, and hurried to the nearest lamp-post to be executed. By the feeble light which then fell upon the group he was at length recognized. "Why," exclaimed one, "this is the Polichinelle of the République!" Polichinelle, as belonging to the theatre in the Rue de Richelieu, was believed to be a sound patriot, and was accordingly borne home with enthusiasm on the shoulders of those who had intended to hang him Arnault, the author of *Marius à Mitnurnes*, met with a precisely similar experience. But neither anarchy nor

carnage nor distress seemed able to damp the proverbial ardour of the French for dramatic entertainments.
Paris boasted of no fewer than twelve playhouses—the
Théâtre de la République, the Opéra, the Opéra Comique,
the Théâtre Feydeau, the Théâtre de l'Égalité, the
Théâtre de la Montagne, the Théâtre des Sans-Culottes,
the Théâtre Lyrique des Amis de la Patrie, the Théâtre
du Vaudeville, the Théâtre de la Cité, the Théâtre du
Lycée des Arts, and the Amphithéâtre d'Astley; and
never were they so well attended as at the time of
those atrocities which sent a thrill of horror and dismay
and indignation throughout the reading world.

Bearing in mind the merciless decision with which
the government struck down its opponents, the most
sanguine friend of the players still in custody could not
have hoped that they would be saved from the scaffold.
After passing nine months in the Madelonnettes, it is
true, they were transferred to a pleasanter prison, the
convent that had been of Pipcus, at the extremity of the
turbulent Faubourg St. Antoine. But this appears to
have been only an amiable device for arming death with
a fresh sting. Collot d'Herbois, now an important part
of the executive, had no intention to let them escape.
" Herewith," he wrote to the Public Prosecutor, Fouquier-Tinville, " the Committee of Public Salvation sends
you, citizen, the documents relating to the *ci-devant*
actors of the Comédie Française. Like all patriots, you

know how counter-revolutionary their conduct has been. You will bring them before the Tribunal on the 13th Messidor." As in all other cases, the trial so ordered was to be nothing but a pretence. In those palmy days of freedom, we learn, the brief against an accused person was marked with a letter in red ink for the guidance of the learned judge, who had simply to give effect in legal form to the wishes of the authorities. " G " stood for the guillotine, " D " for deportation, " R " for a reprieve. The first was affixed to the names of six players—Louise Contat, Dazincourt, Raucourt, Fleury, Lange, and Emilie Contat. "And in all these cases there is to be no appeal," added the gentle Collot. St. Fal and the others were to be banished only; they had shown less fervour than their doomed companions against the Jacobins, and it was thought desirable to limit the number of victims whose fate could not fail to enlist unusual sympathy. " In players," it has been remarked, " the mass of the French people have a special interest; the sight of them off the stage awakens a thousand delightful memories." Hurrying up from the country, Madame Sainville, *née* Fleury, appealed in behalf of her brother to Danton, Robespierre, and Collot, the last of whom, it may be remembered, owed her a heavy debt of gratitude. From each she received a bitter rebuff. " I do not deny," said Collot, "that you interceded for me once. But times have changed. You

intercede with me for another. I can give you no hope ;
Fleury is an aristocrat, and must suffer with the others."

In conformity with the usual practice, the papers
against the condemned players were sent by Fouquier-
Tinville to the Bureau des Pièces Accusatives, at the
dismantled Tuileries. Now, all documents of this kind
had to pass through the hands of a royalist in disguise,
Charles de Labussière, who had accepted a clerkship
in the department as a means of ensuring his safety,
and who, at the imminent risk of his life, took every
favourable opportunity of destroying them. " In the
first instance," he said long afterwards, " I caused all
fathers and mothers to be overlooked in this way,
without reference to the justice or injustice of the
charges against them. Having abstracted the documents, I locked them carefully in a strong oaken drawer.
But it was necessary that the executioner should do
something for his wages unless he wished to be discovered. I therefore left to their fate the captives in
whom I could not venture to interest myself. No
suspicion was aroused, and I came to be regarded as
a most zealous servant of the Republic. How happy I
felt in being able to save a few unfortunate beings from
certain death ! My joy, however, was soon damped
by embarrassment. What should I do with these
voluminous papers ? If I took them away I might be
searched. It was dangerous to burn them; summer

had come, and a blaze of fire would have attracted notice. I racked my brain on the subject, but for some time to no purpose. Suffering from a horrible headache, I began to bathe my temples from a pail of water which had been placed in the apartment to cool our wine at *déjeuner*. Excellent idea! Might I not destroy the papers, or at least diminish their bulk, by soaking them in the water? No sooner thought of than done; the papers became balls of soft paste, and in this form found their way into my pockets. Carrier had had his *noyades* for the work of death; I had my *noyades* for the work of preserving life. I then repaired to the Bains Vigier, subdivided the balls into smaller ones, threw them into the water, and anxiously watched their progress as they floated along the bank of the Place de la Révolution." In this way, it is said, the humane and intrepid official kept from the scaffold as many as eight hundred persons, one of whom was no less a person than Joséphine de Beauharnais.

Labussière's royalist sympathies naturally prompted him to include the players among his protégés. On the 9th Messidor he collected the accusatory papers from the portfolio, and, noiselessly entering his office the same night in the dark, had the audacity to carry them off as they were. Morning not having come, he resolved to walk about until the hour when the Bains Vigier opened. In the Boulevard des Italiens, half worn out by anxiety, he sat down in a reverie on the steps of a café. Before long he was aroused by a heavy slap on the shoulder, and on looking up was startled to find himself confronted by a fierce member of a revolutionary committee. "What are you doing here?" demanded the latter, by name Aillaume. "Taking a walk," was the reply. "Is walking sitting down?" "After a walk one may sit down from fatigue." "But good citizens are not usually abroad at this hour?" "Then we are neither of us good citizens; the hour is not less extraordinary for you than for me." "My name is Aillaume." "I wish to know your name as little as to tell you mine." "Perhaps, then, you may be induced to tell it to somebody else." A patrol coming up, Labussière was conveyed to the nearest lock-up. The critical nature of his position did not affect his presence of mind. He absolutely refused to say who he was. "Why what is this?" cried Pierre, a clerk to the Committee of Public Safety, entering precipitately; "is it a joke?" "On the contrary," replied Labussière, "I am really under arrest." "You under arrest? Nothing ever so droll. My good fellow," said the clerk to Aillaume, "be careful, or you will get yourself into trouble." "Trouble for doing my duty?" cried the revolutionist; "the fellow must be an accomplice. Seize him; he is a suspect." "Do you see this?" said Pierre, discovering under his coat the

badge which all servants of the Committee of Public
Safety wore round their necks. Aillaume began to feel
uncomfortable; he doffed his red cap, looked apprehensively at Labussière, and muttered some words of
apology. "I suppose," he said, "that your friend can
also show a medal?" Labussière could not do that
at the moment, but he boldly drew the terrible papers
from his pocket, and, contriving to keep the super-
scriptions downward, allowed him to see that they bore
official seals and signatures. "Citizen," he added to
Aillaume, "have no fear of me; I have simply done
this to test your patriotism, and shall report your zeal
to the Committee." He was then allowed to go, and
soon afterwards the papers were wholly destroyed at
the baths.

Messidor 13, the day set apart for the trial of the
players, at length arrived. Paris evinced more than
ordinary interest in the event; the quays and bridges
near the Tribunal were alive with spectators, and a
swarm of Vengeances took possession of the court
when the doors opened. Probably this interest, in
most cases hard and vindictive, was deepened by a
whisper that the Government intended to import a
"sort of dramatic effect" into the proceedings. Intense,
therefore, was the disappointment caused at the fifty-
ninth minute by an announcement that the cases would
be put off *sine die,* in consequence of a mysterious

disappearance of the evidence against the accused. How long was this oft-recurring interference with the course of "justice" to continue? Fouquier-Tinville, who had doubtless prepared an elaborate oration for the occasion, could scarcely contain himself. "Citizens," he wrote to the superintendents of the General Police, "the representation made a few days ago to the Convention proves only too true. Le Bureau des Détenus is filled by royalists and counter-revolutionists, who do their best to obstruct the progress of public business. For ten months there has been the utmost disorder as to the documents of the Committee. Of every thirty cases marked out for trial, only ten, or at best fifteen, are brought forward. Everybody has been anticipating the trial of the Comédiens Français. As yet I have received nothing as to this business, and I have to await instructions about it. I can do nothing in the absence of papers giving me the names of the prisoners, the places in which they have been confined, etcetera." And arrangements for the production of such papers were at once made, the Public Prosecutor, who was not disposed to let the players escape, keeping in the meantime a sharp watch upon the workers in the Bureau des Pièces Accusatives.

Before the new brief could be prepared, however, another order of things arose in the State. In fulfilment of a prophecy by Vergniaud, the Revolution, like

Saturn, was continuing to devour its own progeny. Fierce dissensions broke out among the Jacobins soon after they had trampled the Girondists under foot; Danton fell a victim to a few lingering traces of kindness in his nature, and the pitiless Robespierre, in the midst of an attempt to restore the worship of the Deity, was himself sent to the scaffold. In an instant, as though by magic, the funeral pall which had so long hung over the country was gone. Humanity and reason resumed their sway; the distinctive figures of the Terror disappeared like shadows; the era of violence and proscription came to an end. "The dawn of the Arctic summer day after the Arctic winter night; the great unsealing of the waters; the awakening of animal and vegetable life; the sudden softening of the air, the sudden blooming of the flowers, the sudden bursting of whole forests into verdure, is but a feeble type," says Macaulay, "of that happiest and most genial of revolutions, the Revolution of the 9th Thermidor." Some of the Jacobins made despairing attempts to prevent the extermination of the faction, but the Convention proved equal to any emergency. Moral laws again came into force, and were not easily to be set aside. Of the magnitude of this change a glance at the prisons will afford the best proof. About two hundred thousand persons lying there in fear of death recovered their liberty, including, of course, the six players of whom

Collot d'Herbois had so fervently desired to rid the earth.

No such death-roll as that of the Revolution had darkened the pages of history. It amounted to a hundred thousand names. It represented all classes of society, from the erstwhile King and Queen, who met their fate with a fortitude worthy of their birth, down to persons like the little sempstress in *A Tale of Two Cities*. Genius and virtue, beauty and grace, dignity and courage, poverty and wealth, infancy and old age, had alike been sent to the guillotine. But few of the victims specially concern us here. Prominent among them was Danton's impetuous secretary and coadjutor, Fabre d'Eglantine. Incurring the relentless enmity of Robespierre, he was charged with malversation, taken before the Revolutionary Tribunal, and instantly sent to his last account. Dramatic literature could ill-afford to lose him. His continuation of the *Misanthrope*, though unworthy of being named in the same breath as its forerunner, is really an admirable picture of Alceste in after life. If the audience at the first representation came to hiss the author for his presumption, as is alleged, they were soon applauding the piece in spite of themselves. In his last hours, it seems, he was in a cell adjoining that of Camille Desmoulins. "Through a chink in the wall," writes the latter to his Lucile, " I heard the voice of a man in pain. Presently I ventured to speak to him. He asked my name; I gave it. 'O mon Dieu!' he cried. Could he be Fabre d'Eglantine? 'Oui, je suis Fabre,' he replied." Other dramatic writers swallowed up in the vortex were Ronsin and Durozoi, editor of the royalist *Gazette de Paris.* The latter was beheaded by torchlight in the Place du Carrousel. "I rejoice," he said, "in dying on the day of St. Louis, for my religion and my King." At the scaffold he received a letter from a girl to whom he was betrothed. "My soul," she wrote, "is torn; but you know what I have promised you." "Ah!" he murmured, "her sufferings are greater than mine." His head fell; and a few hours later, either from grief or by her own hand, she joined him in the grave.

Few signs of the revulsion of feeling that followed the ending of the Terror are so clear as those supplied by the moods of playgoers as a body. After a much-needed change of scene, the members of the Comédie Française reappeared at their theatre in the Faubourg St. Germain, now called the Théâtre de l'Egalité, on the 29th Thermidor. It was not only in name that the house had been altered. Hatred of social distinctions showed itself in the abolition of the boxes; the decorations and the curtain itself were ornamented with the tricolor in narrow perpendicular lines, and columns surmounted by busts of political martyrs, such as Marat,

graced the sides of the *salle*. *La Métromanie* and the
Fausses Confidences composed the programme. Republican as France remained, the players who had so
pointedly revealed their sympathies with the old *régime*
were received with the utmost warmth by an ample
audience, several lines in the first piece being applied
to them in a flattering sense. Talma, forgetting the
past, came over to congratulate his former comrades,
" toujours ses maîtres," upon their triumph. " Mon
ami," said Louise Contat bitterly, " there would have
been a larger gathering to see us guillotined." Before
long, however, she fell upon his neck in a sort of
ecstasy, as it leaked out that under the sway of Robespierre he had generously expended a large sum to
obtain possession of a document — to wit, a paper
relating to Charlotte Corday — which might have
brought his old enemy Fleury to the scaffold in a few
hours. If it were possible, the enthusiasm of the
audience went to a higher pitch a few nights afterwards,
when Préville came back to the stage for the last time.
His resurrection must have aroused unusual interest.
During the Terror he had lost his reason ; he believed
himself to be in a dungeon ; and it was only by putting
him through a pretended trial in the great hall of
Bresces, with an honourable acquittal to follow, that
the lost balance could be restored. In direct contrast
to the cordiality shown to the aged player and his

companions was the mood of the audience at the Théâtre
de la République.   Murmurs of indignation greeted
nearly all the company there.   Talma, who had been
an object of suspicion to the Jacobins, at length came
forward.   " Citizens," he said, " I have always been,
and am still, a lover of liberty.   But I have always
detested crime ; the reign of Terror has cost me many
tears ; all my friends have perished on the scaffold."
Unless I am mistaken, this energetic little speech, so
well adapted to its purpose, was uttered on the 11th of
September, when Chénier's *Timoléon*, rewritten as soon
as Robespierre fell, was brought out with Talma as the
principal character.

In the winter, amidst the returning sunshine of
freedom tempered with law, the players of the Théâtre
de l'Egalité found it necessary to shift their quarters.
Continued goodwill on the part of the public did not
counterbalance a disadvantage under which they lay.
By a strange freak of fashion, the Faubourg St. Germain,
so long the home in Paris of rank and opulence, had
been abandoned in favour of more central spots.   " Most
of its stately houses," writes a contemporary, " are
tenantless ; grass is flourishing in its comparatively
empty streets."   Moreover, as a result of the existing
free trade in theatrical matters, there were several playhouses within a narrow radius of the Palais Royal, and lazy
residents on that side of the river often preferred them

to one situated near the remote Luxembourg. Now, among these more favoured places of amusement was the Théâtre Feydeau, erected about five years previously for a company of operatic farceurs who had come to Paris from Italy early in 1789 to occupy the famous *salle* at the Tuileries, but who soon had to seek refuge at the Foire Saint Germain. Its present manager was Sageret, one of the most grasping, speculative, and enterprising of men, with a profound contempt for art unless it spelt fortune. Mindful of the injury done to the Egalité company by the desertion of the Faubourg St. Germain, he invited them to appear under his auspices alternately with the Italians, especially as the attractiveness of the latter had appreciably waned. In the end, towards the end of January, the remnant of the old Comédie Française went over to his theatre, which subsequently became known as the Théâtre de la Réaction.

For some time the records of the two companies are of historical rather than literary interest. Echoes of the Revolution were frequently to be heard in each house. Something like a riot occurred at the Théâtre de la République on a first night. In the afterpiece, Lesage's *Crispin*, an actor named Fusil, having been a member of the Revolutionary Commission, was hooted from the stage. Carried away by reactionary fervour, the audience next called upon Dugazon, who remained

an extremist, to sing the "Réveil du Peuple." In reply
he angrily flung his wig at the foremost pittites. Such
insolence could not be endured ; the stage was stormed
by a few ardent spirits, and the player found dis-
cretion the better part of valour. It is pleasant to pass
from this scene to the production of a tragedy by
Ducis, *Abufar,* in which, as Talma, the representative
of the hero, remarks, the transports of a supposed in-
cestuous love "are painted in traits of fire." A comedy
at the Théâtre Feydeau, *Le Tolérant,* introduced a new
dramatist, Demoustier, who combined the utmost
simplicity of manner with an equally conspicuous affectation in his writings. While this piece enforced a
wholesome political moral, the memory of Robespierre
was indirectly assailed in a *Pausanias* by Trouvé, afterwards famous in diplomacy. Lemercier, Arnault, and
Legouvé worked with the best will for the Théâtre de
la République, the first going out of his way so far as
to reproduce Molière's immortal hypocrite as a Jacobin
(*Le Tartuffe Révolutionnaire*). For a sign of the revulsion
of public feeling which emboldened him to undertake
such a task we may note the effect of a revival at the
Théâtre Feydeau of Voltaire's *Mort de César.* Brutus
and his associates awakened much less sympathy
than their victim ; they were accepted as prototypes
of the Terrorists, and their republican fervour was
received with a coldness decidedly favourable to the

military despotism so soon to be inflicted upon the country.

Curiously enough, a schism was caused among the company of the Théâtre Feydeau by a sentiment which might have been expected to draw them more closely together. They had begun to yearn for a re-establishment of the Comédie Francaise on something like its former basis, with their rivals at the Palais Royal among its more prominent members. Moreover, had they not exposed themselves to a sort of degradation in becoming the servants of the speculative Sageret? Mlle. Raucourt, in whose mind this movement seems to have originated, at length abandoned the theatre in the Rue Feydeau for one in the Rue de Louvois, intending to make it the " central point " of the projected reunion. Thither she was followed by Larive, St. Fal, Mlle. Joly, St. Prix, Mlle. Mézerai, Dupont, Naudet, and one or two others; but at least five of the old band—Molé, Mlle. Contat, Fleury, Dazincourt, and Mlle. Lange,—declined to come under the banner which she unfurled. Probably they thought that the time for such an experiment had not yet come. Raucourt sent them an earnest invitation in writing to join her. The arts and humanity, she said, cried out against the subjection under which they had been led to place themselves. It was all in vain; and towards the end of December, after securing desirable recruits in Mlle.

Simon, of the Palais Royal, and Picard, who had as marked a talent for acting as for play-writing, the new company successfully opened their campaign with *Iphigénie*. It is significant of the earnestness with which Raucourt pursued the idea of a revived Comédie Française that she set apart *loges* in her theatre for Talma, Fleury, Dazincourt, and Dugazon.

In one respect, it is clear, the three companies into which the flower of French histrionic talent was now divided found themselves at a marked disadvantage as time passed on. Never had the volatility of the national character been more strongly illustrated than it was in the inevitable reaction against the ferocity of the Revolution. The stern lessons to be learnt from that convulsion were overlooked. In all quarters a demand for frivolous amusement was to be heard. "Eat, drink, and be merry, for to-morrow we may die," appeared to be the prevailing motto. Foppery of the most elaborate kind was again in fashion, and the *incroyables*, as those who descended to it were generically known, became typical figures of the age. Simultaneously, too, there grew up an extreme daintiness of thought, sentiment, and language. Energy and precision in either were deemed more or less repellant. Letters which seemed to have a harsh sound, such as R and G, were temporarily excluded from the alphabet, "paole d'honneu" taking the place of "parole d'honneur" in the utterances and writings of persons with pretensions to refinement. How the contemporary drama was affected by all these changes I need hardly point out. It lost weight, fibre, and colour. Play-writers generally showed a tendency to pass over the great story of human nature in favour of lighter themes, while vigour of expression was often sacrificed to mere euphony and grace. In regard to old plays, Marivaux and Dorat proved more attractive than Corneille, Molière, and Racine, deep as was the admiration which Frenchmen had been taught from infancy to regard that illustrious trio. Even in acting a modification on the wrong side could be observed; Talma kept his bursts of passion within narrower bounds, Contat "softened down her rich and exuberant humour into a tone of elegant *finesse*," and Raucourt found it convenient to intensify a little affectation in her style. One or two writers of genius might have saved the drama from the enervating influences just mentioned, but genius was the quality to which the poets known at the theatres could lay the least claim. In striking contrast to the effect it had in England and elsewhere, the intellectual agitation aroused by the Revolution seemed to benumb rather than quicken the creative faculty in Paris. If the players had not possessed a large and varied repertory they would have been compelled to close their doors.

It would be unprofitable to dwell at length upon the

new pieces prepared in such circumstances as these. In the *Lovelace Français*, a five-act drama, we have the possibly apocryphal story of the seduction by the Duc de Richelieu of his upholsterer's wife, Madame Michelin, whom he leaves to die of a broken heart. Madame Petit represented this sort of Jane Shore with a peculiar depth of sensibility. Though ascribed in part to Monvel, the play seems to have been wholly the work of an erratic member of the company, Alexandre Duval, born at Rennes in 1767. He had been many things by turn but nothing long—soldier, sailor, engineer, architect, secretary to the States of Brittany, teacher at the college in his native town, and a sketcher in Paris of deputies' heads at 6 francs each. In 1790 he began to act at a minor theatre, but left it to fight under Dumouriez. Returning to the capital, he joined the company in the Faubourg St. Germain, shared their vicissitudes during the Terror, and was now settling down at the Palais Royal as a player and dramatist. In the latter capacity he generally succeeded in combining interest of plot with brightness of treatment, while a robust love of virtue and independence found expression in nearly all he wrote. Mlle. Raucourt was fortunate in accepting a tragedy by Legouvé, *Laurence*, the hero whereof was the youth who became enamoured of Ninon de Lenclos without knowing that he was her son. No reasonable expectation as to Lemercier could

have been disappointed by *Agamemnon*, which he sent to
the Palais Royal; it is pervaded throughout by a lofty
spirit, and the acting of Talma and Madame Petit, the
latter as a very impressive Cassandre, completed the
young author's triumph. Beaumarchais, who had been
driven by the Revolution to seek refuge abroad, and
who, after a singular series of incidents, including a
temporary imprisonment in the King's Bench of
London, had lately obtained leave to return to Paris,
there to find his once palatial home wrecked as that
of an aristocrat, was not dead to dramatic ambition. In
1792 he had produced at one of the minor theatres
a piece in his earlier manner, the *Mère Coupable*. It
now reappeared in a slightly improved form, but was
of too revolting and gloomy a nature to please the great
mass of playgoers. His reason for reverting to the
drame may have been a belief, unfortunately well-
founded that his old *verve* had passed away. As to
other pieces, I need direct attention only to *Falkland*,
an adaptation by Laya of *Caleb Williams*, and *Blanche et
Monteassin*, a tragedy on a Venetian subject, by Arnault.

Each of the companies had to bear a serious loss
while they were suffering from the comparative dearth
of attractive novelty. Mlle. Desgarcins, that ideal
Iphigénie and Monime, met with what may be described
as a tragic fate. Devoured by an unreciprocated
passion, she impulsively attempted to destroy herself with

a dagger, but was saved by the arrival of a comrade. Her friends, after restoring her to a better frame of mind, sent her to a country house near Paris for a rest. One night she found herself face to face with burglars; her reason gave way under the shock, and before long she died in a madhouse. Her delicate sensibility on the stage was sorely missed by the frequenters of the Palais Royal. In the next place, Mlle. Lange, though in the heyday of her success as a soubrette, retired in consequence of marrying one Simon, son of a wealthy coachbuilder at Brussels. With this marriage a curious anecdote is connected. Simon's father, puritanical enough in his ideas to be horrified at the prospect of having an actress for his daughter-in-law, came to Paris for the purpose of remonstrating with Lange on the subject. Mlle. Candeille was present at the interview; and her charms made so deep an impression upon the coachbuilder, a widower, that two weddings were solemnized instead of one. Lastly, the town had to deplore the death, all too premature, of another delightful soubrette, Marie Elizabeth Joly, whose health had been permanently impaired by the imprisonment of 1793-4. For her, a devoted wife and mother, the probability of being guillotined must have had peculiar terrors. As she had wished, her remains were buried on a solitary hill near Falaise, where she had passed a portion of her girlhood.

Mingled with the regret excited by the disappearance of these three Graces was a fear that before long
there would be no players at all.   Like the despotisms
it succeeded, the Directory kept a close watch upon the
theatres, and was ready to place arbitrary power above
justice and reason on the slightest provocation.   One or
another of the three principal companies was frequently
forbidden to act, the cause in one case being that
the attendants had acquired the habit of addressing
playgoers as "Monsieur" or "Madame" instead of
"Citizen" or "Citizeness."   Presently the house in
the Rue de Louvois was closed for good, because the
public, with whom the Minister of Justice, Merlin, was
in bad odour, had satirically applauded a line in the
Trois Frères Rivaux—"M. Merlin, you are a rascal."
However, by means unexplained, Raucourt and her
associates, with the versatile Picard, obtained possession
of the former seat of the Comédie Française in the
Faubourg St. Germain, henceforward to be known as
the Odéon.   Not long afterwards the theatre of the
Palais Royal shared the fate of that in the Rue de
Louvois, mainly on account of the too-obtrusive sympathy of its inmates with the Revolution in its more
sombre aspect.   Sageret's energy and love of speculation
were as conspicuous as ever.   He induced the homeless
players to join their brethren in the Rue Feydeau,
reopened the theatre in the Palais Royal, relieved

Raucourt of the management of the Odéon, and then
caused the men and women under his command to
appear at one or another of the houses as in his wisdom
he thought fit.   But this enterprise proved less and less
successful ; and at length, reduced to absolute bankruptcy, the too-ambitious director disappeared.   Some
of the players reassembled at the Odéon, where, among
other things, they produced an adaptation by Madame
Molé of Kotzebue's chief play under the title of *Misanthropie et Repentir.*   In March their theatre was burnt
to the ground ; and Paris, the most playgoing city
in the world, found itself without a temple for the
legitimate drama.

In this hour of misfortune it was asked whether the
idea of restoring the Comédie Française might not be
converted into reality, especially as the Minister of
the Interior, François de Neufchâteau, would give it his
best support.   Surely the animosities created among
the players by the Revolution had been softened by
time and reason and experience ?   Alive to their own
interests, the dramatic authors sent to the government
a petition against the re-establishment of one privileged
theatre, forcibly contending that emulation was necessary to the progress of every art.   If a second Comédie
were formed they would be satisfied.   Beaumarchais
lent them the aid of his name, but was not to have the
chance of doing more.   His eventful and varied career,

which at some points belongs to the history of his country, came to its end a few weeks later,—to be precise, on the 11th of May. Dazincourt espoused the cause of reunion, and, believing that it might be effected with a fair prospect of concord, invited the members of the late companies to dine together under his presidency. Molé, Mlle. Contat, Talma, Mlle. Raucourt, Fleury, Madame Petit, Michot, Mlle. Simon, St. Fal, St. Prix, Mlle. Devienne, Larive, Dugazon, Grandménil—in fine, every player known to fame was present. " How pleasant it was," writes Fleury, " to see that combination of talent and hope, that absorption of conflicting opinions and feelings in a love of art !" Michot presently rose to speak. It was simply, he said, to narrate a little apologue. Some persons once affected to be embarrassed by the simple question how many six and six made. "Twelve," said one to whom they referred. Another, after mature reflection, said " fourteen." " I will be impartial," said a third ; " six and six make thirteen." " Here," continued the comedian, " you have the history of our past opinions, our friendships and antipathies. Six and six make twelve, whatever may be said to the contrary. Let us come together in the best of harmony. I repeat that six and six make twelve, and let all who agree with me hold up their hands." Nearly every hand, writes Fleury, " was raised ; a prolonged *vivat* greeted Michot ; joy and concord

beamed on every countenance.   Talma was profoundly
moved; his magnificent eyes seemed to be looking
into the future; his voice escaped him in a burst of
enthusiasm :—

> Quelle Jérusalem nouvelle
> Sort du fond du désert, brillante de clartés,
> Et porte sur son front une marque immortelle ?
> Peuples de la terre, chantez !
> Jérusalem renait, plus charmante et plus belle !

For my part I was beside myself with delight.   I ran
to a bust of Molière, and, calling upon the company to
vow allegiance to him, embraced it devoutly.   Everybody did the same; the last traces of the old bitterness
were drowned in a common feeling] of reverence.   We
joined hands round the sacred image ; a long compact
of amity was concluded between us ; the Comédie
Française again came into existence !"

My task draws to an end.   The reunited players
instantly obtained possession of the theatre at the
Palais Royal, where they appeared on the 30th of May
in the *Cid* and the *Ecole des Maris*.   Paris felt more
like itself after the event ; and the reorganized Comédie,
further strengthened by the favour of Napoleon, who
in the same year became First Consul, took as high a
place among the institutions of the country as it had
occupied at any time since its formation (*l*).

NOTES.

A, page 13.—*Refléxions sur Lekain et l'Art Théâtral,* by François Joseph Talma.

B, page 33.—*Mémoires de Préville.*

C, page 45.—*Mémoires de Clairon.*

D, page 77.—*Mémoires de Molé.*

E, page 115.—*Les Souvenirs et les Regrets du Vieil Amateur Dramatique; ou, Lettres d'un Oncle à son Neveu sur l'ancien Théâtre Français:* Paris, 1861. An excellent collection of written portraits, with engravings after original miniatures.

F, page 146.—*Beaumarchais et son Temps,* by Louis de Loménie, edition of 1873.

G, page 154.—*Béverley* was the last important work of the adapter, who died in 1781. Bernard Saurin was a son of Joseph Saurin, so prominent a figure in the second affair of the couplets, and in all his tragedies had shown himself to be a pupil of the philosophical school. His *Spartacus* ought not to be forgotten.

H, page 172.—Diderot also wrote two unrepresented bagatelles, *La Pièce et le Prologue* and *Est-il Bon? est-il Méchant?* Though brighter than the *Père de Famille* and the *Fils Naturel,* they are of less importance in literary history than those plays, in which the earliest examples of the *drame* are to be found. Nowadays, however, he is remembered in theatrical circles chiefly as the author of the *Paradoxe sur le Comédien,* so exactly reproduced in English by Mr. Walter Pollock.

I, page 197.—*Mémoires de Fleury: publiés par J. B. Lafitte:* second edition, 1835. It is often assumed that these memoirs are apocryphal. In point of fact they are partly genuine. Fleury undoubtedly left behind him a sheaf of autobiographical papers. Some years afterwards they passed into the possession of Lafitte, who, not content with being merely an editor, rewrote them in his lively way, amplified them from published memoirs and correspondence, and generally turned them into a striking picture of the time in question. My quotations from his book, therefore, are limited to passages which either seem to bear internal evidence of Fleury's authorship or are capable of corroboration.

J, page 206.—*Mémoires de Fleury.*

K, page 315.—Madame Préville, a sister of the actor Drouin, first appeared at the Comédie in 1753.

L, page 421.—Full accounts of the plays produced between 1789 and 1799 are given in *L'Histoire du Théâtre Français pendant la Révolution,* by Etienne and Martainville, 1802.

ERRATA.

Vol. I., pages 346 and 348. Grandval, having pressed his right of seniority, became the first representative of Mahomet in Paris. The eulogies bestowed by Voltaire upon Lanoue were evoked by his acting of the part elsewhere. Vol. II., page 36, *for* "Ximénès," *read* "Ximènès." Pages 163 and 164, *for* "Mouvel," *read* "Monvel."

CHRONOLOGY OF THE FRENCH STAGE.

1699—1799.

1699.

La Veuve, one-act comedy in prose, by Champmêlé, July 30.
La Noce Interrompue, one-act comedy in prose, by Dufresny, Aug. 19.
Athénaïs, tragedy, by Lagrange-Chancel, Nov. 20.

1700.

Thésée, tragedy, by Lafosse, Jan. 5.
Démocrite, comedy, by Regnard, Jan. 12.
Le Retour Imprévu, one-act comedy in prose, by Regnard, Feb. 11.
Mlle. Durieu retired, Easter.
Philippe Poisson appeared, Aug.
L'Esprit de Contradiction, one-act comedy in prose, by Dufresny, Aug. 29.
Mlle. Guérin (formerly Mlle. Molière) died, Nov. 3.
Hubert died, Nov. 19.
Le Capricieux, comedy, by J. B. Rousseau, Dec. 17.

1701.

Mlle. Raisin retired.
Les Trois Gascons, one-act comedy in prose, by Lamotte and Boindin, June 4.
Devilliers died, July 14.
Champmêlé died, Aug. 22.
Ponteuil appeared, Sept. 5.
Roselis retired.
Boursault died, Sept. 15.
Colin Maillard, one-act comedy in prose, by Dancourt, Oct. 28.
Amasis, tragedy, by Lagrange-Chancel, Dec. 13.
Esope à la Cour, comedy, by Boursault, Dec. 16.
Durieu died.

1702.

Le Point d'Honneur, comedy in prose, by Lesage, Feb. 3.
Montézume, tragedy, by Ferrier, Feb. 14.
Le Double Veuvage, three-act comedy in prose, by Dufresny, March 8.
Legrand appeared, March 21.
Arie et Pétus, tragedy, by Mlle. Barbier and Pellegrin, June 3.
Le Bal d'Auteuil, one-act comedy in prose, by Boindin, Aug. 22.
La Matrone d'Ephèse, one-act comedy in prose, by Lamotte, Sept. 23.
L'Opérateur Barri, one-act comedy in prose, by Dancourt, Oct. 11.

1703.

Cornélie, tragedy, by Mlle. Barbier and Pellegrin, Jan. 5.
La Mort de Néron, tragedy, by Péchantrés, Feb. 21.
Le Faux Honnête-Homme, three-act comedy in prose, by Dufresny, Feb. 24.
L'Andrienne, comedy, by Baron, Nov. 16.
Corésus et Callirhoé, tragedy, by Lafosse, Dec. 7.
Alceste, tragedy, by Lagrange-Chancel, Dec. 19.

1704.

Les Folies Amoureuses, three-act comedy in verse, by Regnard, Jan. 15.
Hypermnestre, tragedy, by Riupérous, April 1.
Madame Beauval, her husband, and Lecomte retired, Easter.
Le Port de Mer, one-act comedy in prose, by Boindin, May 29.
Institution of a formal censorship of plays.
Le Galant Jardinier, one-act comedy in prose, by Dancourt, Oct. 22.
Cosroès, Rotrou's tragedy retouched by Dussé de Valentiné, Nov. 20.

1705.

Les Adelphes, comedy, by Baron, Jan. 3.
Saül, tragedy, by Nadal, Feb. 27.
Polydore, tragedy, by Pellegrin, Nov. 6.
Les Ménechmes, comedy, by Regnard, Dec. 4.
Idoménée, tragedy, by Crébillon, Dec. 29.

1706.

Cyrus, tragedy, by Danchet, Feb. 23.
Sallé died, March.
L'Avocat Patelin, three-act comedy in prose, by Brueys, June 4.
Tomyris, tragedy, by Pellegrin and Mlle. Barbier, Nov. 23.
Mlle. Debrie died.

1707.

Atrée et Thyeste, tragedy, by Crébillon, March 14.
César Ursin, comedy, and *Crispin Rival de Son Maître*, one-act comedy in prose, both by Lesage, March 15.
Danaé, one-act comedy in irregular verse, by Lafont, July 4.
Hauteroche died, July 14.
Le Faux Instinct, three-act comedy in prose, by Dufresny, Aug. 2.
Le Diable Boiteux, one-act comedy in prose, by Dancourt, Oct. 8.
Le Second Chapitre du Diable Boiteux, two-act comedy in prose, by Dancourt, Oct. 20.
Les Tyndarides, tragedy, by Danchet, Dec. 16.
Madame Dangeville appeared, Dec. 23.

1708.

Madame Quinault-Denesle appeared, Jan. 4.
Le Légataire Universel, comedy, by Regnard, Jan. 9.
La Critique du Légataire Universel, one-act comedy in prose, by Regnard, Feb. 19.
Le Jaloux Honteux, five-act comedy in prose, by Dufresny, March 6.
Mlle. d'Ennebaut died, March 27.
Lafosse died Nov. 2.
Electre, tragedy, by Crébillon, Dec. 14.

1709.

Turcaret, comedy, by Lesage, Feb. 14.
Hérode, tragedy, by Nadal, Feb. 15.
Péchantré died, March.
Regnard died, Sept. 5.
La Foire St. Laurent, one-act comedy in verse, by Legrand, Sept. 10.
La Mort de César, tragedy, by Pellegrin and Mlle. Barbier, Nov. 26.
Thomas Corneille died, Dec. 13.
Le Jaloux Désabusé, comedy, by Campistron, Dec. 13.
Beauval died, Dec. 29.

1710.

Devisé died, July 8.
Les Agioteurs, three-act comedy in prose, by Dancourt, Sept. 26.
Le Curieux Impertinent, comedy, by Destouches, Nov. 17.
Joseph, tragedy, by Genest, Dec. 19.

1711.

Roselis died.
Rhadamiste et Zénobie, tragedy, by Crébillon, Jan. 23.
L'Epreuve Réciproque, one-act comedy in prose, by Alain and Legrand, Oct. 6.
Etienne Baron died, Dec. 9.

1712.

L'Ingrat, comedy, by Destouches, Jan. 28.
Absalon, tragedy, by Duché de Vancy, April 7.
Jean Baptiste Rousseau expelled from France, April 7.
Jean Baptiste Quinault appeared, May 6.
Dufresné appeared, Oct. 7.
L'Amour Vengé, one-act comedy in verse, by Lafont, Oct. 14.

1713.

L'Irrésolu, comedy, by Destouches, Jan. 15.
Cornélie Vestale, tragedy, by Hénault and Fuzelier, Jan. 27.
Ino et Mélicerte, tragedy, by Lagrange-Chancel, March 10.
Les Trois Frères Rivaux, one-act comedy in verse, by Lafont, Aug. 4.
Madame Quinault-Denesle died, Dec. 22.

1714.

Mlle. Quinault the elder appeared, Jan. 1.
Xerxès, tragedy, by Crébillon, Feb. 7.
Jonathas, tragedy, by Duché de Vancy, Feb. 26.
Habis, tragedy, by Madame de Gomez, April 17.
Mahomet II., tragedy, by Châteaubrun, Nov. 13.

1715.

Caton d'Utique, tragedy, by Deschamps, Jan. 25.
Le Médisant, comedy, by Destouches, Feb. 23.
La Coquette de Village, three-act comedy in verse, by Dufresny, May 27.
Marius, tragedy, by Hénault and Decaux, Nov. 15.

1716.

Sémiramis, tragedy, by Madame de Gomez, Feb. 7.
First representation of Racine's *Athalie* in Paris, March 3.

Revival of the Comédie Italienne.
Le Triple Mariage, one-act comedy, by Destouches, July 7.
Mlle. Gautier appeared, Sept. 3.
L'Aveugle Clairvoyant, one-act comedy in verse, by Legrand, Sept. 18.
Sophonisbe, tragedy, by Lagrange-Chancel, Nov. 10.

1717.

Sémiramis, tragedy, by Crébillon, April 10.
Adrienne Lecouvreur appeared, May 14.
Guérin d'Etriché's last appearance, July 25.
L'Obstacle Imprévu, comedy in prose, by Destouches, Oct. 18.
Cléarque, tragedy, by Madame de Gomez, Nov. 28.
La Métempsycose des Amours, ou les Dieux Comédiens, three-act comedy in irregular verse, by Dancourt, Dec. 17.
Duchemin appeared, Dec. 27.

1718.

Dancourt, Beaubourg, Mlle. Desbrosses, and Madame Beaubourg retired, April 3.
Artaxare, tragedy, by Pellegrin, May 3.
Abeille died, May 22.
Mlle. Quinault appeared, June 14.
Ponteuil died, Aug. 15.
L'Ecole des Amants, three-act comedy in verse, by Jolly, Oct. 18.
Œdipe, tragedy, by Voltaire, Nov. 18.
Le Roi de Cocagne, three-act comedy in irregular verse, by Legrand, Dec. 31.

1719.

Electre, tragedy, by Longepierre, Feb. 22.
La Réconciliation Normande, comedy, by Dufresny, March 7.
Le Dédit, one-act comedy in verse, by Dufresny, May 12.
Le Faucon, one-act comedy in verse, by Pellegrin and Mlle. Barbier, Sept. 7.
Momus Fabuliste, ou les Noces de Vulcain, one-act comedy in prose, by Fuzelier, Sept. 26.
Genest died, Nov. 19.
Les Héraclides, tragedy, by Danchet, Dec. 29.

1720.

Plutus, three-act comedy in verse, by Legrand, Feb. 7.
Artémire, tragedy, by Voltaire, Feb. 15.
Madame Beauval died, March 28.
Madame Dancourt retired, Easter.
Baron the elder reappeared.
Annibal, tragedy, by Marivaux, Dec. 16.

1721.

Le Mariage Fait et Rompu, three-act comedy in verse, by Dufresny, Feb. 14.
Les Machabées, tragedy, by Lamotte, March 6.
Longepierre died, March 31.
Mlle. Desmares retired.
First representation of Racine's *Esther* in Paris, May 8.

Pandore, one-act comedy in verse, by Saint-Foix, June 13.
Mlle. Labat appeared, Aug. 2.
La Rivale d'Elle-même, one-act comedy in prose, by Boissy, Sept. 19.
Cartouche, three-act comedy in prose, by Legrand, Oct. 21.
La Vengeance de l'Amour, comedy, by Jolly, Dec. 14.
Mlle. Raisin, Palaprat, and Ferrier dead.

1722.

Romulus, tragedy, by Lamotte, Jan. 8.
L'Oracle de Delphes, tragedy, by Moncrif.
A. M. Lathorillière received, April 9.
Philippe Poisson retired, April.
Mlle. Dangeville appeared, April 17.
L'Opiniâtre, comedy, by Brueys, May 19.
F. A. Poisson appeared, May 21.
Le Nouveau Monde, three-act comedy in irregular verse by Pellegrin,
    Sept. 11.
Les Machabées, tragedy, by Nadal, Dec. 16.

1723.

Mlle. Gautier retired, Jan.
Mlle. Quinault the elder retired, Feb. 1.
Nitétis, tragedy, by Danchet, Feb. 11.
Armand appeared, March 2.
Inès de Castro, tragedy, by Lamotte, April 6.
Campistron died, May 11.
Lachapelle died, May 29.
Mlle. Lamotte appeared, Oct. 1.
Brueys died, Nov. 25.

1724.

Mariamne, tragedy, by Voltaire, March 6.
Paul Poisson retired, April 1.
Dufresny died, Oct. 6.
Le Dénouement Imprévu, one act comedy in prose, by Marivaux, Dec. 3.

1725.

Mariamne, tragedy, by Nadal, Feb. 15.
Lafont died, March 20.
La Force du Sang, three-act comedy in prose, by Brueys, April 21.
Madame Dancourt died, May 11.
Le Babillard, one-act comedy in verse, by Boissy, June 16.
L'Indiscret, one-act comedy in verse, by Voltaire, Aug. 1.
Madame Quinault-Dufresne appeared, Nov. 7.

1726.

Œdipe, tragedy in prose, by Lamotte, March 18.
Voltaire exiled to England, April.
Pyrrhus, tragedy, by Crébillon, April 29.
Montménil (Lesage) appeared, May 8.
Le Pastor Fido, three-act pastorale-héroïque in irregular verse, by Pellegrin
    Sept. 7.
Dancourt died, Dec. 6.

1727.

La Nouveauté, one-act comedy in prose, by Legrand, Jan. 13.
Le Philosophe Marié, comedy, by Destouches, Feb. 15.
L'Envieux, one-act comedy in prose, by Destouches, May 3.
Le Français à Londres, one-act comedy in prose, by Boissy, July 3.
L'Ile de la Raison, three-act comedy in prose, by Marivaux, Sept. 20.
Les Amazones Modernes, three-act comedy in prose, by Legrand and
    Fuzelier, Oct. 29.
Mlle. Balicourt appeared, Nov. 29.
La Surprise de l'Amour, three-act comedy in prose, by Marivaux, Dec. 31.

1728.

Guérin d'Etriché died, January.
Legrand died, Jan. 7.
Le Procureur Arbitre, one-act comedy in verse, by Philippe Poisson,
    Feb. 25.
Montménil reappeared, May 18.
Le Faux Savant, three-act comedy in verse, by Duvaure, June 21.
L'Ecole des Bourgeois, three-act comedy in prose, by Allainval, Sept. 20.
L'Ecole des Pères, comedy, by Piron, Oct. 10.

1729.

Sarrazin appeared, March 3.
Return of Voltaire to Paris.
La Boëte de Pandore, one-act comedy in verse, by Philippe Poisson,
    March 20
L'Impertinent Malgré Lui, comedy, by Boissy, May 14.
Banières appeared, June 9.
Les Philosophes Amoureux, comedy, by Destouches, Sept. 26.
Grandval appeared, Nov. 19.
Baron died, Dec. 22.

1730.

Mlle. Dangeville's formal début, Jan. 28.
Callisthène, tragedy, by Piron, Feb. 18.
Adrienne Lecouvreur died, March 20.
La Tragédie en Prose, one-act comedy in prose, by Dauvigny, May 9.
Brutus, tragedy, by Voltaire, Dec. 11.

1731.

Mlle. Gaussin appeared, April 28.
L'Italie Galante, comedy, by Lamotte, May 11.
Le Faux Sincère, comedy, by Dufresny, June 26.
Lathorillière died, Sept. 18.
La Réunion des Amours, one-act heroic comedy in prose, by Marivaux,
    Nov. 9.
Le Chevalier Bayard, heroic comedy, by Autreau, Nov. 25.
Erigone, tragedy, by Lagrange-Chancel, Dec. 17.
Lamotte died, Dec. 26.

1732.

Le Glorieux, comedy, by Destouches, Jan. 18.
Eryphile, tragedy, by Voltaire, March 7.
Les Serments Indiscrets, comedy in prose, by Marivaux, June 8.
Zaïre, tragedy, by Voltaire, Aug. 13.
Cassius et Victorinus, tragedy, by Lagrange-Chancel, Oct. 6.
Le Complaisant, five-act comedy in prose, by Pont-de-Veyle, Dec. 29.

1733.

Gustave Vasa, tragedy, by Piron, Feb. 6.
Jean Baptiste Quinault and Mlle. Labat retired, March.
Le Paresseux, three-act comedy in verse, by Delaunay, April 25.
Le Rendezvous, one-act comedy in verse, by Fagan, May 27.
Pélopée, tragedy, by Pellegrin, July 18.
La Fausse Antipathie, three-act comedy in verse, by Lachaussée, Oct. 12.
Introduction of the *comédie attendrissante*.

1734.

Adélaïde Duguesclin, tragedy, by Voltaire, Jan. 18.
La Grondeuse, one-act comedy in prose, by Fagan, Feb. 11.
La Critique de la Fausse Antipathie, one-act comedy in irregular verse, by
  Lachaussée, March 11.
Didon, tragedy, by Lefranc de Pompignan, June 21.
La Pupille, one-act comedy in prose, by Fagan, July 5.
Les Courses de Tempé, one-act pastoral in verse, and *L'Amant Mystérieux*,
  three-act comedy in verse, both by Piron, Aug. 30.
Le Petit-Maître Corrigé, three-act comedy in prose, by Marivaux, Nov. 6.
Les Mécontents, one-act comedy in irregular verse, by Labruère, Dec. 1.
Sabinus, tragedy, by Richer, Dec. 29.

1735.

Le Réveil d'Epiménide, three-act comedy in verse, by Philippe Poisson,
  Jan. 7.
Le Préjugé à la Mode, comedy, by Lachaussé, Feb. 3.
La Magie de l'Amour, one-act pastoral comedy in verse, by Autreau,
  May 9.
Abenéaïd, tragedy, by Leblanc, July 29.
Les Acteurs Déplacés, one-act comedy in prose, by Lathchard and Panard,
  Oct.
L'Amitié Rivale, comedy, by Fagan, Nov. 16.
Téglis, tragedy, by Morand, Nov. 19.
Artaxerxe, tragedy, by Deschamps, Dec. 19.

1736.

Alzire, tragedy, by Voltaire, Jan. 27.
Mlle. Duclos retired, March 17.
Madame Quinault-Dufresne retired, March.
Le Legs, one-act comedy in prose, by Marivaux, June 11.
Pharamond, tragedy, by Gébanon, Aug. 14.
L'Enfant Prodigue, comedy, by Voltaire, Oct. 10.
Dubois appeared, Oct. 19.
Childéric, tragedy, by Morand, Dec. 19.

1737.

Les Deux Nièces, comedy, by Boissy, Jan. 17.
L'Ecole des Amis, comedy, by Lachaussée, Feb. 25.
L'Ambitieux et L'Indiscrète, comedy, by Destouches, June 14.
Les Caractères de Thalie, three-act comedy in prose, each act a distinct
  piece, by Fagan, July 15.
Mlle. Dumesnil appeared, Aug. 6.
Achille à Scyros, three-act tragi-comedy in verse, by Guyot de Merville,
  Oct. 10.

1738.

La Métromanie, comedy, by Piron, Jan. 10.
Maximien, tragedy, by Lachaussée, Feb. 28.
Mlle. Balicourt retired, March 22.
Le Fat Puni, one-act comedy in prose, by Pont-de-Veyle, April 7.
Le Pouvoir de la Sympathie, three-act comedy in verse, by Boissy, July 5.
Le Consentement Forcé, one-act comedy in prose, by Guyot de Merville,
    Aug. 13.
Les Epoux Réunis, three-act comedy in verse, by Guyot de Merville, Oct. 31.

1739.

Marié sans le Savoir, one-act comedy in prose, by Fagan, Jan. 8.
La Somnambule, one-act comedy in prose, by Pont-de-Veyle, Jan. 19.
Mahomet II., tragedy, by Lanoue, Feb. 23.
Madame Dangeville retired, March 14.
L'Ecole du Monde, one-act comedy in irregular verse by Voisenon, preceded
    by a prologue entitled *Le Retour de l'Ombre de Molière*, by the same
    writer, Oct. 14.

1740.

Edouard III., tragedy, by Gresset, Jan. 22.
Les Dehors Trompeurs, five-act comedy in verse, by Boissy, Feb. 18.
L'Oracle, one-act comedy in prose, by Saint-Foix, March 22.
Zulime, tragedy, by Voltaire, June 8.
Joconde, one-act comedy in prose, by Fagan, Nov. 5.

1741.

Deucalion et Pyrrha, one-act comedy in prose, by Saint-Foix, Feb. 20.
Jean Baptiste Rousseau died, March 17.
Mlle. Quinault, Dufresne, and Duchemin retired, March.
Mélanide, five-act comedy in verse, by Lachaussée, May 12.
Paulin appeared, August 5.
Nadal died, August 7.
Sylvie, one-act bourgeois tragedy in prose, by Landois, August 17.
La Belle Orgueilleuse, one-act comedy in verse, by Destouches, Aug. 17.
L'Amour Usé, five-act comedy in prose, by Destouches, Sept. 20.

1742.

L'Amour pour Amour, three-act comedy in irregular verse, by Lachaussée,
    Feb. 16.
Lanoue appeared, May 14.
Madame Drouin appeared, May 30.
Mahomet, tragedy, by Voltaire, Aug. 9.
Roselli appeared, Oct. 24.

1743.

Mérope, tragedy, by Voltaire, Feb. 20.
Zénéide, one-act comedy in irregular verse, by Cahusac, May 13.
L'Ile Sauvage, three-act comedy in prose, by Saint-Foix, July 5.
Mlle. Balicourt died, August 4.
La Mort de César, tragedy, by Voltaire, Aug. 29.
Montménil died, Sept. 8.
L'Algérien, three-act comedy ballet in irregular verse, by Cahusac, Sept. 14.

Clairon appeared, Sept. 19.
Philippe Poisson died.
Paméla, comedy, by Lachaussée, Dec. 6.

1741.

Fernand Cortez, tragedy, by Piron, Jan. 6.
L'Ecole des Mères, five-act comedy in irregular verse, by Lachaussée, April 27.
Drouin appeared, May 20.
Les Grâces, one-act comedy in prose, by Saint-Foix, July 23.
La Dispute, one-act comedy in prose, by Marivaux, Oct. 19.
L'Heureux Retour, one-act comedy in verse, by Fagan, Nov. 6.
Le Quartier d'Hiver, one-act comedy in verse, by Bret, Dec. 4.
Jean Baptiste Quinault dead.

1745.

La Princesse de Navarre, three-act comedy ballet in verse, by Voltaire, at Versailles, Feb. 25.
La Fête Interrompue, one-act comedy in prose, by Lachaussée, April 20.
Sidney, three-act comedy in verse, by Gresset, May 3.
Les Souhaits pour le Roi, one-act comedy in verse, by Valois and others, Aug. 3.
Le Temple de la Gloire, three-act opera ballet, by Voltaire, at Versailles, Nov. 27.
Pellegrin, Mlle. Barbier and Autreau dead.

1746.

Le Rival de Lui-même, one-act comedy in irregular verse, by Lachaussée, April 20.
Le Préjugé Vaincu, one-act comedy in prose, by Marivaux, Aug. 6.
Mlle. Laballe appeared, Sept. 15.
Julie, one-act comedy in prose, by Saint-Foix, Oct. 20.
Venise Sauvée, tragedy, by Laplace, Dec. 15.

1747.

La Gouvernante, comedy, by Lachaussée, Jan. 18.
Le Méchant, comedy, by Gresset, April 27.
La Rivale Suivante, one-act comedy in verse, by Pierre Rousseau, Aug. 3.
Egérie, one-act comedy in prose, by Saint-Foix, Sept. 9.
Ribou appeared, Nov. 6.
Lesage died, Nov. 17.

1748.

Denis le Tyrant, tragedy, by Marmontel, Feb. 15.
Danchot died, Feb. 21.
Sémiramis, tragedy, by Voltaire, Aug. 29.
Mlle. Laballe disappeared, Oct. 31.
Catilina, tragedy, by Crébillon, Dec. 12.
Mlle. Duclos dead.

1749.

L'Ecole de la Jeunesse, comedy, by Lachaussée, Feb. 22.
Mlle. Beaumenard appeared, April 17.

Aristomène, tragedy, by Marmontel, April 30.
Nanine, comedy in ten-syllable verse, by Voltaire, June 16.
La Colonie, three-act comedy, by Saint-Foix, Oct. 25.

1750.

Oreste, tragedy, by Voltaire, Jan. 12.
La Force du Naturel, comedy, by Destouches, Feb. 11.
Caliste, tragedy, by Laplace, April 27.
Cléopatre, tragedy, by Marmontel, May 20.
Cénie, comedy in prose, by Madame de Grafigny, June 25.
Lekain appeared, Sept. 14.
Bellecourt appeared, Dec. 21.
Roselli slain in a duel, Dec. 22.
Flight of Ribou.

1751.

Zarès, tragedy, by Palissot, June 3.
Mlle. Hus appeared, July 26.
Antipater, tragedy, by Portelance, Nov. 25.
Boindin died, Nov. 30.

1752.

Rome Sauvée, tragedy, by Voltaire, Feb. 24.
Les Héraclides, tragedy, by Marmontel, May 24.
Le Duc de Foix (*Adelaïde Duguesclin*), tragedy, by Voltaire, Aug. 17.
Fuzelier died, Sept. 19.
L'Amant de Lui-Même, one-act comedy in prose, by Jean Jacques Rousseau.
Aménophis, tragedy, by Saurin, Nov. 12.

1753.

Mlle. Hus reappeared, Jan. 22.
Allainval died, March 2.
Le Dissipateur, comedy, by Destouches, March 23.
F. A. Poisson died, Aug. 25.
Mlle. Desmares died, Sept. 12.
Préville appeared, Sept. 20.
Madame Préville appeared, Dec. 28.

1754.

Paros, tragedy, by Mailhol, Jan. 21.
Les Adieux du Goût, one-act comedy in irregular verse, by Patu and
     Portelance, Feb. 13.
Lachaussée died, March 14.
La Créole, one-act comedy in prose, by the Chevalier de la Morlière.
Les Méprises, one-act comedy in irregular verse, by Pierre Rousseau, April 25.
Destouches died, July 5.
Les Tuteurs, two-act comedy in verse, by Palissot, Sept. 2.
Molé appeared, Nov. 7.
Duchemin died, Nov. 15.
Le Triumvirat, tragedy, by Crébillon, Dec. 23.
Labruère died.

1755.

Drouin retired, Jan. 1.
Fagan died, April 8.
Le Jaloux, comedy, by Bret, May 15.
Guyot de Merville died, May.
L'Orphelin de la Chine, tragedy, by Voltaire, Aug. 20.

1756.

La Coquette Corrigée, comedy, by Lanoue, Feb. 23.

1757.

Fontenelle died, Jan. 9.
Lanoue retired, March 26.
Sarrazin ceased to play.
Adèle de Ponthieu, tragedy, by Laplace, April 28.
L'Impatient, one-act comedy in verse, by Poinsinet.
Iphigénie en Tauride, tragedy, by Latouche, June 4.
Brizard appeared, July 30.
Morand died, Aug. 5.

1758.

Le Faux Généreux, comedy, by Bret, Jan. 18.
Astarbé, tragedy, by Colardeau, Feb. 27.
Boissy died, April 19.
La Fille d'Aristide, five-act comedy in prose, by Madame de Grafigny,
   April 29 ; death of the author, Dec. 12.
Hypermnestre, tragedy, by Lemierre, Aug. 31.
Lagrange-Chancel died, Dec. 27.

1759.

Titus, tragedy, by Debelloy, Feb. 28.
La Fausse Agnès, three-act comedy in prose, by Destouches, March 12.
Sarrazin, Lathorillière, and Mlle. Lamotte retired, *clôture*.
Mlle. Rosalie appeared, March 14.
Abolition of seats on the stage.
Rotrou's *Venceslas*, altered by Marmontel, April 30.
Mlle. Dubois appeared, May 30.
Cahusac died, June 11.
Briséïs, tragedy, by Poinsinet de Sivri, June 25.
Lathorillière died, Oct. 23.
Madame Quinault-Dufresne dead.

1760.

Zulica, tragedy, by Dorat, Jan. 7.
Molé reappeared, Jan. 28.
Latouche died, Feb. 10.
Spartacus, tragedy, by Saurin, Feb. 20.
Les Philosophes, three-act comedy in verse, by Palissot, May 2.
Dauberval appeared, May 11.
L'Ecossaise, comedy, by Voltaire, July 26.
Tancrède, tragedy, by Voltaire, Sept. 3.
Caliste, tragedy, by Colardeau, Nov. 12.

1761.

Madame Molé appeared, Jan. 21.
Le Père de Famille, drame, by Diderot, Feb. 18.
Térée, tragedy, by Lemierre, March 25.
Lanoue died, Nov. 15.

1762.

L'Ecueil du Sage, comedy in ten-syllable verse, by Voltaire, Jan. 18.
Julie, three-act comedy in prose, by Marin, March 3.

Zelmire, tragedy, by Debelloy, May 6.
Crébil'on died, June 17.
Les Méprises, five-act comedy in ten-syllable verse, by Palissot, June.
Sarrazin died, Nov. 15.
Heureusement, one-act comedy in verse, by Rochon de Chabannes, Nov. 29.
Bouret appeared, Dec. 2.
Eponine, tragedy, by Chabanon, Dec. 16.

1763.

Dupuis et Desronais, three-act comedy in irregular verse, by Collé, Jan. 17·
Marivaux died, Feb.
Mlle. Gaussin and Mlle. Dangeville retired.
Théagène et Chariclée, tragedy, by Dorat, March 21.
Auger appeared, April 14.
Mlle. Doligny appeared, May 3.
La Mort de Socrate, tragedy in three acts, by Sauvigny, May 9.
Mlle. Luzi appeared, May 26.
Blanche et Guiscard, tragedy, by Saurin, Sept. 25.
Le Comte de Warwick, tragedy, by Laharpe, Nov. 7.

1764.

Mlle. Fanier appeared, Jan. 11.
Idoménée, tragedy, by Lemierre, Jan. 13.
L'Amateur, one-act comedy in irregular verse, by Barthe, March 3.
Olympie, tragedy, by Voltaire, March 17.
La Jeune Indienne, one-act comedy in verse, by Champfort, April 30.
Feulie appeared, May 8.
Cromwell, tragedy, by Duclairon, June 7.
Les Triumvirs, tragedy, by Voltaire, July 5.
Timoléon, tragedy, by Laharpe, Aug. 1.
Le Cercle, one-act comedy in prose, by Poinsinet, Sept. 7.

1765.

Le Siége de Calais, tragedy, by Debelloy, Feb. 13.
Imprisonment of five players for refusing to act.
Armand retired, March.
Dubois expelled, April.
Clairon retired, May.
Panard died, June 3.
Pharamond, tragedy, by Laharpe, Aug. 14.
Le Tuteur Dupé, comedy in prose, by Cailhava, Sept. 30.
Le Philosophe sans le Savoir, comedy in prose, by Sédaine, Nov. 2.
Armand died, Dec.

1766.

La Partie de Chasse d'Henri Quatre, three-act comedy in prose, by Collé, Feb. 4.
Gustave Wasa, tragedy, by Laharpe, March 3.
Mlle. Sainval the elder appeared, May 5.
Guillaume Tell, tragedy, by Lemierre, Dec. 17.

1767.

Eugénie, drame in five acts, and in prose, by Beaumarchais, Jan. 29.
Quinault-Dufresne died, Feb.
Les Scythes, tragedy, by Voltaire, March 28.
Hirza, tragedy, by Sauvigny, May 27.

Mlle. Gaussin died, June 9.
Cosroès, tragedy, by Lefevre, Aug 26.
Les Deux Sœurs, two-act comedy in prose, by Bret.
Mlle. Labat dead.

1768.

Amélise, tragedy, by Ducis, Jan. 3.
Les Fausses Infidélités, one-act comedy in verse, by Barthe, Jan. 25.
Les Valets Maîtres de la Maison, one-act comedy in prose, by Rochon de
    Chabannes, Feb. 11.
Grandval retired.
Béverley, tragedy, by Saurin, May 7.
La Gageure Imprévue, one-act comedy in prose, by Sédaine, May 27.
Les Deux Frères, comedy, by Moissy, July 27.
Madame Vestris appeared, Dec. 19.

1769.

Julie, three-act comedy in prose, by Denon, Jan. 14.
Poinsinet died, June 7.
Hamlet, tragedy by Ducis, Sept. 30.

1770.

Les Deux Amis, drame in prose, by Beaumarchais, Jan. 13.
Le Marchand de Smyrne, one-act comedy in prose, by Champfort, Jan. 13.
Paulin died, Jan. 19.
Migration of the players to the theatre of the Tuileries, April 24.
Monvel appeared, April 28.
La Veuve du Malabar, tragedy, by Lemierre, July 30.
Hénault died, Nov. 21.
Larive appeared, Dec. 3.
La Veuve, one-act comedy in prose, by Collé, Dec. 29.

1771.

Gaston et Bayard, tragedy, by Debelloy, April 24.
Dugazon appeared, April 29.
Le Fils Naturel, drame, by Diderot, July 26.
Le Bourru Bienfaisant, three-act comedy in prose, by Goldoni, Nov. 4.
La Mère Jalouse, three-act comedy in verse, by Barthe, Dec. 23.

1772.

Les Druïdes, tragedy, by Leblanc.
Pierre le Cruel, tragedy, by Debelloy, May 24.
Mlle. Sainval the younger appeared, May 27.
Roméo et Juliette, tragedy, by Ducis, July 23.
Mlle. Raucourt appeared, Sept. 23.
Les Chérusques, tragedy, by Beauvin, Sept. 26.
Desessarts appeared, Oct. 4.

1773.

Piron died, Jan. 21.
Le Centenaire, one-act comedy in irregular verse, by Artaud, Feb. 18.
Mlle. Dubois retired, July 3.
Régulus, tragedy, and *La Feinte par Amour,* one-act comedy in verse, both
    by Dorat, July 31.
Pont-de-Veyle dead.

1774.

Sophonisbe, Mariet's tragedy, retouched by Voltaire, Jan. 15.
Fleury appeared, March 7.
Adélaïde de Hongrie, tragedy, by Dorat, Aug. 26.
School of Declamation founded.

1775.

Le Barbier de Séville, three-act comedy in prose, by Beaumarchais, Feb. 2.
Debelloy died, March 5.
Le Célibataire, comedy, by Dorat, Sept. 20.
Pygmalion, one-act comedy in prose, by Jean Jacques Rousseau, Oct. 30.

1776.

Louise Contat appeared, Feb. 3.
Mlle. Dumesnil retired, May.
Saint-Foix died, Aug. 25.
La Manie des Drames Sombres, one-act comedy in prose, by Cubières,
    Oct. 29.
Dazincourt appeared, Nov. 21.
Le Malheureux Imaginaire, by Dorat, Dec. 7.

1777.

Gresset died, June 17.
Vanhove appeared, July 2.
Gabrielle de Vergy, tragedy, by Debelloy, July 12.
L'Amant Bourru, three-act comedy in verse, by Monvel, Aug. 14.
Mustapha et Zéangir, tragedy, by Champfort, Dec. 15.

1778.

Lekain died, Feb. 6.
Irène, tragedy, by Voltaire, March 16.
Fleury reappeared, March 20.
Apotheosis of Voltaire, March 30.
Death of Voltaire, May 30.
Jean Jacques Rousseau died, July 2.
Les Barmécides, tragedy, by Laharpe, July 11.
L'Impatient, one-act comedy in prose, by Lantier, Sept. 3.
Bellecourt died, Nov. 19.
Œdipe chez Admète, tragedy, by Ducis, Dec. 4.

1779.

Les Muses Rivales, by Laharpe, Feb. 1.
Grammont appeared, Feb. 5.
Médée, tragedy, by Clément, Feb. 19.
L'Amour Français, by Rochon de Chabannes, April 17.
Agathocle, tragedy, by Voltaire, May 31.
Strike of dramatists against the Comédie Française.
Quarrel between Madame Vestris and Mlle. Sainval the elder, terminating
    in the banishment of the latter.
Pierre-le-Grand, tragedy, by Dorat, Dec. 1.

1780.

Les Etrennes de l'Amour, by Dorvigny, Jan. 1.
Madame Hus retired, *clôture*.
Dorat died, April 29.

Dauberval retired, July 1.
Mlle. Olivier appeared, Sept. 26.
Monvel left for Stockholm.
End of the dramatic authors' strike, December.

1781.

Mlle. Luzi retired.
Mlle. Joly appeared, May 1.
Richard III., tragedy, by Durozoi, July 6.
Saurin died, Nov. 17.
Jeanne de Naples, tragedy, by Laharpe, Dec. 12.

1782.

Mlle. Quinault died.
Molière, by Laharpe, April 12.
Agis, tragedy, by Laignelot, May 6.
St. Fal appeared, July 8.
Les Courtisanes, comedy, by Palissot, July 26.
St. Prix appeared, Nov. 9.
Migration of the Comédie Française to a new theatre in the Faubourg St.
    Germain, April.

1783.

Le Roi Léar, tragedy, by Ducis, Jan. 20.
Auger died, Feb.
Mlle. Doligny retired.
Le Séducteur, by the Marquis de Bièvre, Nov. 8.
Collé died, Nov. 29.
Les Brahmes, tragedy, by Laharpe, Dec. 15.

1784.

Macbeth, tragedy, by Ducis, Jan. 12.
Coriolan, tragedy, by Laharpe, March 2.
Le Mariage de Figaro, comedy in prose, by Beaumarchais, April 27.
Diderot died, June.
Naudet appeared, Sept. 22.
Grandval died, Sept. 24.
Émilie Contat appeared, Oct. 5.
Lefranc de Pompignan died, Nov. 1.

1785.

La Morlière died, February.
Mlle. Devienne appeared, April 7.
La Comtesse de Chazelles, comedy, by Madame de Montesson, May 6.
Barthe died, June 17.
Mlle. Candeille appeared, Sept. 19.
Mlle. Vanhove appeared, Oct. 8.
Pierre Rousseau died, Nov.
Céramis, tragedy, by Lemierre, Dec. 29.

1786.

Préville, Brizard, Madame Préville, and Mlle. Fanier retired, April 1.
L'Inconstant, comedy, by Colin d'Harleville, June 13.
Virginie, tragedy, by Laharpe, July 22.
Les Amours de Bayard, by Monvel, Aug. 24.
Azémire, tragedy, by Chénier, Nov. 6.

1787.

La Fausse Inconstance, comedy, by Madame de Beauharnais, Jan. 31.
L'Ecole des Pères, comedy, by Pièyre, July 19.
Mlle. Olivier died, Sept. 21.
La Maison de Molière, by Mercier, Oct. 20.
Talma appeared.

1788.

L'Optimiste, comedy, by Harleville, Feb. 22.
Mlle. Desgarcins appeared, May 24.
La Jeune Epouse, comedy, by Cubières, July 14.
Mlle. Lange appeared, Oct. 2.
L'Entrevue, comedy, by Vigée, Dec. 6.
Larive temporarily retired.

1789.

Le Présomptueux, comedy, by Fabre d'Eglantine, Jan. 7.
Les Châteaux en Espagne, comedy, by Harleville, Feb. 7.
Auguste et Théodore, two-act comedy in prose, March 6.
Beginning of the Revolution, May 5.
Charles IX., tragedy, by Chénier, Nov. 4.
Le Paysan Magistrat, comedy, by Collot d'Herbois, Dec. 7.

1790.

Players declared entitled to all the rights of citizens.
L'Honnête Criminel, five-act drame in verse, by Falbaire, Jan. 4.
Les Dangers de l'Opinion, five-act drame in verse, by Laya, Jan. 19.
Le Philinte de Molière, ou La Suite du Misanthrope, comedy, by Fabre
    d'Eglantine, Feb. 22.
Le Couvent, one-act comedy, by Lanjon.
Larive reappeared, May 4.
Barneveldt, tragedy, by Lemierre, June 30.
Momus aux Champs Elysées, one-act piece in verse, July 14.
Grandménil appeared, Aug. 31.
The monopoly of the Comédie Française broken down.
Calas, drame, by Laya, Dec. 18.

1791.

La Liberté Conquise, ou le Despotisme Renversé, drame in five acts, by
    Harvy, Jan. 4.
Dorval, ou le Fou Par Amour, one-act drame in verse, by Ségur, Jan. 29.
Brizard died, Jan. 30.
Rienzi, tragedy, by Laiguelot, March 2.
M. de Crac dans son Petit Castel, one-act comedy in verse, by Harleville,
    March 4.
Les Victimes Cloîtrées, four-act drame in prose, by Monvel, March 29.
Beginning of a second Théâtre Français at the Palais Royal, April 27.
Henri VIII., tragedy, by Chénier, Palais Royal, April 27.
Marius à Minturnes, three-act comedy, by Arnaud, Théâtre de la Nation
    (Comédie Française), May 19.
Mlle. Simon appeared, June 14.
L'Intrigue Epistolaire, comedy, by Fabre d'Eglantine, Palais Royal, June 15.
Jean Santerre, tragedy, by Ducis, Palais Royal, June 28.
Calas, ou l'Ecole des Juges, tragedy, by Chénier, Palais Royal, July 7.
Washington, ou La Liberté du Nouveau Monde, four-act tragedy in verse,
    by Sauvigny, Théâtre de la Nation, July 13.

Mlle. Mezerai appeared, July 20.
La Prise de la Bastille, three-act drame in verse, Palais Royal, Aug. 25.
L'Héritière, comedy, by Fabre d'Eglantine, Palais Royal, Nov. 11.
Retirement of Mlle. Sainval the younger.
Mélanie, tragedy, by Laharpe, Palais Royal, Dec. 7.

1792.

Paulin et Clairette, one-act comic opera, music by Dézède, Théâtre de la
  Nation, Jan. 5.
Caius Gracchus, tragedy, by Chénier, Palais Royal, Feb. 7.
Le Vieux Célibataire, comedy, by Harleville, Théâtre de la Nation, Feb. 24.
Bret died, Feb. 25.
La Mort d'Abel, three-act tragedy in verse, by Legouvé, Théâtre de la
  Nation, March 6.
Le Sot Orgueilleux, ou l'Ecole des Elections, comedy, by Fabre d'Eglantine,
  Palais Royal, March 7.
Lovelace, five-act drame in verse, by Lemercier, Théâtre de la Nation,
  April 20.
Lucrèce, tragedy, by Arnaud, Théâtre de la Nation, May 4.
Baptiste the younger appeared, May 5.
L'Amour et l'Intérêt, by Fabre d'Eglantine, Palais Royal, May 5.
Fall of the Monarchy, August 10.
Othello, tragedy, by Ducis, Palais Royal, Nov. 26.
La Matinée d'une Jolie Femme, one-act comedy in verse, by Vigée,
  Théâtre de la Nation, Dec. 29.

1793.

L'Ami des Lois, comedy, by Laya, Théâtre de la Nation, Jan. 2.
Le Général Dumouriez à Bruxelles, four-act comedy in prose, by Madame
  Degouges, Palais Royal, Jan. 23.
Le Conteur, ou les Deux Postes, three-act comedy in prose, by Picard,
  Théâtre de la Nation, Feb. 4.
Fénélon, drame, by Chénier, Palais Royal, Feb. 9.
Baptiste the elder appeared.
Robert Chef de Brigands, drame, Palais Royal, April 3.
La Vivacité à l'Epreuve, three-act comedy in verse, by Vigée, Théâtre de
  la Nation.
Mutius Scaevola, tragedy, by Luce de Lancival, Palais Royal, July 23.
Lemierre died, July.
Paméla, ou la Vertu Récompensée, comedy, by Neufchâteau, Théâtre de la
  Nation, Aug. 1.
Suspension of the Comédie Française by the imprisonment of nearly all its
  members, Sept. 2.
Death of Desessarts.
Le Jugement Dernier des Rois, drame, by Sylvain Maréchal, Oct.
La Moitié du Chemin, three-act comedy in verse, by Picard, Oct. 25.
Le Modéré, drame, Oct. 30.
Arétaphile, ou la Révolution de Cyrène, by Ronsin.
La Vraie Bravoure, one-act comedy in prose, by Picard and Duval.

1794.

Les Contres Révolutionnaires Jugés par Eux-mêmes, three-act comedy in
  verse, by Dorveau, Jan. 7.
L'Expulsion des Tarquins, ou la Royauté Abolie, tragedy, by Leblanc,
  Jan. 13.

Epicharsis et Néron, ou la Conspiration pour la Liberté, tragedy, by Legouvé, Feb. 5.
Fabre d'Eglantine guillotined, April 5.
Rose et Picard, one-act comedy in verse, by Harleville, June 16.
Execution of Robespierre, July 29.
Release of the imprisoned members of the Comédie Française.
Timoléon, tragedy, by Chénier, Palais Royal, Sept. 11.
Le Bienfait de la Loi, one-act comedy in verse, by Forgeot, Théâtre de l'Egalité.
Cincinnatus, ou la Conjuration de Spurius Mellius, three-act tragedy in verse, by Arnault, Théâtre de la République (Palais Royal).

1795.

Opening of a theatre in the Rue Feydeau.
Galathée, one-act melodrama, by Poulher, Feb.
Pausanias, tragedy, by Trouvé, Rue Feydeau, March 28.
Abufar, tragedy, by Ducis, Palais Royal, April 12.
Le Tolérant, comedy, by Demoustier, Rue Feydeau, April.
Le Tartuffe Révolutionnaire, three-act comedy in verse, by Lemercier, Palais Royal, June.
Quintus Fabius, three-act tragedy in verse, by Legouvé, Palais Royal, Aug. 30.
Les Conjectures, comedy, by Picard, Rue Feydeau, Oct. 20.
Les Amis de Collége, three-act comedy in verse, by Picard, Dec. 12.

1796.

Le Lévite d'Ephraim, three-act tragedy in verse, by Lemercier, Palais Royal.
Mlle. Dangeville died, March.
Caton d'Utique, tragedy, by Saint-Marcel, Palais Royal, April 16.
Oscar, tragedy, by Arnault, Palais Royal, June 2.
L'Original, one-act comedy in verse, by Hoffman, Rue Feydeau, July 30.
Le Chanoine de Milan, one-act comedy in prose, by Duval, Théâtre de la République, Sept.
Les Artistes, comedy, by Harleville, Théâtre de la République, Nov. 9.
Les Deux Voisins, ou Etre et Paraître, comedy, by Harleville, Rue Feydeau, Nov.
Les Héritiers, ou le Naufragé, one-act comedy in prose, by Duval, Théâtre de la République, Nov. 27.
Opening of a theatre in the Rue de Louvois, Dec. 23.
Les Deux Sœurs, one-act comedy in verse by Laya, Rue de Louvois, Dec.
Le Lovelace Français, ou la Jeunesse du Duc de Richelieu, five-act drame in prose, by Monvel and Duval, Théâtre de la République, Dec.

1797.

Le Mari Jaloux, comedy, by Desforges, Théâtre de la République, Jan. 31.
Les Trois Fils, ou l'Héroïsme Filial, four-act drame in verse, by Demoustier, Théâtre Feydeau, Feb.
Verseuil et St. Elmont, drame, by Ségur the younger, Rue de Louvois, Feb. 12.
Laurence, tragedy, by Legouvé, Rue de Louvois, March.
Junius, ou le Proscrit, by Monvel the younger, Théâtre de la République, April.
Agamemnon, tragedy, by Lemercier, Théâtre de la République, April 24.
La Mère Coupable, five-act drame in prose, by Beaumarchais, May 5.
Mlle. Desgarcins died.

Œdipe à Colonne, tragedy, by Ducis (his *Œdipe chez Admète* recast),
    Théâtre de la République, May 15.
Sédaine died, May 17.
Géta, tragedy, by Petitot, Rue de Louvois, May 25.
Le Journaliste, ou l'Ami des Mœurs, one-act comedy in verse, by Delangres,
    Théâtre de la République, July 5.
Méliocre et Rampant, comedy, by Picard, Rue de Louvois, July 19.
Fernandez, tragedy in three acts, by Luce de Lancival, Sept. 4.
Closure of the Théâtre Louvois, Sept.
La Prude, comedy, by Lemercier, Théâtre Feydeau, Dec.
Retirement of Mlle. Lange.
Théâtre de la République closed.

1798.

Reopening of the theatre in the Faubourg St. Germain (Odéon).
Falkland, drame, by Laya, Théâtre Feydeau, May 25.
Les Projets de Mariage, one-act comedy in prose, by Duval, Théâtre
    Feydeau, Aug. 5.
Théâtre Feydeau closed.
Thémistocle, tragedy, by Larnac, March 1.
Reopening of the Théâtre de la République (Sept. 19).
Madame Joly died, May 5.
Blanche et Montcassin, tragedy, by Arnault, Théâtre de la République, Oct.
Michel Montaigne, comedy, by Guy, Théâtre de la République, Nov. 12.
Ophis, tragedy, by Lemercier, Dec. 22.
Misanthropie et Repentir, drame from Kotzebue, by Madame Molé, Odéon,
    Dec. 28.

1799.

Une Journée du Jeune Néron, two-act comedy in prose, by Laya, Odéon,
    Feb. 15.
The Odéon destroyed by fire, March 18—19.
Death of Beaumarchais, May 19.
Reunion of the players: restoration of the Comédie Française, May 30.

INDEX.

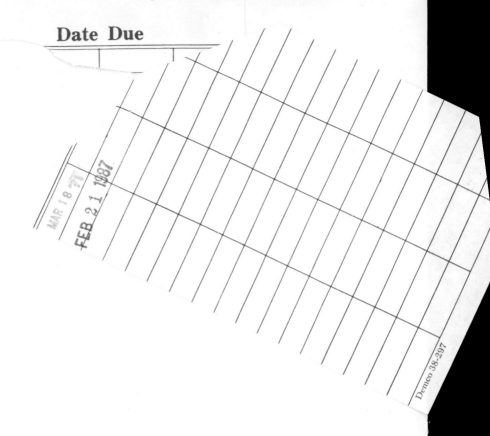